Death beyond Disavowal

Difference Incorporated

Roderick A. Ferguson and Grace Kyungwon Hong
Series Editors

Death beyond Disavowal

The Impossible Politics of Difference

GRACE KYUNGWON HONG

Difference Incorporated

UNIVERSITY OF MINNESOTA PRESS

MINNEAPOLIS · LONDON

A portion of the Introduction was previously published as "Neoliberalism," *Critical Ethnic Studies* 1, no. 1 (Spring 2015); reprinted by permission. An earlier version of chapter 1 was published as "Fun with Death and Dismemberment: Irony, Farce, and the Limits of Nationalism in Oscar Zeta Acosta's *Revolt of the Cockroach People* and Ana Castillo's *So Far from God,*" in *Strange Affinities: The Gender and Sexual Politics of Comparative Racialization* (Durham: Duke University Press, 2011); reprinted by permission. A portion of chapter 2 was published as "Existentially Surplus: Women of Color Feminism and the New Crises of Capitalism," *GLQ* 18, no. 1 (2012): 87–106; reprinted by permission. An earlier version of chapter 4 was published as "'The Future of Our Worlds': Black Feminism and the Politics of Knowledge in the University under Globalization," *Meridians* 8, no. 2 (2008): 95–115; copyright Smith College; reprinted by permission from Indiana University Press.

Excerpt from Cherríe Moraga, "I Was Not Supposed to Remember," from *The Last Generation,* copyright 1993 by Cherríe Moraga, reprinted with permission. All rights reserved.

Published by the University of Minnesota Press
111 Third Avenue South, Suite 290
Minneapolis, MN 55401-2520
http://www.upress.umn.edu

Library of Congress Cataloging-in-Publication Data
Hong, Grace Kyungwon.
    Death beyond disavowal: the impossible politics of diﬀerence /
Grace Kyungwon Hong. (Diﬀerence Incorporated series)
Includes bibliographical references and index.
ISBN 978-0-8166-9526-3 (hc)
ISBN 978-0-8166-9530-0 (pb)
    1. Feminist theory. 2. Racism. 3. Discrimination. 4. Death—Political aspects. I. Title.
HQ1190.H665 2015
305—dc23   2014046941

UMP LSI

Contents

Neoliberal Disavowal and the Politics of the Impossible

In a relatively unheralded essay from *Sister Outsider* called "Learning from the 60s," Audre Lorde presents her relationship to the dead in which seemingly mutually exclusive orientations to life and death converge.[1] Lorde begins this essay, a transcript of a speech at the "Malcolm X Weekend" organized by the Harvard-Radcliffe Black Students Association in 1982, in this manner: "Malcolm X is a distinct shape in a very pivotal period of my life. I stand here now—Black, Lesbian, Feminist—an inheritor of Malcolm and in his tradition, doing my work, and the ghost of his voice through my mouth asks each one of you here tonight: Are you doing yours?"[2] With this opening, Lorde launches a speech that performs a series of contradictory double functions. She *both* reinscribes a temporality of inheritance ("an inheritor . . . in his tradition"), with the associated affects of mourning, obligation, and the implication of a singular lineage, and instantiates an alternative heterogeneous temporality that fractures and makes multiple the possible futures that Malcolm X's memory could invoke ("Black, Lesbian, Feminist"). She both memorializes Malcolm and gestures to the dangers of memorialization; she insists on the importance of inheritance while simultaneously undermining patrilineage.

By asserting that she is Malcolm X's inheritor, Lorde acts audaciously, situating her lesbian feminist self as no less assuredly and authentically Black as any male in Malcolm's lineage, against a quickly ossifying memorialization of Malcolm as a charismatic, masculine, and patriarchal figure.[3] She refuses to cleave "Black" from "Lesbian" and "Feminist," working against the "pressure to express only one [part] to the exclusion of all others,"[4] and in so doing, insisting that Malcolm's legacy enables the suturing of these identities rather than their mutual exclusivity. In the context of what she described in an earlier essay as "the enormous energy . . . being wasted in the Black community today in anti-lesbian hysteria,"[5] we can see that the forceful beginning to this speech is a deliberate intervention into a developing normative definition of Blackness in part constituted through a Black nationalist memorialization of Malcolm X—an effect, if not the overtly stated goal, of events like "Malcolm X Weekend." She refuses any nostalgia about the 1960s, observing that while it was "a time of promise and excitement," it was also "a time of isolation and frustration from within." She specifically names disciplining and monolithic definitions of Blackness as contributing to that isolation, describing her sense at the time that "it was [her] own fault—if [she]was only Blacker, things would be fine."[6] She accordingly warns her audience of the present-day consequences of 1960s nostalgia, particularly as it coalesces around such figures as Malcolm X:

> For while we wait for another Malcolm, another Martin, another charismatic Black leader to validate our struggles, old Black people are freezing to death in tenements, Black children are being brutalized and slaughtered in the streets, or lobotomized by television, and the percentage of Black families living below the poverty line is higher today than in 1963.[7]

In so doing, Lorde analyzes the 1980s as a Benjaminian "moment of danger" in which minority nationalist memorialization of the social movements of the 1960s can become the fuel for a multiculturalist manifestation of neoliberal power.[8]

And yet she goes further: she not only refuses any narrative that might dismiss her as an inauthentic subject (not Black enough because of her lesbianism or feminism) but also situates herself as the speaking authority, channeling "the ghost of his voice through [her] mouth" so as to demand "are you doing yours?"[9] It is not Malcolm's ghost but the "ghost of his voice" that comes through Lorde's mouth. It is a double remove, where not only is Malcolm gone but so too, potentially, is his "voice," which exists only as a ghostly residue in her "mouth." As Avery Gordon says of ghosts, "It is not a case of dead or missing persons sui generis, but of the ghost as a social figure. It is often a case of inarticulate experiences, of symptoms and screen memories, of spiraling affects, of more than one story at a time, of the traffic in domains of experience that are anything but transparent and referential."[10] Insofar as Lorde situates herself—Black, lesbian, feminist—as the exact nexus that Black nationalism must repress in order for its imagined community based on Blackness to cohere, she is unrepressing, and is thus coming back to haunt. The fact that she herself, Black, lesbian, feminist, is a sign of the "more than one story at a time" or the "spiraling affects" makes *her* the ghost. But she situates herself not so much as the ghost that haunts Malcolm but rather as one of the two ghosts that haunt the present formations of Black community. In this way, she implies that Malcolm X is himself "more than one story at a time" and that his ghost demands that we understand his legacy as discontinuous, contradictory, and multifarious. In so doing, she signals a connection between herself and Malcolm that is, in Gordon's words, "anything but transparent and referential."

Having "reclaimed" Malcolm X as her ancestor from those who would define his lineage more narrowly, Lorde goes on to support this assertion by re-reading the trajectory of his political vision. She writes, "In the last year of his life, Malcolm X added a breadth to his essential vision that would have brought him, had he lived, into inevitable confrontation with the question of difference as a creative and necessary force for change."[11] This breadth, she observes, spurred him to reconsider several key beliefs: the role of women, his relationship to Martin Luther King and politics of nonviolence, and, most importantly for her essay and for this book, separatism, because he was in the process of rethinking "the societal conditions under which *alliances* and *coalitions* must indeed occur."[12]

Lorde goes on to argue that in order for Malcolm's vision of coalition to cohere, it means letting go of a monolithic conception of Blackness and accepting the multiplicity of his legacy. This does not mean dismissing the shared history of racial violence that binds Black people. For while a heroic mode of minority nationalist memorialization can be incorporated into neoliberal power, so too can the dismissal of racialized violence or a containment narrative that posits Malcolm X's death as instigating, only to resolve, a U.S. national crisis of conscience. As such, rather than negate a Black nationalist impulse to mourn Black death as a consequence of a uniquely anti-Black violence, she affirms, redirects, and enlarges it. The murder of Malcolm X is a loss that must be thus memorialized, for the forces that murdered him are in no way lessened, but rather exacerbated in the moment of her speech. If mourning Malcolm means rededicating oneself to a critique of "the forces which dehumanize us from the outside,"[13] she is certainly mourning him. Indeed, she characterizes Black history as "four hundred years of survival as an endangered species."[14] In so doing, she identifies minority nationalist narratives of Black homogeneity as an important response to racist violence, writing, "Historically, difference had been used so cruelly against us that as a people we were reluctant to tolerate any diversion from what was externally defined as Blackness."[15] Yet this response to violence can become a replication of the violence it is meant to protect Black people from. "In the 60s . . . a small and vocal part of the Black community lost sight of the fact that unity does not mean unanimity."[16] Taking Malcolm's ghost and the multiplicity of his legacy seriously means acknowledging that "Black" is already a coalition of diverse constituents: "Unity implies the coming together of elements which are, *to begin with,* varied and diverse in their particular natures."[17] This is the basis for her assertion that she, as a Black lesbian feminist, can speak with Malcolm's voice; to imply as she does that Malcolm's legacy is multifaceted is to imply that Black communities are already varied. And if Black communities are not homogeneously unified but are themselves made up of diverse and heterogeneous entities, they are themselves always already coalitional. As such, Lorde acknowledges the violence of anti-Blackness not to situate Black death as the ultimate injury, whether it be that upon which political claims can be anchored,[18] or alternatively, that which cannot ever be remedied and thus subverts the very notion of the political,[19] but to undermine any sense that any one people or history has cornered the market in suffering and violation.

Instead, her theorization of difference *within* Black communities leads to a theorization of coalition *across* boundaries of race, class, and nation; and for Lorde, this is particularly important in the 1980s. The aftermath of the revolutionary struggles in the 1960s means increased conservatism, retrenchment, and the incorporation of previously radical politics and actors into the structures of power in the 1980s. Coalitional practice, then, is "the force we need to face the multidimensional threats to our survival in the 80s. There is no such thing as a single-issue struggle because we do not live single-issue lives."[20]

The diversity of Black communities, which we can recognize through the acceptance of the multiplicity of Malcolm X's legacy, is far from being a liability to the unity of the race. Instead, it is the very quality from which coalitional strategies emerge. Lorde writes, "Each one of us here is a link in the connection between antipoor legislation, gay shootings, the burning of synagogues, street harassment, attacks against women, and insurgent violence against Black people."[21] However, this connection requires an honest appraisal of the stakes of coalition, an appraisal of exactly what one might have to give up in order to advance the cause of social justice. She continues:

> I ask myself as well as each one of you, exactly what alteration in the particular fabric of my everyday life does this connection call for? . . . In what way do I contribute to the subjugation of *any part of those who I call my people?* Insight must illuminate the particulars of our lives: who labors to make the bread we waste, or the energy it takes to make nuclear poisons which will not biodegrade for one thousand years; or who goes blind assembling the microtransistors in our inexpensive calculators?[22]

Rather than define racialization as only a shared and uniform devaluation in comparison to whiteness, or along a fixed scale of devaluation with Blackness as the ultimate and exemplary category of abjection, Lorde demands that those in the audience—and, implicitly, we as readers— all take into account our own complicities with power over and against others. In so doing, Lorde articulates a politics that is not based on the protection of self-interest or claims to injury, but on a critique of the uneven but connected dispersion of death and devaluation that make self-protective politics threaten to render others precarious. Speaking to Black students in the 1980s, Lorde marks the importance of "Learning from the 60s," asking them to consider those who pay the costs of their inclusion. Referencing the social movements of the 1960s that made possible their presence at institutions like Harvard and Radcliffe, the epitome of racial and class exclusion, she exhorts them to remember—now that they have access, however fragile and contingent, to the college educations and white-collar jobs that would have been near unthinkable prior to desegregation and affirmative action—who makes the "inexpensive calculators" they may be using at those schools and at those jobs.[23]

In observing that inequities and forms of devaluation exist within and between racial groups, Lorde does not dismiss the brutal history of racial violence and devaluation that subtends racial categorization but rather calls attention to new configurations of power that, in contingently extending protection and value to formerly categorically marginalized identities, "are unevenly sutured to older categories of race, gender, and sexuality."[24] Lorde provides a rigorous, deeply materialist analysis that extends beyond Black communities as well as the boundaries of the United States, providing a transnational analysis of the material costs of our own comfort. However, rather than allow this insight—that any politics of self-protection requires subjecting others to violence—to foreclose political possibility, Lorde instead crafts an alternative vision of a politics not based on self-interest. An alternative imagination of community that does not depend on identification or equivalence is neither easy nor utopian, for a truly relational vision of community must mean being willing to jeopardize one's own security for that of others. In so doing, she casts Malcolm X's life and death in different terms; rather than allow the brutal fact of his death to limit the politics of Blackness to a circumscribed set of people, she defines Blackness as an analytic that allows us to see the ways in which power puts us all in unequal relation to each other. In so doing, Lorde wields Black feminism as a comparative method.[25]

I begin with this moment from Lorde's work because it offers a sense of political (im)possibility attuned to the manifestations of power in our moment. Attempting to name what Lorde is doing, I realized that Lorde had a word for it herself: difference. "Difference," as Lorde and others used it, has had many different meanings. For the purposes of this book, I use the term to reference a cultural and epistemological practice that holds in suspension (without requiring resolution) contradictory, mutually exclusive, and negating impulses. "Difference" names an epistemological position, ontological condition, and political strategy that reckon with the shift in the technologies of power that we might as well call "neoliberal."

I define neoliberalism foremost as an epistemological structure of disavowal, a means of claiming that racial and gendered violences are things of the past. It does so by *affirming* certain modes of racialized, gendered, and sexualized life, particularly through invitation into reproductive respectability, *so as to* disavow its exacerbated production of premature death. Historically, it emerged as a response to the liberation movements of the post–World War II period—by which I mean movements for decolonization, desegregation, and self-determination, within and outside of the territorial bounds of the United States. As I describe in more detail below, these movements challenged the ideological tenets of white supremacy and Western civilization that undergirded settler colonialism, Jim Crow segregation, and franchise colonialism all over the world. In response to these movements, a new neoliberal order arose based on the selective protection and proliferation of minoritized life *as the very mechanism* for the brutal exacerbation of minoritized death. Neoliberal ideologies hold out the promise of protection from premature death in exchange for complicity with this pretense. In the pages that follow, *Death beyond Disavowal* finds the memories of death and precarity that neoliberal ideologies attempt to erase.

What I am calling "difference," as Lorde and other women of color feminists wielded it, emerged as a political and ethical rejoinder to this neoliberal move that both brutalizes *and* affirms. Knowing that oppositional critiques of the state as wielded through minority nationalisms can become incorporated into the neoliberal discourses of the 1980s, for example, potentially through such events as "Malcolm X Weekend," but also understanding that such oppositional critiques are still vitally important against a consistently and increasingly violent state, Lorde attests to the importance of sustaining two oppositional political, epistemological, and ethical practices at the same time. This deployment of difference is particularly necessary in the contemporary moment in which the protection of racialized and gendered life ironically produces exacerbated death. This book is thus about how death can and indeed must be the basis of a politics in the contemporary moment, impossibly alongside the antagonistic pursuit of a politics based on the preservation of life. The theoretical and political practice of "difference" holds in suspension the ostensibly mutually exclusive states of life and death. In so doing, it remembers the exacerbated dispersal of minoritized death that neoliberalism disavows.

In the case of Lorde's speech, difference inheres in her ability to both mark the uniqueness of anti-Black violence as well as insist that it is possible to connect this violence to those experienced by other racialized, gendered, devalued peoples. Difference inheres in her acknowledgement of Malcolm X's significance to a Black people, while at the same time challenging the notion that there is "a" Black people, and in so doing, widening his legacy to include others. Further, Lorde's mobilization of a politics based on self-critique over one based on self-interest is an example of a politics of difference that radically rethinks self and community. Jeopardizing one's own security is always a fraught exercise, but it has particular significance and stakes at this historical moment, because security—or lack thereof—becomes exactly the site where power operates in the wake of the social movements of the post–World War II period.

In so doing, Lorde offers a politically useful alternative to racial exceptionalism—that is, the belief that the histories and conditions of particular racial groups are unique and incomparable, and that relational or comparative analyses between racial groups must necessarily eradicate or disenable an understanding of racial specificity.[26] Indeed, as many have argued, the self-consciously named "women of color feminism" or "Third World feminism" of the 1970s and 1980s, of which Lorde is an important contributor, emerged precisely to enable such a political analytic able to articulate coalitional practice based on, rather than in spite of, historical and material differences between and within racial groups.[27]

The fact that Lorde makes this political intervention at an event named after Malcolm X is apropos: the assassination of Malcolm X is often deployed as the climactic event in a familiar narrative of those social movements, one that characterizes the liberation movements of the post–World War II period as radical, heroic (implicitly, or sometimes explicitly, masculine) resistance to white supremacy brutally crushed by state repression, assassination, and violence, and that consequently understands the period of the 1980s onward as apolitical and rudderless. Alternatively, the liberal, official nationalist narrative is one in which the crises marked by these social movements have been resolved, and those once-radical figures either have been incorporated into the U.S. security state or rendered "terrorists."[28]

I see this historical period somewhat differently—namely, as the latest phase of what Cedric Robinson has called "racial capitalism."[29] As I go on to explain in more detail in chapter 1, these movements engaged in heterogeneous struggles against the conditions that bound racialized, gendered, and sexualized difference to forms of social and physical death. As Sylvia Wynter has argued, these "multiple anti-colonial social-protest movements and intellectual challenges of the period to which we give the name, 'The Sixties,'"[30] were a challenge to a Western bourgeois conception of Man that colonizes the very definition of the human itself, and in so doing, required racialized categories of the nonhuman. Wynter continues, "One of the major empirical effects . . . would be 'the rise of Europe' and its construction of the 'world civilization' on the one hand, and, on the other, African enslavement, Latin American conquest, and Asian subjugation."[31] Wynter notes that these movements were "co-opted, reterritorialized" in modes both "sanitized" and "harshly intensified."[32] This book traces how this reterritorialization happened precisely within these movements' engagement with the "master code of symbolic life and death."[33] At the same time, it identifies the discontinuous, ghostly, but not entirely devastated, remains of these struggles' challenge to the symbolics of life and death, which I argue reemerge through *culture*.

In this process of reterritorialization, certain minoritized subjects and populations became recognizable as protectable life (what Michel

Foucault might call "biopolitics") for the first time.[34] As I will go on to explore in chapter 1, while many of the struggles of the liberation movements were predicated on the notion that life and death were not mutually exclusive but were always mutually constitutive, those aspects of these movements were erased, dismissed, or outright extinguished. These social movements of the post–World War II period were so fundamentally concerned with the life/death binary because this binary was exactly what made racialized, gendered, and sexualized difference coterminous with social devaluation and vulnerability to physical death in the earlier era of racial capital. These social movements of the post–World War II period undermined the legitimacy of this form of racial capitalist modernity, exposing liberal democracy as a hypocritical ideological formation undergirded by white supremacy. In so doing, they inaugurated a new neoliberal racial order under which it became possible for some sectors of populations previously only relegated to death also to be recognized as worthy of life. These movements were made up of a number of differentiated and sometimes contradictory impulses and tactics, but this heterogeneity was occluded in the resulting incorporative phase, whether it came in the form of state-based civil rights in Western nations or postcolonial Global South nation-states managed by native elites. The management and containment of desegregation movements (which were themselves heterogeneous and strains of which were rooted in radical, labor, and internationalist organizing traditions), through the codification of civil rights legislation and the dominant narrative of civil rights respectability, became the technology through which radical movements, both within the United States and abroad, were disciplined.[35] Further, the more radical aspects of these movements were subjected to brutal state violence and repression, including assassination, incarceration, infiltration, and vilification.[36] Thus, while the project of making racialized life recognizable as a form of life that must be protected and encouraged to proliferate was only one of a number of connected tactics (and by no means the most important of such strategies), such a politics of recognition has become legitimated and institutionalized, so much so that it has become how these movements are remembered.[37]

Thus, the varied strategies of these movements are narrowly re-membered as contained by the most recognizable and articulable goals, commensurate with the logic of political modernity: that of claiming for oneself (and by extension, one's "people," imagined as discrete, coher-ent, and unified) the status of protectable life. As I argue in the section below entitled "Gender, Race, and Sexuality at the Neoliberal Shift," pro-tectable life became sutured to reproductive respectability, with all the attendant gendered and sexualized implications. As far as these social movements were invested in respectable reproduction, they replicated the investments of modernity. The reaction to these radical social move-ments was thus twofold: the brutal crackdown by the forces of the state as well as the incorporation and affirmation of those aspects of these movements that were appropriable—that which replicated the norma-tive investments of political modernity.

These critiques of race in turn became the vocabulary for a new mode of power that narrowly acceded to these social movements by extending biopolitical protection to certain legible and visible sectors of formerly marginalized groups. Thus, currently, we see racialized, gendered, and sexualized subjects with access to capital and citizenship in ways that were previously unimaginable, whether through the emergence of a global Asian technological and professional class that utilizes citizenship "flex-ibly" (and that are accorded forms of pastoral care whether or not they are actually citizens of a particular nation), through the creation of a class of elite Global South nationalist state managers and bureaucrats in the wake of decolonization (a class that facilitates the neocolonial extraction of wealth from the Global South to the Global North), or through the creation of a post–civil rights–era African American middle class through the establishment of new categories of jobs in social welfare, policing, and government administration that positioned them as conduits for state violence against and disciplining of the racialized and immigrant poor.[38] Similarly, this era also witnesses the emergence of homonorma-tive gay and lesbian identities that mark themselves as parents, tourists, homeowners, and taxpayers.[39] The existence of these formations do not alleviate, but rather exacerbate the conditions that lead to the devaluation of poor, racialized, and sexual- and gender-deviant populations, and the relegation of these populations to premature death.

In other words, the liberation movements of the post–World War II period put the older political mode in crisis, but the reestablishment of a life-affirming politics by those aspects of these movements that have captured the dominant imaginary has meant that the mutually constitutive relationship between life and death—the fact that life for some must mean death for others—remains disavowed and thus unchallenged. The selective protection of certain racialized, gendered, and sexualized subjects actually *further* obfuscates this mutually constitutive relationship between protectable life and ungrievable death.

Counter to conventional wisdom, the existence of these protected categories do not prevent, but rather exacerbate, the devaluation of others and their consequent relegation to death. This modality of power is particularly striking in the way in which racialized, sexualized, and gendered differences are both invisible *and* entirely structuring. Those whose lives are unprotectable, whose social and political statuses are so negligible that they do not merit recognition or protection, are referenced by terms like "prostitute" or "drug dealer." "Homeless" or "welfare cheat" or "illegal" or "immigrant" are other such terms.[40] Only the most willfully naive of us could overlook the ways in which these categories are deeply racialized and gendered, yet in ways that allow for the disavowal of race, gender, and sexuality as criteria for precarity. Such names legitimate the wholesale violence against and criminalization of the racialized poor, all the more terrifying because such racialized violence happens without having to explicitly invoke racial, gendered, or sexualized discourse. The most obvious example of one whose life cannot be respected is the "terrorist," which Sohail Daulatzai has observed is the twenty-first-century version of "savage."[41] The deployment of this name underwrites the violence of U.S. military devastation in the Middle East, the Pacific, Latin America, and Africa, and constitutes the illegibility of Palestinian deaths. This condition—whereby certain lives are deemed lives and others not, and certain deaths appear able to be mourned, and others not at all—is the generalizable condition of contemporary power, manifested globally.[42]

This neoliberal technology of power, which Roderick Ferguson has so aptly called the "affirmation of difference,"⁴³ is one through which certain racialized, gendered, and sexualized populations are protected and certain "antiracist" ideas become acceptable and indeed even hegemonic. It does not supplant as much as it supplements, and thus enables, the more established role of racialized, gendered, and sexualized difference as the process by which death is dispersed.⁴⁴ In the wake of the liberation movements of the post–World War II period we have seen a new form of power that both affirms racialized, gendered, and sexualized difference, yet through this affirmation, is able to levy even more brutally exacerbated forms of death and destruction to poor, racialized, and sexually "deviant" populations. At the same time, decrying these deathly conditions can be institutionally incorporated, as I am acutely aware as someone who makes a living as a scholar and teacher of ethnic and gender studies. In this context, the racialized and colonized poor are rendered vulnerable so as to produce them as a form of surplus labor, and are also imagined as backward, homophobic, and patriarchal as a means of rendering them as morally bankrupt and excluded from a privileged liberal subjecthood.⁴⁵ These conditions are symptomatic of new epistemological and "commonsensical" ways of reading racial, gender, and sexual difference that emerged out of and as a reaction to the liberation movements of the post–World War II period: the cultivation of "color blindness" as well as outright racist hate, and correspondingly, greater discursive avenues to represent whiteness as victimization;⁴⁶ the racialization of ideologies as well as the racialization of bodies;⁴⁷ the establishment of white liberalism alongside white supremacy;⁴⁸ and the commodification and affirmation of minority difference alongside its repression.⁴⁹ Alongside this new form of (bio)power that "lets die," outright deadly, necropolitical regimes that "make die" also proliferate. These two forms of legitimated death are not separable, but exist alongside each other. Prison abolitionist scholars and activists, for example, importantly remind us of one institution that is undergirded by the idea that certain populations are dangerous for societal security and quality of life.⁵⁰ Both are enabled by the limited incorporation and affirmation of certain forms of racialized, gendered, or sexualized difference, insofar as this incorporation and affirmation preserves the fundamental process of Western political modernity—the ostensible protection of lives that enables the dispersal of death.

In this way, formerly uniformly devalued categories are now populated with those whose lives are protectable and those whose lives are not, but the basic bifurcation of life and death still remains. As such, the life/death binary retains its ability to legitimate the deaths of some to protect the lives of others. As to be expected, those subjects who were unruly toward the normativizing tendencies within these social movements—women of color and queer of color formations foremost among them—described exactly the dangers of this developing duality of power, and importantly, provided a strategy against it, based on the inevitability of complicity with power and the repudiation of protection. A recent generation of social movements scholarship[51] that focuses on the interventions of queer and feminist activists highlights what Lorde herself also makes manifestly clear with her introduction of herself as "Black, Lesbian, Feminist"—that is, that the lives of those rendered marginal by race, gender, and sexuality are never only or entirely protected by those particular aspects of these social movements that limit themselves to claims for the protection of life. Thus, while acknowledging this moment as a violent state assault on radicalism, feminist and queer formations within these movements also understand this moment as requiring new kinds of politics and a different definition of what a movement is that address both the repression *and* incorporation of difference. As Lorde implies when she asserts that "the raw energy of Black determination released in the 6os . . . is still being felt in movements for change among women, other peoples of Color, gays, the handicapped—among all the disenfranchised peoples of this society,"[52] positing the 1980s as a period of decline erases the vibrancy of the activist efforts in the era, many of which were instigated and led by women of color and queers, from welfare rights to reproductive justice to prison abolition to a renewed politicization of culture and art.[53]

Lorde's reminder of the forgotten, fetishized labor that produced the calculators used by the Harvard-Radcliffe BSU reveals how presciently she predicted the precise technology of our contemporary conditions.

Lorde's question to the BS—"In what way do I contribute to the subjugation of *any part of those who I call my people?*"—is an example of "difference" as a cultural practice that pushes past the limits of the political as it is conventionally defined. It articulates "difference" as a contradictory, *impossible* political and representational strategy that brings together and holds in suspension the conflicting goals of the preservation or protection of the political subject *and* the recognition of the others at whose expense that subject is protected. In other words, Lorde's query insists on remembering those whose deaths are necessary but forgotten, so that others may live.

In using "impossible" in this way to define Lorde's politics, I take up Gayatri Gopinath's and Kara Keeling's theorizations of impossibility. Gopinath defines the politics of impossibility as referencing "the range of oppositional practices, subjectivities, and alternative visions of collectivity that fall outside of the developmental narratives of colonialism, bourgeois nationalism, mainstream liberal feminism, and mainstream gay and lesbian politics and theory."[54] Keeling elegantly suggests why such alternative visions might be so impossible and yet so necessary by gesturing to the utility of affect, which while "bound to the ethico-political context of our times. . . . points toward the ways that whatever escapes recognition, whatever escapes meaning and valuation, exists as an impossible possibility within our shared reality . . . and therefore threatens to unsettle, if not destroy, the common senses on which that reality relies on for coherence as such."[55] That is, affect is one of the forces that somehow manages to exceed the present-day conditions of possibility to gesture to "a different epistemological, if not ontological and empirical, regime."[56] The shift to the interrogative mode, as I have observed elsewhere, can be a shift into the realm of the impossible, the unanswerable, and the epistemologically unstable.[57] Lorde launches the impossible but necessary politics of "difference" by posing a question that can never be answered, but that must be continually addressed, enacting a temporality of suspension rather than a resolution.

Following theorists like Lorde, this book attempts to keep in dialectical tension two contradictory political imperatives: that of mourning death and of understanding death as proliferative. First, how do we describe the ways in which racialized, gendered, and sexualized difference are produced currently? I propose that we track how these systems of difference operate by tracking how death gets deployed. How are some populations rendered more vulnerable to death? How populations are subjected to death still occur along the lines of race, gender, and sexuality, but in different configurations than in the era before the liberation movements of the post–World War II period. Yet there is a second problem: what does this mean, and how do we address it? What "politics" can adequately account for and address our current condition, and how is this even possible when the very definition of modern "politics" is based on the notion of self-preservation? This is to say that when we ask this question, we abut the question of what death means, what it means to be vulnerable. If we stop with only the first question, with what we are able to *track*, what we are able to *know*, we run the risk of relegating these vulnerable populations to being merely a problem to be fixed. We see them only as those we must bring into the realm of the living, rather than those who, in and through their very condition of vulnerability to death (their deathly existence) produce their own forms of meaning(lessness) and new definitions of (non)existence that expand our own narrow sense. Insofar as our ability to live protected lives *depends upon* their inability to do so, a politics that registers vulnerability to death simply as something to be eradicated and sees these deathly subjects simply as those we have yet to bring into the protection of life merely advances the validation of life that legislates their deaths. In so doing, we replicate the conditions that create these deathworlds by making *life* the only site of meaning or political possibility. This project thus asks: What are the various and proliferating meanings of death? What kinds of social (non)existence does "death" describe? Put another way, what kinds of knowledges, modes of being, affects, memories, temporalities, embodiments do these populations that are marked for death, that inhabit what Zygmant Bauman calls "death in life,"[58] produce? And how may we apprehend those products? Are these different deathly modes of knowing and being always observable? Do they register on us not as presence, but as absence, or what Avery Gordon calls "ghosts"?[59] Is it (im)possible to build a politics around them? If so, how must we redefine what the political is and can be?

Race, Gender, and Sexuality at the Neoliberal Shift

Neoliberalism is a structure of disavowal, an epistemological framing, a way of seeing and not seeing. It claims that protected life is available to all and that premature death comes only to those whose criminal actions and poor choices make them deserve it. This neoliberal disavowal legitimates the proliferation and exacerbation of what Ruth Wilson Gilmore has described as "the state-sanctioned and/or extra-legal production and exploitation of group-differentiated vulnerabilities to premature death, in distinct yet densely interconnected political geographies."[60] This exacerbated proliferation of death is by turns hidden and justified by an unprecedented access to protectable life for more and more sectors of populations once categorically denied access to this protection because of race, gender, or sexuality.

This neoliberal disavowal is a reaction against the crises brought on by the social movements of the post–World War II era. As Roderick Ferguson and I explain in a recent essay, while neoliberalism has been defined more narrowly to reference the espousal of a "free market" approach to governance most famously championed by Milton Friedman and the Chicago School, or more broadly to reference the extension of economistic definitions of value to all sectors of social and political life, we might more expansively define this term to reference the ideological and epistemological shift that occurred with the emergence of the current stage of racial capital following the worldwide liberation movements of the post–World War II period, movements that encompassed struggles for decolonization, desegregation, and revolutionary engagements over the state.[61] These movements were, importantly, ideological and representational contests over the legitimacy of colonial and racial modes of power, upon which capitalist extraction of value was dependent. In the wake of World War II, the global imperial vacuum left by the decimation of Europe opened the way for decolonization movements across the globe. As Cedric Robinson has argued, "While the official world contestation, the Cold War, has been taken to have subsumed all other conflicts, it is now possible to cast the competition between the two imperial hegemons, the United States and the Soviet Union, as a historical sidebar to the struggles to obtain or vanquish racial domination."[62] In this context, as Derrick Bell Jr. and Mary Dudziak have argued, the U.S. nation-state had to reckon with movements for racial liberation at home if it were to seem credible as a force for antiracism in a rapidly decolonizing world.[63] Thus began an era of what Jodi Melamed has called "official antiracism," in which the U.S. nation-state and capital affirmed the rhetoric and some-times the figureheads of liberation movements, while outright suppress-ing their redistributive aims.[64]

What is often not considered in the scholarship on neoliberalism is the centrality of Black women's sexuality to this shift. Here, we are indebted to Black feminist scholarship, which has importantly highlighted the ways in which discourses of respectability and the gendered and sexualized pathologization and criminalization of Black communities have under-girded neoliberal politics.[65] As many such scholars have documented, racial capital in the nineteenth and early twentieth century was premised on systems of enslavement and Jim Crow segregation that required the Cult of True Womanhood and Victorian ideals of sexual propriety, reserved for white women, and corresponding images of Black female deviance.[66] In the post–social movements moment, Black women are still narrated as sexually deviant, albeit in service of a different set of geopolitical and economic structures. Candice Jenkins observes that "the perceived inability of African Americans to conform to middle-class understandings of family and appropriate sexual behavior has hardly diminished since its origins during the ante-bellum period."[67] Through precise, devastating readings of the 1965 policy brief known as the Moynihan Report and the 1996 Personal Responsibility and Work Opportunity Reconciliation Act of 1996, Jenkins outlines the conditions that make intimacy doubly vulnerable for Black people. I bring her analy-sis to bear on the conversation on neoliberalism as context for why such punitive discourses of Black pathological sexuality circulate so steadily to this day.

Toward this end, I also return to the Moynihan Report, or more for-mally, "The Negro Family: A Case for National Action," authored by sociology professor and Assistant Secretary of Labor Daniel Patrick Moynihan, and published by the U.S. Department of Labor. While much ink[68] has been spilled on critiques and defenses of the Moynihan Report and its ideological ilk that blame a host of social problems, from poverty to crime to violence, on the ostensible reproductive and domestic failings of poor Black women, it is not a conversation that has intersected much with those on neoliberalism.[69] However, I find in the Moynihan Report perhaps the clearest symptomatic distillation of the shifts in technologies of power that mark the past four decades, that era that has been called neoliberal. To restate, my definition of neoliberalism is as an epistemological response on the part of global racial capital to the growing illegitimacy of then-dominant modes of social relation, based on exclusion from institutions of citizenship and nationalism: Jim Crow segregation as the aftermath of chattel slavery, franchise colonialism, and settler colonialism. Worldwide movements for decolonization, desegregation, and self-determination challenged the viability of these social relations and the discourses of white supremacy and Western civilizations that subtended them. The response, of which the Moynihan Report is an exemplary case, was to not only invest racialized communities with what Foucault has called deductive or repressive power but also induct such communities into affirmative, productive biopower.[70] Neoliberalism thus can be characterized by the coexistence of diverse forms of power—both repressive and affirmative, necropolitical and biopolitical—at the same time.

In describing neoliberalism in this way, as a change in the distribution of respectability in response to the crises in racial capital as marked by the social movements of the post–World War II period, I contribute to contemporary scholarship on the nature of global capital.[71] I do so by re-narrating a shift that has been explained as instigated by everything from changes in communication technology, to a crisis among Cold War superpowers, to the development of the atom bomb; in my re-narration, I center mid-twentieth-century movements for liberation.

As can be seen in the Moynihan Report, a crucial element of incorporating Black communities in the United States into biopolitics was to constitute them as populations requiring help and care (by narrating them as presently deviant), and in particular, help in attaining reproductive and domestic respectability and security. Access (or lack thereof) to gendered and sexual respectability becomes the dividing line between those who are rendered deviant, immoral, and thus precarious and those whose value to capital has been secured through a variety of norms. The invitation to respectability becomes a way of regulating and punishing those populations it purports to help; thus, in the neoliberal moment, "care" becomes the conduit for violence, both epistemological and physical. The Moynihan Report warns of a grim future for African Americans that might not improve despite the passage of the Civil Rights and Voting Rights Acts because of the "breakdown in the Negro family." This "breakdown," by which Moynihan meant the high rates of mother-headed or "matriarchal" families without the presence of Black men, produces a variety of ills, which he described in the infamous phrase "tangle of pathologies." Strengthening the Black family by encouraging patriarchally organized, heteroreproductive domesticity thus must be a priority for "national action," according to the report.

While this aspect of the Moynihan Report is quite familiar, other less-analyzed parts of the report make explicit certain connections that we today might have forgotten—that is, that the regulation of Black female sexuality as ostensibly a means of bringing Black communities into the fold of respectable national culture was motivated by the United States' precarious position in a Cold War struggle that became split along racial lines. The report opens:

> It is in no way a matter of chance that the nonviolent tactics and philosophy of the movement, as it began in the South, were consciously adopted from the techniques by which the Congress Party undertook to free the Indian nation from British colonial rule. It was not a matter of chance that the Negro movement caught on fire in America at just that moment when the nations of Africa were gaining their freedom. Nor is it merely incidental that the world should have fastened its attention on events in the United States at a time when the possibility that the nations of the world will divide along color lines seems suddenly not only possible, but even imminent.
>
> (Such racist views have made progress within the Negro community itself—which can hardly be expected to be immune to a virus that is

endemic in the white community. The Black Muslim doctrines, based on total alienation from the white world, exert a powerful influence. On the far left, the attraction of Chinese Communism can no longer be ignored.)

It is clear that what happens in America is being taken as a sign of what can, or must, happen in the world at large.[72]

Moynihan situates struggles for desegregation and civil rights (what he calls the "Negro movement") within the context of decolonization worldwide (including India and "the nations of Africa"), highlighting the internationalist imaginaries of U.S.-based movements (e.g., the potential influence of "Black Muslims" and "Chinese Communism") as a threat to U.S. global power, or in other words, the United States' influence over the terms of resource extraction and capital accumulation within the new world order.[73]

The Moynihan Report thus makes perfectly evident its own context within a field of power that was reacting to the seismic shifts in social relations caused by the movements for liberation of the twentieth century. The Moynihan Report's focus on what Sara Clarke Kaplan calls the "Black reproductive"[74] and its fixation with regulating Black female sexuality is no accident, but is symptomatic of a shift away from earlier social relations that produced racialized subjects as *universally* exempt from normative modes of reproduction, intimacy, and sexuality.[75] Instead, the Moynihan Report redistributed value and vulnerability *within* racialized communities. This did not diminish the allure of what Jenkins calls the "salvific wish" in Black culture, a strategy of protecting Black communities from the violences legitimated by narratives of Black sexual deviance by ascribing to propriety and respectability. Instead, the salvific wish became incorporated as a neoliberal mechanism through which categories of the devalued and unprotectable were produced, categories into which Black populations were predominantly relegated. Jenkins observes that the "productive (or affirmative) nature of power exists precisely at those moments when African Americans participate in their own victimization through the project of self-imposed sexual and familial propriety."[76]

The establishment of white liberal state policy and the conditional invitation of certain formerly marginalized populations into respectability has been bolstered by, and has enabled, a discourse of rationality that equates capitalist development with political and social freedom. As I go on to elaborate in chapter 2, this invitation into respectability enables the more efficient extraction of surplus value in forms both economic and affective from populations rendered marginal and deviant. Such invitations to respectability have had different manifestations and effects in different parts of the globe. The United States (and other white settler colonial states) has "reformed" itself along the lines of what Jodi Melamed has called "a formally antiracist, liberal-capitalist modernity whose driving force has been a series of successive official or state-recognized U.S. antiracisms,"[77] or the development of white liberalism as an official state policy. This state-recognized nominal antiracism has the effect of eliding and thus exacerbating, rather than mitigating, state violence against racialized populations, becoming the foundational part of neoliberal disavowal. At the same time, a neocolonial world order contains formerly colonized territories (now nation-states in the wake of decolonization) through international debt and structural adjustment on the one hand, and militarism, increasingly narrated as a form of humanitarianism, on the other.[78] Liberal feminism and normative notions of respectable heteropatriarchal sexuality are now crucial to legitimating such relations of domination.[79] The process by which capital is extracted from the poor and redistributed upward, called "structural adjustment" in countries of the Global South, is often accomplished through what is called "privatization" in North America and Western Europe. A transnational Asian "model minority" and a new Black bourgeoisie, for example, can only now exist because of U.S. militarism in Asia, on the one hand, and the rendering surplus of poor people of color, warehoused in prisons or punitively regulated through welfare "reform," on the other.[80] Alongside such brutal demonstrations of state violence, scholars have noted that NGOs and what has been termed the "non-profit industrial complex" are crucial to managing populations marked as deviant, and demonstrate the dispersal of regulation and governance beyond the literal apparatuses of the state.[81]

In this context, respectability, increasingly defined by the attainment of monogamous couplehood, normative reproductivity, and consumerist subjectivity, has become indispensible for determining those who are protected and those who are precarious.[82] Given this, we can now recognize the Moynihan Report as an exemplary document of neoliberalism. Roderick Ferguson has usefully situated the Moynihan Report as producing a discourse that legitimates the regulation of working-class women of color within a new global division of labor that took shape within neocolonial and neoliberal political economies based increasingly on a feminized proletariat and on domestic and service labor.[83] In conjunction with this argument, we can read the report as performing a *rhetoric* of care for Black communities that renders such communities more deviant and punishable.

In the face of this, what it means to struggle is immensely complicated. Fortunately, we have a rich tradition of thought and practice that attends to the ways in which, as Patricia Williams attests, "that life is complicated is a fact of great analytical importance."[84] This tradition, upon which I rely heavily, has been called "women of color feminism,"[85] and this practice of engaging the complexity of life has been called "intersectionality." It is in this context of neoliberalism that I reconsider the interventions of women of color feminism and queer of color critique, as articulated in activism, theory, and cultural production. Women of color feminism emerged out of this moment to articulate the violences of biopolitical incorporation. The major intervention of women of color feminism is not only the critique of the exclusion of minoritized populations from protectable life, but a critique of the dialectic of life/death that structures political modernity. I began this book with Lorde as an exemplary model of all three, but Lorde is one of a number of theorists and artists since the 1960s who have taken on these particular configurations of power. In challenging the politics of respectability, women of color feminists make a crucial intervention into the foundations of neoliberalism. Women of color feminism's engagement with the liberation movements of the post–World War II era thus not only provides a localized critique of the masculinism and sexism of minority nationalist movements and of the racism and classism of mainstream white feminism but also offers an analysis of a broad historical process that was incorporating those elements of nationalist and feminist movements into a new modality of power at that very moment.

Of course, women of color feminism itself was not impervious to marginalization and containment, as in the late 1980s and 1990s, when the rise of multiculturalism misread women of color feminism as espousing a celebratory definition of "difference." Referencing an even earlier era, Nick Mitchell demonstrates that the category "woman of color," or "Third World women," rather than creating a barrier to the domestication and management of feminism by the academy, enabled the institutionalization of women's studies departments and programs within universities.[86] Women of color feminism, often referred to obliquely through the invocation of "intersectionality," can thus be interpreted narrowly only as this defanged version, and dismissed as identitarian, antitheoretical, essentialist, or irrelevant.[87] I would argue that the techniques of neoliberal multiculturalism in the wake of the social movements of the 1960s and 1970s to incorporate, minimalize, misread, or neglect powerful antiracist, feminist, and queer critiques was honed precisely against "women of color" as a category. This book is a part of ongoing efforts by a number of scholars and activists to challenge such revisionist misreadings.[88] Returning to Jenkins, the literary texts that she examines in her study are just a part of a larger field of political and discursive projects against neoliberal deployments of respectability as the legitimating principle for the distribution of life and death. We might think of such disparate but connected modes of Black feminist and women of color feminist activism as welfare reform, prison abolition, anti-sterilization campaigns, gender violence, and other such struggles as refusing the "salvific wish" for respectability and placing at its center the most devalued and nonnormative subjects.

In this way, I understand what Roderick Ferguson has called "queer of color critique" as a related and coincident formation to women of color feminism.[89] If we think of "queer" not as an identity category but as a politics that eschews gender and sexual normativity, we must include not only those subjects who engage in same-sex sexual practices but also "a range of dissident and non-heteronormative practices and desires"[90]— in other words, the "welfare queens" as well as the "punks" and "bulldaggers" of Cathy Cohen's foundational essay.[91] The central figures and texts of those we call women of color or Black feminist—Audre Lorde,

Barbara Smith, Cherríe Moraga, the Combahee River Collective, and so on—explicitly self-identify as lesbian and name a challenge to heterosexism and homophobia as central tenets of their political and intellectual practice.

Life and Death at the Foundations of Modernity

These conditions, in which adherence to and deviance from criteria of value (meaning life for some at the expense of others), in particular those constituted through reproductive respectability, are not new, but comprise the contradictions of the modern political order at its most logical extension. We know from the work of Michel Foucault that the modern political order is defined by exactly its politicization of life and death. In Foucault's analysis, it is differentiated from the earlier regime by its claim to protect and proliferate the lives of its subjects. Foucault observes that, beginning in the eighteenth century, modern political power became legitimated not only by its right to kill as in the earlier formation of "sovereignty" but also by a new biopolitical function to "make live," which meant taking up the proliferation and protection of life as its responsibility.[92] Giorgio Agamben extends this idea to argue that, by creating a category of political life that is different from the simply biological or physical state of life, the modern state produces a new form of "bare life," in which one is physically alive, but one's life is politically unprotectable.[93] Agamben traces the implications of the separation between biological and political life in Western politics through the figure of the *homo sacer* in Roman law, the subject who can be killed but can not be sacrificed to the gods. In this figure, "human life is included in the juridical order . . . solely in the form of its exclusion (that is, its capacity to be killed)."[94] Both theorists thus level devastating critiques of liberal claims that the state exists to preserve life, instead demonstrating the ways in which the modern political sphere's creation of a category of protectable life implies a category of unprotectable life. For Foucault, for example, the very move to protect and proliferate life allows it to more efficiently disperse death through the *withdrawal* of this protection.[95] In Agamben's formulation, the once obscure and exceptional political figure of the *homo sacer* and its corresponding status of "bare life" comes to characterize the function of the entire modern political order, with the Holocaust as its exemplary event. As such, the only allowable and legible goal or aim in this formation of the political order is to make claims on life, or, in other words, to act in the preservation of one's own life, which is always at the expense of others'.

While the uneven and limited extension of life to *certain* sectors of racialized, gendered, and sexualized populations that were previously unrecognizable as protectable life is a new maneuver, such a maneuver simply reconfirms the modern political order that makes the protection of life its primary legitimation. That is, this particular relation between life and death is not new, but is utterly commensurate with the structuring binary of racial capitalist modernity, which captured the symbolics of life and death such that they are not simply *biological* states of existence or nonexistence, but are powerful constructs that connect these physical states with political agency, epistemological legibility, and ontological coherence, or the lack thereof. When the social movements of the post–World War II period challenged the relationship between race and death, they exposed and addressed the foundational dialectic that structures modern politics: a disavowal of the ways in which the political protection of life is always predicated on the dispersal of death. The neoliberal incorporation of difference simply responded to this challenge by rendering uneven the relationship between death and racialized, gendered, and sexualized difference, but in so doing, reconfirmed the underlying relationship between life and death.

This process whereby the lives of some are protected at the expense of others is thus inherently, primarily, and always a racial and colonial project, a condition that scholars such as Orlando Patterson and Achille Mbembe have described. As Mbembe has observed, the condition of possibility for the European political entities's claims to protect life is to displace onto the colony the death-dealing upon which such entities depend.[96] Mbembe writes, "All manifestations of war and hostility that had been marginalized by a European legal imaginary find a place to reemerge in the colonies."[97] In other words, for Foucault, biopolitics produces death through the withdrawal of protection of life. Mbembe reminds us that the biopolitical order in Europe is dependent not on simply a withdrawal of protection of life, but the outright production of death in the colonies. In a similar vein, Patterson demonstrates that the category of physical life that cannot be politically protected (what Agamben calls "bare life") was invented through slavery. He observes that enslavement is characterized by a condition of "social death" wherein the enslaved exist socially only through the master; in other words, in Patterson's formulation, the *slave* is the paradigmatic figure that allows for the separation of physical and social life (and the corresponding category of "social death").[98] While slavery as a form of social death exists in many societies, the difference between Western and non-Western societies is an epistemological one, in that Western societies *disavow* the dependence relationship between the two existential states of enslavement and freedom, social death and social life.[99] This disavowal allows such political imaginaries to erase its racial and colonial brutalities and thus legitimate its self-definition as defenders of freedom and protectors of life. If the mode of legitimation for modern power is based on a disavowal of its power to inflict death in its very protection of life, this process is intimately dependent on producing such sites of disavowal through colonization and racialization. The histories of race and colonialism thus best exemplify the operations of modern power described by Agamben and Foucault, but are displaced by their focus on Europe.

While Patterson and Mbembe helpfully provide a critique of the blind spots of Western political theory, feminist and queer analyses best describe the contradictory structure of political modernity, which is organized not only through being the structuring exception but also by eradication through incorporation.[100] This is because the structure of eradication through incorporation is best exemplified by racialized reproduction and the related contradictions of consanguinity. As I have already observed, the Moynihan Report is an exemplary document of neoliberalism; the emphasis on racialized reproduction is not unique to the neoliberal moment, but subtends political modernity itself. Agamben argues that the "decisive event of modernity"[101] is the moment when physical life becomes politicized through its *entrance* into the political sphere *as that which is excluded,* in a state of inclusion as the figure of exclusion, in particular, from the paternal consanguinity that underlies Western law.[102]

However, as Scott Morgensen observes in a brilliant feminist critique of Agamben, this definition of bare life as "an exception (which is simultaneously an inclusion)"[103] in actuality best describes a condition that Agamben does not account for: the gendered and sexual histories of settler colonialism.[104] Morgenson writes that such histories constitute that which is "unimaginable in [the] theory of biopower."[105] Settler colonial states, Morgensen argues, eradicated Native peoples not simply by excluding Native communities from the patriarchal consanguinity of national belonging through outright physical killing. It also did so by forcibly making Native women and their children "non-Native" in the eyes of the patriarchal state, by coercing Native women into consanguineous relations through rape and forced intermarriage, and through the foreclosure of Indian tribal identity under nineteenth-century Canadian law for Native women who out-married and for their children. In this way, "Western law incorporates Indigenous peoples into the settler nation by simultaneously pursuing their elimination."[106]

Morgensen describes this positioning of Indigenous populations within modern Western law as that of the "incompletely consanguineous,"[107] a term that I find immensely useful as a descriptor for the ways in which modernity is predicated on the disavowal of its racialized, colonized, and gendered conditions of possibility. Black feminists, for example, have described the gendered and racialized processes that have constituted Black women in the modern capitalist system as a kind of *forced* consanguinity that does not guarantee the protections of the state, but instead consigns Black women to the condition of "that zero degree of social conceptualization."[108] Indeed, Hortense Spillers goes so far as to attest that "trying to understand how the confusions of consanguinity worked becomes the project, because the outcome goes far to explain the rule of gender and its application to the African female in captivity."[109] As I will go on to examine in more detail in chapter 3, scholars such as Spillers, along with Hazel Carby, Jennifer Morgan, and others have theorized the implications of the property system of eighteenth- and nineteenth-century chattel slave societies in which enslaved peoples were definitionally unable to inherit, or, in other words, were outside of consanguinity, *except as* they inherited their enslaved status from their mothers.[110] Through this

principle of *partus sequitur ventrem,* enslaved women were incorporated
into the structures of inheritance for the precise purpose of disinheriting
them and their children, for constituting them as exemplary exclusions.[111]
When taking into consideration the *gendered* and *sexualized* nature of
racialization, settler colonialism, and enslavement, we can see that the
condition of bare life was constituted through a process that did not
place these populations simply *outside* of the paternal consanguinity of
the law, but by what Spillers has described as the "powerful 'No,' the
structuring exception."[112] Spillers's definition renders the Black *female*
enslaved subject the most exemplary representative of the contradictory
nature of political modernity.

Listening to the Dead: Memory and Haunting in the Neoliberal Nexus

As we have seen through such documentary traces as the Moynihan
Report, these racialized and gendered contradictions of political modernity are not curious historical remnants, but rather deeply structure
our moment. Critics of neoliberalism have astutely observed that the
"neo" in neoliberalism falsely implies that it constitutes a complete
break from the past, which of course replicates the very disavowal of neoliberalism. In my view, our moment be characterized neither as a clean
break from the past nor by a direct cause-and-effect relationship between
past and present. The relationship between past and present is best
described as haunting, in which certain elements of the past—and therefore, the present—are repressed and disavowed, but never entirely or
successfully. Avery Gordon famously calls haunting "what it feels like to
be the object of a social totality vexed by the phantoms of modernity's
violence."[113] Neoliberalism can be seen as that social totality, a totality
that is always paradoxically incomplete *because* it is vexed by its phantoms, the trace or residue of that which can never be fully erased, yet cannot speak. Because neoliberalism is so centrally a refusal to recognize its
own violence, and a stubborn pretense that the racial, gendered, and
sexual basis for the distribution of protected life and premature death has
been remedied and leveled, it is structured by a deep disavowal. It holds
out the promise of protection from premature death—most exemplarily
in the form of reproductive respectability—in exchange for complicity

with this pretense. It's a difficult—impossible—bargain to refuse, given the stakes; it is what Gayatri Spivak has called, in a different context, that which "we cannot not want."[114]

Neoliberalism's erasure of the connections between the violences of the past and those of the present gives it its power. Saidiya Hartman beautifully articulates the tragedy of the erasure of this connection between past and present. In an essay about the impossible desire to know the female experience of the Middle Passage, Hartman writes, "We stumble upon her in exorbitant circumstances that yield no picture of the every-day life, no pathway to her thoughts, no glimpse of the vulnerability of her face or of what looking at such a face might demand. We only know what can be extrapolated from an analysis of the ledger or borrowed from the world of her captors and masters and applied to her."[115] All we have left of this girl—who is of course not just a girl, but is in Avery Gordon's words "a social figure"[116]—is what the archive holds, and because the archive is constituted of the documents of those who enslaved her, "the archive is, in this case, a death sentence, a tomb, a display of the violated body, an inventory of property."[117] Any narration of the past is thus impossible not because of our distance from it, but because the contours of our present depend on its erasure. Hartman writes, "I too live in a time of slavery, by which I mean I am living in the future created by it . . . the perilous conditions of the present establish the link between our age and a previous one in which freedom too was yet to be realized."[118] In our moment, the exacerbated dispersal of racialized, gendered, and sexualized death is erased and legitimated by the pretense that such un-equal relationships to precarity are entirely in and of the past.

Yet if there is anything we have learned from the many beautiful theories of haunting, it is that this pretense is impossible, for the forcibly forgotten dead are never content to stay buried. If the archive is "a death sentence, a tomb," then what this book tries to add is that death is not only an end, but also a beginning, that death can be proliferative and that we can converse with ghosts. As Lorde implies when she says that Malcolm's message was "amplified"[119] by his death, and as she enacts when she situates his legacy as multiple, complex, and proliferative, death pro-duces a variety of (im)possibilities. Hartman herself says as much when she goes on to say, "I want to do more than recount the violence that deposited these traces in the archive. I want to tell a story about *two girls* capable of retrieving what remains dormant—the purchase or claim of their lives on the present—without committing further violence in my own act of narration."[120] Her way of enacting this desire is to "tell an impossible story and to amplify the impossibility of its telling,"[121] a contradictory project that I would call aligned with the project of *difference* as Lorde and others theorized it.

For while our own desire resurrects these ghosts, and we thus are implicated whenever we tell the stories that we want to tell, we are also haunted by what these ghosts themselves demand that we speak. As Grace M. Cho observes, "The haunting effect is produced not so much by the original trauma as by the fact of its being kept hidden."[122] The repression, the disavowal, can never fully succeed; instead, it produces the haunting, which disorganizes any narrative even as it demands it. As such, if the dead speak, they do so in a way that simultaneously speaks and gestures to the impossibility of speaking, in ways that hold in tension these contradictory forces simultaneously, what I've earlier described as "difference."

Each chapter of this book thus identifies neoliberalism's modes of erasure and arrays cultural texts as ways of remembering—albeit in fragments and riven with ellipses—what neoliberalism attempts to forget: that is, that the protection of life is predicated on the dispersal of death. I start in chapter 1 by situating radical and revolutionary movements and their contradictory relationship to the life/death binary inherent to liberal modernity. In this chapter, I provide a genealogy of Chicana feminist responses to the ways in which certain minority nationalist elements of these movements mobilize a demand for a particular affect of mourning as a way to discipline feminist and queer critiques. I connect these Chicana feminist responses to two literary texts—Oscar Zeta Acosta's *Revolt of the Cockroach People* and Ana Castillo's *So Far from God*—by situating the deployment of literary form (in particular, irony) as a mode through which these texts articulate the contradictory imperatives of recognizing death while valuing life. Through the use of irony—and, in turn, the refusal to be ironic—Acosta's and Castillo's texts *both* mourn death in ways that align with minority nationalist affect *and* humorously puncture an overinflated sense of nationalist outrage over death when that outrage is used as a mode of discipline and control. *Difference* as aesthetic form inheres in these texts in the simultaneous existence of mourning and skepticism about mourning.

In chapter 2, I move to analyses of works by Audre Lorde and Cherríe Moraga, which likewise interrogate the moralism that infuses those aspects of social movements that become invested in respectability and legibility. Since neoliberal disavowal of gendered, sexual, and racialized precarity is so centrally predicated on respectability as the only avenue to security, a refusal of respectability is a powerful repudiation of neoliberal modes of power. I thus posit Lorde and Moraga as paradigmatic of woman of color feminist / queer of color theories of the onset of neoliberalism in the 1980s, which I argue is marked by the exacerbated extraction of surplus value from populations, modes of surplus value based not only on the economic but also the affective. Extending my engagement with Lorde in the introduction, I read several key essays from *Sister Outsider* to highlight the ways in which Lorde theorizes the importance of affect in enabling devaluation and abandonment in a neoliberal economy of surplus. In other words, Lorde argues that an economy dependent on devalued people uses affects like terror and loathing to create them; her response is to likewise wield affect as a source of power. I connect Lorde's politics of affect with Moraga's refusal to be morally defensible on any terms, whether normative or radical, as a means of critiquing respectability and legibility. I read two of Moraga's texts—*The Last Generation*, a collection of poetry and prose, and *Waiting in the Wings: Portrait of a Queer Motherhood*—for how they engage with generationality and reproduction. In *The Last Generation*, Moraga theorizes writing as a mode of historical transmission for queer women like herself who are not biologically reproductive and thus cannot claim motherhood as a mode of gendered valorization. While her subsequent book *Waiting in the Wings*, which documents her pregnancy and motherhood, might seem to contradict her claims in *The Last Generation*, Moraga documents the ways in which, as a queer Chicana butch, her experience of motherhood is always one of nonnormativity and inadequacy.

Because reproductive respectability is, as I have argued, such an important mode by which political and social legibility and value becomes sutured to literal physical life, chapter 3 extends this analysis to examine queer possibilities and futurities that might emerge from Black feminism's theorization of reproduction and the queerness of what Orlando Patterson has called natal alienation. In particular, I interrogate why a slew of texts from the 1980s and 1990s, including Gayl Jones's novel *Corregidora*, Isaac Julien's film *Looking for Langston*, Inge Blackman's *B.D. Women*, and Rodney Evans's *Brother to Brother*, look to the blues and jazz aesthetic of improvisation as a way of imagining a connection to foreclosed pasts and futures marked by contingency. Improvisation, which has been theorized as both invention and tradition, is an apt metaphor and method for describing the ways in which Blackness has been constituted through a simultaneously forced and foreclosed relationship to reproductive normativity. In this chapter, improvisation is my example of difference.

Chapter 4 meditates on how such a theory of queer reproduction might help us engage with the material and epistemological violences of the university, particularly as they manifest around the exclusion and extermination of Black feminist lives alongside the institutionalization of Black feminism. Following the lead of Barbara Christian, this chapter asks, what happens when academic generationality is interrupted by both cutting off of future generations of Black feminists through the abolishment of affirmative action and the premature death of Black feminists in the academy? This chapter examines the university itself as a biopolitical institution, and finds in Black feminism a vision for a different relationship to knowledge, futurity, and the political. Finally, in a brief epilogue to the book, I return to the questions that instigated this study in the first place, questions about the ethics of raising the dead, of inhabiting a temporality of progression and return and simultaneity, and of our responsibility to those whose deaths enable our lives.

In turning to women of color feminism as a framework and theory and to cultural production that remembers the continuing racialized, colonized, and gendered violences that neoliberalism disavows, this project means to find something else besides despair or disavowal when faced with the ubiquity of death. To end this introduction where I began, I turn again to Lorde, who sets us on a task (in its simplest terms) to take seriously her characterization of "how infinitely complex any move for liberation must be."[123] The pages that follow take inspiration from Lorde and bend toward the project of pursuing a complex liberation without any guarantee of a certain or knowable future.

CHAPTER ONE

Fun with Death and Dismemberment

Irony, Farce, and Nationalist Memorialization

Ana Castillo's novel *So Far from God* begins: "La Loca was only three years old when she died."[1] While the death of a child is not usually the stuff of comedy, the first chapter recounts, with the novel's characteristic dry wit, the miraculous resurrection of La Loca at her own funeral and the ensuing panicked argument among the parishioners about whether the event is an act of God or the devil. This, we find out, is but the first of many deaths that occur throughout Castillo's book, along with assorted dismemberments, diseases, ritual self-mutilations, and other embodied distresses. Oscar Zeta Acosta's loosely autobiographical novel *The Revolt of the Cockroach People,* which documents his involvement in the Chicano movement in the late 1960s and early 1970s, is likewise fascinated with death, albeit in a different affective register that moves between earnestness and glibness.[2] As befitting someone who, in legal terms, was the first to argue for "Mexican American" as a distinct racial category different from "white" because of the relationship to what Ian Haney López calls "legal violence, encompassing both judicial mistreatment and police brutality,"[3] Acosta writes about death in *The Revolt of the Cockroach People* in a properly memorializing nationalist fashion. However, this text simultaneously laments the ways in which nationalism becomes the only available language for making sense of death. *So Far from God* approaches this question in a different way but ends up with a similar response to death. Castillo's novel undermines a number of metanarratives, one of the most important of which is the metanarrative of nationalism, both official state and minority nationalisms. As such, *So Far from God* has been read as a postmodern text that undermines all sense of certainty through the deployment of irony. Yet the novel at moments defends the fixity of meaning and the sanctity of death and, in so doing, insists on the necessity, at particular moments, of an earnest memorialization attributable to nationalist sentiment. Both texts enact a complex and ambivalent rereading of oppositional nationalist ideologies of the social movements of the 1960s and 1970s.

In so doing, these texts share a project with Audre Lorde's active intervention into the Malcolm X weekend with which I began this book and echo her challenge to remember the 1960s in multiple and contradictory ways. In this chapter, I elaborate upon these projects of rememorialization, arguing through readings of Castillo's and Acosta's texts that these ambivalent re-readings operate not only in *what* they remember but *how* they remember. These texts must refuse the traditional genres of heroism or elegy, which are themselves deeply nationalist formal strategies, and mobilize new, hybrid, or debased formal strategies that remember social movements differently. In Castillo's and Acosta's texts, these formal strategies might be called irony. Yet at the same time, like Lorde, both Castillo and Acosta refuse to jettison the mournful affects of nationalism entirely, insisting that there are moments that require a straightforward and un-ironic challenge to official nationalist distribution of racialized death. As such, I will elaborate, their form of irony cannot be encapsulated either by the bourgeois literary notion of irony as constitutive of a knowing subject or by the postmodern variant that purports to shatter that knowing subject. Rather, Castillo's and Acosta's ironic representations of nationalist culture, both oppositional nationalism and official state nationalism, emerge from the racialized and gendered contradictions of nationalism itself. In particular, Castillo's and Acosta's dis-identification with nationalism emerges through an ironic relationship to its primary idiom: death.

While engaging with nationalism treads on well-worn ground, I do so here to describe the ways in which nationalism is newly redeployed by neoliberal power. If, as I have been arguing, neoliberalism is foundationally an epistemological formation organized around erasure and disavowal, that gesture of disavowal is only possible with the appropriation of the social movements of the post–World War II era. An important aspect of this appropriative gesture is to misremember that moment as entirely subsumed under a cultural nationalist claim to injury. Certainly, one of the tactics of those social movements was to make racialized death visible as something to be memorialized, in order to reveal the hypocrisy of liberal claims to the equivalence of death as the epitome of the equality ostensibly guaranteed by citizenship. Yet in the neoliberal appropriative gesture, the politicization of racialized death becomes removed from this critique and ossified simply into a claim to rights. Challenging this misremembering, a number of texts written in the 1980s and thereafter—Acosta's and Castillo's texts among them—undermine the ways in which only certain aspects of oppositional nationalist discourse become visible and legible within a regime of power that becomes neoliberal in the moment when it recognizes racialized death as a problem to be solved. Acosta's and Castillo's re-narrations of that moment work to undermine that operation of power, and also to describe different relationships to death.

As Lisa Lowe has argued, citizenship exceeds the political field, operating as an ideological process that attempts, incompletely and in fragmented fashion, to displace the contradictions between capital's needs and those of the nation-state.[4] If national culture attempts to eradicate material inequalities through the promise of political equality, that equality is exemplified by death. Donald Lowe observes that the rise of bourgeois society necessitated a notion of death as the endpoint of temporality.[5] That is, if the nation-state is based on "empty, homogeneous time," death is that which marks the end of this time, as opposed to an earlier, feudal temporality where death exists within a temporality capable of differentiation in which life has one kind of temporality and death another kind, albeit in the realm of God. In contrast, the bourgeois sense of death meant the end of temporality for the individual altogether. In the liberal notion, death is the final, unknowable end, and must be memorialized as such. It is in this way that nationalism establishes itself so powerfully within a seemingly secular imagination. In *Imagined Communities,* Benedict Anderson notes that nationalism's power lies in its ability to mobilize structures of feeling more commonly associated with religions than with political ideologies. In particular, religion gives meaning to human mortality and vulnerability by "transforming fatality into continuity (karma, original sin, etc.)."[6] In other words, in Anderson's narration, the nation-state replaced religion as the primary means of dealing with death. Unlike the nonsecular "estate [feudal] societies" that Donald Lowe describes, however, national culture establishes death as a form of equivalence that ends every life in the same way.

In Anderson's analysis, various national incarnations of the Tomb of the Unknown Soldier—a focal point for mourning that he observes is unique to nationalism—quintessentially illustrate how the nation-state interpellates citizens into its narrative history.[7] The Tomb of the Unknown Soldier commemorates not a specific death but a generalizable death that calls to the citizen, rather than the individual, as mourner. The connection to the dead that allows the living to mourn is not familial or individual but national. The mourner is not the friend, parent, spouse, or child of an individual, particular soldier, but is the citizen of a nation for whom the soldier ostensibly gave his life. But even that is too facile: shared grief binds the citizenry, not by *transcending* the claims of friendship or family but by harnessing them to the nation-state. The Unknown Soldier's sacrifice sutures the individual and known soldier's sacrifice for a particular family, spouse, children, or parents with the protection of the nation's families, indeed, for the protection of a nation's ability and right to have families at all. This is, at base, a struggle over meaning and truth: nationalism claims a community, by providing one irrefutable meaning for, and one possible affect—earnestness, mournfulness, grief—toward, death. The death of the Unknown Soldier has only one possible interpretation, one that mobilizes his sacrifice in defense of the nation and incorporates individual soldiers' deaths into that narrative. Any difference between that particular soldier, that particular family, and the Unknown Soldier and the national family is exactly what must be repressed. Any other meanings that the particular soldier's death—and, by extension, life—might have had in contradiction to the nationalist narrative of heroic sacrifice are rendered illegible.

Yet this difference is never perfectly repressed, and we might see oppositional nationalist movements as one way of expressing these differences.

The Chicano antiwar movement—and the Chicano Moratorium in particular—was organized precisely around the difference between the racialized specificity of the Chicano soldier and the supposedly universal soldier as the ultimate citizen of the U.S. nation-state. In so doing, the Chicano Moratorium was the "return of the repressed" of the nationalist sentiment inspired by the Unknown Soldier. Initiated by concerns over the disproportionately high rates of Chicano enlistment and fatality in the Vietnam War, the Chicano Moratorium movement eventually grew to encompass a transnational connection to, and identification with, the deaths of the Vietnamese as fellow anti-U.S. imperialist fighters. Cofounded by UCLA student body president Rosalío Muñoz and UCLA graduate student Ramsés Noriega, the National Chicano Moratorium Committee, in concert with the Brown Berets and other movement groups, organized a series of demonstrations and marches, most infamously the march of August 20, 1970, at which the L.A. County Sheriff's officers murdered the *Los Angeles Times* journalist and KMEX-TV general manager Ruben Salazar, among others. As the historian Lorena Oropeza recounts in her history of the Chicano antiwar movement, the Chicano Moratorium brought together Chicanos/as with a diversity of political viewpoints and made antiwar protest central to the Chicano movement at that moment.[8]

From its inception, the Chicano Moratorium's critiques of the Vietnam War were based on the hypocrisy of the United States' universalist narratives of death. This movement ultimately associated the United States with the dispersal of death rather than with the protection of life. Revealing the hypocrisy of a nation-state that claimed to protect life universally but actually operated as the very agent of death for some, the Chicano antiwar movement revealed race to be exactly that process by which people were rendered differentially vulnerable to death. In noting that Chicanos were recruited to serve as soldiers at greater rates and died in battle in greater rates as well, the Chicano antiwar movement undermined the claim implicit in the Tomb of the Unknown Soldier. If the Tomb of the Unknown Soldier claimed that citizens were all interpellated similarly and that the Unknown Soldier could represent any or all of the war dead, the Chicano Moratorium attested that this was not the case. Rather than suturing Chicanos to the U.S. nation-state, the deaths of Chicano soldiers instead revealed the incommensurabilities between Chicanos and the U.S. citizen-subject. As Chicano/a activists revealed, such incommensurabilities stemmed from material histories of labor exploitation, disenfranchisement, and dispossession.

Rosalío Muñoz's speech refusing to enlist at his September 16, 1969, induction explicitly connected the military projects of the United States with the greater exploitation of Chicanas/os. In a speech later widely reprinted in Chicano movement newspapers, Muñoz said, "Specifically, I accuse the draft, the entire social, political, economic system of the United States of America of creating a funnel which shoots Mexican youth into Viet Nam to be killed and to kill innocent men, women, and children."[9] Targeting the "educational system," "welfare system," and "law enforcement agencies" as working in concert to give Chicano youth no better alternative than the military, Muñoz's speech re-narrated Chicano soldiers' deaths, wresting them away from any narrative that might represent them as heroes of the U.S. nation-state and recasting them as martyrs for the nation of Aztlán. This characterization was not limited to Muñoz alone: one group, Las Adelitas de Aztlán, marched in the Moratorium demonstration in black mourning clothes, carrying crosses emblazoned with the names of male family members who had died in Vietnam, symbolically mobilizing mourning as a means of producing Chicano/a nationalist identification.[10]

The events of the Chicano Moratorium march and demonstration of August 29, 1970, underscored even further the hypocrisy of the U.S. nation-state toward Chicano lives and deaths. Initially a peaceful protest of between twenty and thirty thousand people through East Los Angeles, culminating in a demonstration and speeches at Hollenbeck Park, the march was ended by rampant police brutality, including the LAPD in full riot gear assaulting unarmed protesters, and ultimately killing four. Most infamously, a sheriff's deputy fired a high-velocity tear gas projectile without warning into the open doorway of a local bar, striking the journalist Ruben Salazar and killing him instantly.

A special issue of *La Raza* published in the aftermath of the inquest into this murder is replete with images of the state's contradictions in the face of Chicano death.[11] Contradicting official state accounts of police behavior, the journal printed dozens of photographs, many taken by editor Raúl Ruiz himself, that depicted complete disregard for Chicano life on the part of the LAPD and the Los Angeles County sheriff. Ruiz happened to be across the street from the Silver Dollar as the episode leading to Salazar's death was occurring, and he took a particularly chilling series of photographs documenting the entire police action, photographs that belie official accounts. Yet despite the evidence entered at the inquest, including eyewitness testimony by Chicanos, the district attorney declined to prosecute Thomas Wilson, the sheriff's deputy who fired the tear gas projectile.

In the wake of this decision, *La Raza* compiled a "special issue," which republished a number of documents previously seen in earlier issues of *La Raza* (including letters to the editor, photographs, articles in Spanish and English, and poetry/song lyrics), alongside new documents. A number of articles in the volume point out that Wilson's and other sheriff's representatives' testimony clearly contradict the physical evidence, and that the hearing officer Norman Pittluck continually turned the questioning toward unruly behavior on the part of Chicano/a demonstrators, not only at the Moratorium but in other contexts, in an effort to represent the use of deadly force by the police as necessary and appropriate.

As such, the special issue's defining logic is less reportage that attempts to document ongoing events than an alternative record in which the editors enter into "evidence" a variety of materials that were excluded from the inquest process and that, because of the results of the inquest, would never be entered into the records of the trial that would never take place. This special issue, in other words, comprises an alternative juridical institution that, in introducing new "evidence," highlights the hypocrisy of the state's claims to legal impartiality.

In *La Raza's* reportage, the inquest is repeatedly called a "farce," referencing a broadly comic, performative theatrical form that entertains by presenting, in straight-faced fashion, improbable, credulity-straining scenarios.[12] In deploying the trope of farce, the authors of *La Raza* reveal the contradiction within U.S. national culture: while claiming to mourn death equally, the state deploys and values death differentially along the lines of race. Naming the inquest a farce highlights the ways in which the state itself does not take seriously its own claims to universally value and protect life for all citizens regardless of race. The U.S. nation-state does not truly mourn or grieve Chicano death; instead, *La Raza* claims, the state uses the genre of farce to legitimate violence against Chicanos. By using the term *farce*, which implies multiple levels of meaning— straight-faced presentation, on the one hand, combined with a winking acknowledgment of the absurdity of the scenario presented, on the other—to describe the U.S. nation-state, the articles in *La Raza* demonstrate that the mobilization of memorialization on the part of U.S. national culture produces racialized difference at the very moment it claims to transcend that difference.

In response to the state's hypocrisy, Chicano/a movement activists created an alternative system of valuation in which Chicano deaths mattered and were memorialized rather than dismissed or subjected to derision. In this special issue of *La Raza*, this memorialization solidifies around the martyred figure of Ruben Salazar. The last page of the special issue features a photograph of Salazar's face on a black background. The facing page, also on a black background, is inscribed with the words "murieron injustamente" ("they were unjustly murdered") and Salazar's name followed by two others—Gilberto Diaz and Lyn Ward—also killed that day. While not the only casualty of police violence, Salazar is most definitely figured as the epitome of Moratorium martyrdom. Salazar's face is open, slightly smiling, eyes cast upward, a representation of hope brutally stalled, glowing with an incandescence that comes from the contrast between his light skin, further lightened by photographic overexposure, and the black background. This particular photograph shows him to be well groomed, with short, conservatively cut hair, and his formal, respectable dress—shirt collar, jacket lapel, and necktie—is just visible below his face. In this final image, the special issue of *La Raza* brings into being an alternative form of memorialization that ensures that if the U.S. nation-state would not take Chicano deaths seriously, Chicanos/as would instead. *La Raza's* memorialization of Chicano death made visible the difference between the state's claims about the sanctity of death and its farcical dismissal of Chicano death. By insisting on the fixity of the meaning of death—that is, by demanding that that Chicano death be memorialized and grieved—Chicano/a nationalists exposed the duplicity of a U.S. national culture that deployed dual meanings for death: memorialization and grief as a privilege of whiteness, farce as a register of the devaluation of Chicanos.

In so doing, these movements highlighted the conditions of extreme exploitation and racialized violence operating for Chicano communities. Norma Alarcón notes that Mexican nationalism and Chicano nationalism (like European bourgeois nationalisms) emerged against "feudal mode[s] of power," both "the Hispanic New World 'feudal mode of power' (which in Mexico gave way to the construction of mestizo nationalism)" and "an Anglo-American 'feudal mode of power' in the isolation of migrant worker camps and exchange labor (which in the United States gave rise to Chicano nationalism of the 1960s)."[13] Alarcón notes that Chicano nationalism is a mode of "defeudalization"—or, in other words, a struggle against these feudal modes of repression. Because feudal modes of power against Chicano/a communities not only continue to exist but are exacerbated by global processes of hyperexploitation and concomitant state violence, this process of defeudalization is necessary and ongoing.[14]

Chicano/a movement discourses such as that seen in *La Raza* engaged in a process of defeudalization by revealing the *farce* and *falsity* of official nationalist deployments of mourning. That is, they highlighted the hypocrisy inherent in the condition in which the state mobilized a feudal mode of power—brute force and violence—against Chicano/a communities at the same time as it maintained the fiction of universal citizenship. Yet movement discourses did so by figuring Chicano/a martyrs as the real bearers of a singular truth—that is, of the value of Chicano life—erased by official nationalism. Mourning can be mobilized to produce varied meanings, some that mask the limits of nationalism, others that trace its fissures and contradictions. Yet oppositional nationalist memorialization often trafficked in the same dialectic of power and abjection that marks official state nationalism, with all its attendant reinscriptions of belonging and expulsion. In the case of the *La Raza* special issue, for example, the memorialization of Ruben Salazar was possible because of the ways in which he was already valuable: because of his respectability as a journalist and community figure. This value both highlights the injustice of racial violence, and also occludes other forms of violence that do not manifest out of a sheriff's tear gas launcher and that occur against those who are not valuable and visible in the same ways. Thus, while the continuing existence and allure of minority or oppositional nationalisms signal the ways in which the feudal mode of power still operates, this feudal mode of power exists *alongside* neoliberal modes of power that mobilize what Jodi Melamed has called an official state antiracism. These neoliberal modes of power are supported, rather than undermined, by minority nationalisms. As such, Alarcón notes, Mexican and Chicano nationalisms (which she describes as a "'communal form of power' under the sign of the cultural nationalist family"), while important critiques of the feudal mode of power, "may be bankrupt, especially for female wage-workers."[15]

Alarcón's observations are supported by historical events, as this enforcement of community boundaries happened most violently, though not exclusively, against Chicana feminists. As Maylei Blackwell has documented, the historic first national conference of Chicana movement activists in Houston, Texas, in May 1971, exemplifies the disciplining uses of Chicano nationalist definitions of death.[16] Organized by Elma Barrera, the conference drew over six hundred Chicanas from twenty-five states. While largely succeeding in bringing Chicanas together to outline issues of importance for Chicanas in the movement—including reproductive rights, sexual agency, and critiques of the Catholic Church, as well as immigration laws, political prisoners, police brutality, and the welfare system—the conference is largely remembered for the divisive walkout staged by a number of participants on the last day. The leaders of the walkout accused the YWCA, who had helped to organize the conference, of racism, and maintained that organizing around women's issues was misguided. The feminist critiques generated at the conference were, they claimed, trivial when compared to the plight of marchers on César Chávez's pilgrimage from Delano (who were getting shot at) and the increasing deaths of Chicanos in the Vietnam War. Worse, they were deflecting attention and energy away from these *more important* issues.

In other words, because Chicano nationalism constituted itself so reso-
lutely around a critique of official state nationalism's hypocrisy about
Chicano death, the sanctity of Chicano death came to be the delimit-
ing boundary for Chicano/a identity and community, which had to be
defined in a singular way, brought together through shared memorialization and grief around Chicano death. Chicana feminism's interrogation of community boundaries was then figured as the ultimate betrayal:
as insufficiently respectful of Chicano death.

Within this gendered economy of belonging and betrayal, any understanding of life and death as mutually imbricated and the line between
them blurred and complex becomes narrated as treachery. These con-
stitutions of community wreaked violence against feminist and queer
subjects who, in turn, developed thoughtful and analytical critiques of
this violence. One of the earliest Chicana feminist theorists, Ana Nieto
Gomez, for example, is precise about the ways in which Chicano nationalism delineated gendered and sexualized definitions of what properly
constituted Chicano/a community: "I am a Chicana feminist. I make
that statement very proudly, although there is a lot of intimidation in our
community and in the society in general against people who define themselves as Chicana feminists. It sounds like a contradictory statement,
a *Malinche* statement—if you're a Chicana you're on one side, if you're
a feminist, you must be on the other side. . . . In fact, the statement is
not contradictory at all, it is a very unified statement."[17] As Blackwell
observes, Nieto Gomez's defiance of the gender and sexual norms of
Chicano nationalism did not go unpunished, resulting in reprisals by
Chicano nationalist men, from her being buried in effigy on the Cal State
Long Beach campus as an undergraduate student leader to being denied
tenure in Chicano studies at Cal State Northridge years later.[18]

Because Chicano/a nationalism had its most brutal and normativizing effects on women and queer subjects, Chicana feminist and queer
critiques provide the most cogent and nuanced engagement with Chicano
nationalism and so offer us a critique of both feudal and liberal modes of
power.[19] According to Wahneema Lubiano, while this recourse to a common culture is central to nationalism in general, it is particularly useful
for minority nationalisms, as severe political and economic alienation

produces culture as the only consistently productive site of contestation.[20] Chicana feminists, within a tradition of women of color feminism,
have long noted the ways in which oppositional nationalisms deploy the
idea of culture as a means of naturalizing masculinism and patriarchy.
In so doing, Chicana feminists disidentify with the dialectic of power
and abjection that inheres in patriarchal nationalism. Nationalism interpellates subjects by assuming the subject's injury insofar as subjects
approach the state to regain a power to which it presumes it is entitled
but has lost.[21] This loss permeates nationalism, producing mourning
as its primary affect.[22] In the context of Chicano oppositional nationalism, the ultimate symbol of this loss is the very real deaths of Chicanos
from economic exploitation as an agricultural peonage class, brutal police
violence, and war, to name just a few examples. Under this rubric, compensation for this loss (or, in Rosalind Morris's words, "the fantasy of
return") comes with the reassertion of one's "rightful" place as patriarch
of a family, narrated as the regaining of "traditional" culture.[23]

Under such a regime, as Norma Alarcón observes, there are two roles
for women: the "unquestioning transmitter of tradition" and the "'betrayer'
of tradition, of family, of what is ethically viewed as 'pure and authen-
tic.'"[24] In the Chicano/a context, Alarcón writes, these roles are figured
as the Virgen de Guadalupe, the "silent mediator," and her "monstrous
double," La Malinche, who subjects the community and culture to the
indignities of the process of translation, which by definition can never be
faithful or accurate.[25] The historical personage upon whom the La Malinche
figure is based was the literal translator (and consort) of Hernan Cortés;
she becomes the figure for the speaking subject that rejects "ritualized repetition" of tradition for "interpretive language."[26] In a context in which "traditional culture," organized around the Chicano male subject's entitlement
to his patriarchal power, acts as the compensatory mechanism for that
subject's losses, undermining this sense of tradition constitutes betrayal,
an ostensible complicity with the forces of colonialism and neocolonialism, state violence, and labor exploitation that produced such losses.

Chicana feminists negotiated such disciplinary regimes with subtlety
and complexity, crafting an alternative political imaginary that took seriously the injuries attendant to racialization (via the feudal mode of power)

but that did not depend on a static and desubjectivizing position for women as part of the compensation for these losses (a sense of compensation that by its very existence implied the internalization of a neoliberal mode of power). Chicana feminism did so through rethinking the dialectic of power and abjection. Rather than attempting to resolve or compensate for the losses wrought upon Chicano/a communities by the racial state and capital and in this way overcome the state of abjection, Chicana feminism instead politicized abjection. Many found themselves doing so through a critical recuperation of La Malinche, as we see in the passage above from Nieto Gomez.

Alarcón reads this recuperation of La Malinche as part of a larger Chicana feminist relationship to the figure of the "native" woman, which she understands as quite different from the way this figure operates within Mexican mestizo nationalism or Chicano nationalism. These nationalisms use the native woman as the figure for barbarity, savagery, and backwardness to forge a "consensus for most others, men and women," over and against her.[27] Alarcón writes, "It is worthwhile to remember that the historical founding moment of the construction of mestizo(a) subjectivity entails the rejection and denial of the dark Indian Mother as Indian, which has compelled women to collude in silence against themselves."[28] In the nationalist ideology of "actually deny[ing] the Indian position even as that position is visually stylized and represented in the making of the fatherland," Alarcón argues that nationalism must sanitize the Indian woman, evacuating her of her "noncivilized" nature and "*barbarie* [savagery]" to situate her as the foundation of a mestizo civilization.[29] In this perverse fashion, the figure of the Indian woman is used to reproduce the very ideologies that situate her as backward; for her to represent the mestizo nation, she must be rescued from her own abjection. In contrast, Chicana feminists identified with the native woman *as* excluded and abject. Unlike mestizo nationalism, Chicana feminist use of the figure of the native woman was not a project of representation or visibility but one that critiqued such projects.

Chicana feminist critiques of Chicano nationalism thus operate as a powerful critique of neoliberalism that incorporates oppositional nationalism. Yet as I argued in the introduction, neoliberal incorporation or affirmation does not signal the end of the repressive "feudal" modes of exploitation that inspires the minority nationalist critique. Emerging out of this very moment, Ana Castillo's *So Far from God* and Oscar Zeta Acosta's *Revolt of the Cockroach People* represent the social movements of the 1960s and 1970s as not simply about the redress of injury but about exploring the limits of such a politics and attempting to advance a new definition of the political. In so doing, there are moments when each text insists on the importance of oppositional nationalist modes of mourning because the conditions of state-sponsored violence, agricultural and industrial peonage, and ideological demonization that make Chicanos and Chicanas particularly vulnerable to death are still painfully present. The process of defeudalization that inspired oppositional nationalisms has not concluded.

Thus, while nationalism was an important epistemological and ideological formation for social movement politics in the 1960s and 1970s, it was neither monolithic nor unchallenged. The most forceful critique of oppositional nationalism came from women of color feminists, and we see that this is the case within the Chicano/a movement as well. In the next chapter, I engage with the works of an iconic Chicana feminist: Cherríe Moraga. Yet other subjects also tested the limits of nationalist discourse, and the analytic offered by Chicana feminism allows us to read a variety of texts and formations. While no one would accuse Acosta of being a feminist—quite the opposite, actually—his text indexes the inherent contradictions within nationalism, contradictions that inhere in Chicano versions, by simultaneously validating and lamenting the limits of nationalist memorialization.[30] While a strange and unsolved (probable) demise marks Acosta's own biography, this curious relationship to death is also quite evident in his fictional work.[31]

Not only a now-canonical text within Chicano studies, Acosta's follow-up to his *Autobiography of a Brown Buffalo* is also explicitly a narrative of his politicization through radical Chicano movements in the late 1960s and early 1970s. In the same "gonzo journalism" style of *Brown Buffalo*, Acosta resurrects the masculinist, hedonistic, hypersexualized persona first introduced in the earlier text: "A dope addict, a bum like me with all my vices, with my love of wild women and song"—a depiction that has become a cliché of early Chicano movement machismo.[32] A fictional-ized rendering of Acosta's experiences as a somewhat reluctant lawyer for the Brown Berets and the Católicos por la Raza (CPLR), the narrative oscillates between representing Acosta as a central figure to the move-ment and a peripheral one. The novel follows Acosta's literary alter ego, Buffalo Zeta Brown, as he defends movement participants in the 1968 blowouts, in which thousands of Chicano/a high school students walked off their campuses in protest of racist teachers and curricula and poor conditions, the 1969 St. Basil protest against racism in the Los Angeles Catholic diocese, and the Chicano Moratorium. Hereafter, I refer to the author as Acosta and to the narrator-character in the novel as Zeta.

Staged as a narrative of politicization or even conversion, the novel opens with a description of Zeta's role in the St. Basil demonstration, when members of the Católicos por la Raza stage a protest at the church during midnight Mass on Christmas Eve of 1969. The novel then flashes back two years, with Zeta returning to Los Angeles after sobering up from the drug- and drink-fueled excesses that made up the narrative ele-ments of this novel's predecessor, *Autobiography of a Brown Buffalo*. On a purely self-motivated mission to "find 'THE STORY' and write 'THE BOOK' so that [he] could split to the lands of peace and quiet where people played volleyball, sucked smoke, and chased after cool blondes," Zeta hears about the Chicano militants and is drawn to them, more in the hopes that they will provide the meat of his narrative than because he has any political investment.[33] Indeed, he writes, "Politically I believe in absolutely nothing. I wouldn't lift a finger to fight anyone."[34] As he gets increasingly drawn into the ranks of Chicano militants, however, he struggles with movement politics and his own cynicism. Practically stumbling into participation in the school blowouts, Zeta asks, "All around me is a new breed of savages, brown-eyed devils who shout defiantly to the heavens. And what am I to do? Is this all to write some story? Do up-and-coming great men march at the command of a wretched voice over a bullhorn? Is this the place for a lone buffalo? Will they bust me for passing out Camels? I am divided against myself, torn in two."[35]

This state of being "torn in two" characterizes Zeta throughout the book. As in this passage, in which Zeta's interrogation of the integrity of his political commitments is interrupted by a flippant aside about a much more prosaic and petty concern regarding being caught giving cigarettes to minors, the tone of the book as a whole oscillates between the mournfully earnest affect of radical nationalist politics and the caricaturing of that affect. Zeta is unable and unwilling to take lightly the all-too-real deaths, at the hands of the LAPD, of Robert Fernandez and Roland Zanzibar (a thinly veiled version of Ruben Salazar, killed by police during the Chicano Moratorium march). Yet neither can he remain completely and uncritically within the idioms of nationalist belonging that would turn these men into martyrs for *la raza*. The entire narrative explores both the seductions and limits of nationalist modes of belonging.

The Revolt of the Cockroach People at times cannot avoid turning such men into martyrs. In his own life, Acosta did indeed represent the family of a young man who died under suspicious circumstances while in police custody.[36] In the narrative, the same happens to Robert Fernandez, and his family attempts to contest the initial autopsy that rules it suicide. In his role as lawyer for the family, Zeta is forced to direct the second autopsy, which brutally dismembers and violates Fernandez's body, an experience Acosta describes as "death as a world of art."[37] At the end of the description of the autopsy, he addresses a moving prayer to the dead Robert Fernandez. This prayer lifts Fernandez to the status of a martyr, a Christ figure whose suffering saves the race or, in Acosta's language, the "living brown":

> I, Mr. Buffalo Z. Brown. Me, I ordered those white men to cut up the brown body of that Chicano boy, just another expendable Cockroach. . . . Forgive me, Robert, for the sake of the living brown. Forgive me and forgive me. I am no worse off than you. For the rest of my born days, I will suffer the knowledge of your death and your second death and your ashes to my ashes, your dust to my dust. . . . Goodbye, *ese*. Viva la Raza![38]

Robert functions in this text as the focal point of mourning that knits together the imagined community of "la Raza." In this context, mourning Robert's death is a way of protesting the violence of the state toward racialized bodies, as represented by police violence (Robert's first death) and again by the autopsy (his "second death"). We might see this prayer-like address as figuratively creating a Tomb of the Chicano (Street) Soldier. This portrayal of Fernandez's sacrificial death operates to call a Chicano into being, as the Tomb of the Unknown Soldier calls a citizen into being. These examples demonstrate the ways in which a common oppositional nationalist narrative that bases the notion of a universal racialized experience through the violence of the nation-state does so through interpellative mechanisms. In other words, what it means to be racialized is to experience the state not as the institution that guarantees the universal protection of life but rather as one that is the very agent of death.

Chicano nationalism challenges this notion of protection of life for all by exposing the ways in which the state is the agent of death for racialized people. In this vein, Acosta mobilizes the rhetoric of Third World solidarity that narrates a connection between Chicano racialization and U.S. imperialist war: "We are the Viet Cong of America. Tooner Flats is Mylai. . . . The Poverty Program of Johnson, the Welfare of Roosevelt, Truman, Eisenhower and Kennedy, the New Deal and the Old Deal, the New Frontier as well as Nixon's American Revolution . . . these are further embellishments of the government's pacification program."[39]

Yet while Acosta's narrative is certainly articulated through an oppositional nationalist idiom, it is not consistently so. It often strays from the dictates of nationalist affect. As such, although Acosta articulates Fernandez's death in this moment within a nationalist frame, his death produces an excess that expresses nationalism's limits, as conveyed in the increasingly hysterical description of the autopsy. The autopsy is presented as one side of a dialogue between the doctors doing the autopsy and Zeta, whose permission is needed to guide the doctor's knives as they cut into Fernandez's body:

Uh oh! Now we get really serious. If he died of strangulation . . . We'll have to pull out the . . . uh, neck bone.
   Go right ahead, *sir!* Pull out that goddamn gizzard.
   Uh, we have to . . . take the face off first.
   Well, Jesus Christ, go ahead!

> Slit. One slice. Slit. Up goes the chin. Lift it right up over the face . . .
> the face? The face goes up over the head. The head? The head is the face.
> Huh? *There is no face!*
> What do you mean?
> The face is hanging down the back of the head. The face is a mask.
> The mouth is where the brain . . . The nose is at the back of the neck. The
> hair is the ears. The brown nose is hanging where the neck . . . Get your
> goddamn hand out of there.
> My hand?
> That is the doctor's hand. It is inside the fucking face.
> I mean the head.[40]

Acosta's text certainly mourns the racialized violence by the state that forecloses access to a universal version of life for racialized Chicano subjects. Yet as we can see by the foregoing passage, it also mourns the fact that *there is no language* through which to understand death and dismemberment in any way but as loss. As he narrates the event, his ability to convey the dismemberment through language starts to break down, signaling the failure of language to represent the horrific and surreal nature of state violence against racialized bodies. Yet this very failure is exactly what conveys the tone of horror and despair. This passage is marked by the slippage of meaning of head and face, of hair and ears, the nose and neck, mouth and brain. Dismemberment disorganizes language, making it impossible to describe a dismembered body precisely and accurately, because the very words one might use to describe it— head, face, hair, ears—imply a whole body, with one universal order and relationship between the various parts. At one moment, Zeta is confused about what to even call the corpse: "This ain't Robert no more. It's just a . . . no, not a body . . . body is a whole."[41] When the wholeness and order of the body are disrupted, language fails in its descriptive duty—it is impossible to call a head without a face a head, or a body that is dismembered a body. In other words, this passage does not merely mourn the inability to ascribe to a definition of subjectivity dependent on a universal sense of life; rather, it mourns the fact that there is no alternative language for subjectivity but this language of life.

This failure of language pervades the entire scene, affecting not only Fernandez but Zeta himself. The violation of the sanctity of the body describes both Fernandez and Zeta at this moment. By being forced to direct this autopsy, he becomes the state's surrogate, which begins to blur his sense of the divide between self and other. Although cast as a dialogue, the passage lacks quotation marks and identifying language, making the coroner's words and Zeta's responses seem more like an internal debate taking place within one subjectivity. At a particular moment, Zeta loses any sense of difference between himself and the coroner: "Get your goddamn hand out of there. My hand? That is the doctor's hand." Here is perhaps the clearest illustration of the contradiction inherent in the term "Chicano lawyer" and, by extension, "Chicano nationalist." The antagonism toward the state that impelled his involvement in this case and constituted his desire to try the state for violence against Chicano bodies is the very thing that puts him in this situation where he becomes a surrogate for the state, demanding and directing the autopsy that enacts the further gruesome violations of Fernandez's body that constitute his "second death." The prayer that Zeta directs toward Fernandez at the end of the passage, then, must be read as mourning the fact that Chicano nationalism, born out of a critique of the U.S. nation-state for Fernandez's "first death," becomes the context for Fernandez's "second death." This prayer thus does not merely interpellate the Chicano but also mourns the *limits* of such an interpellation, a response to the violence of the state that replicates that violence, and in the end, leaves nothing but an apology. The passage mourns the ways in which there is no other language besides that of oppositional nationalism to address the violence of state nationalism.

Similarly, *The Revolt of the Cockroach People* not only describes the power of nationalist affect but also simultaneously and consistently highlights Zeta's failure to fully inhabit this affect. In so doing, the novel conveys the process of abjection that is the necessary corellary to the heroic narrative. That is, if figures such as Fernandez are to be mourned as the sacrificial and "good" dead, there must be by implication the morally flawed, the selfish, those unwilling to sacrifice all for the common good. That morally flawed being is Zeta himself, whose commitment to the radical struggle of Chicano nationalist politics is always tinged with doubt, failure, uncertainty, and resentment.

Zeta's inability to be a properly nationalist Chicano is certainly not represented as any fault of Chicano nationalism, which is all the more powerful for its being organized around death and mourning. Staged as a narrative of conversion, *The Revolt of the Cockroach People* is populated by a number of "savior" figures, men like Fernandez whose sacrifice and martyrdom give meaning to Chicano identity and around whom an ostensibly unified Chicano collectivity may be constituted. One figure is, predictably, César Chávez, who is depicted as saintly and Christlike. Arriving in Delano, Zeta must pass through a chapel to arrive at the room where Chávez is on his twenty-fifth day of a fast. From an author known for his vivid and earthy descriptions of embodiment, both his and others, this passage is remarkable for how absolutely it refrains from describing Chávez's embodied form, especially given the implication that Chávez was suffering from the effects of a long hunger strike. Rather, the narrative's representation of Chávez is almost as a disembodied voice who, being halfway between life and death, is already a kind of ghost. In this text, Chávez is figured as a frail, gentle figure whose pacifist politics are represented as a form of martyrdom: "The height of manhood, Cesar believes, is to give of one's self."[42] Acosta's recounting of a poem that hangs at the door of the chapel heightens the comparison between Chávez and Christ. The poem reads, in an echo of the familiar story of Christ dying for mankind's sins: "Life is not as it seems, / Life is pride and personal history, / Thus it is better that one die / and that the people should live, / rather than one live and the people die."[43] A tearful and heartfelt conversation with Chávez seals Zeta's conversion and inspires his commitment to the struggle.

But the conversion never really sticks. The interpellative power of nationalist affect always creates an unrealizable ideal. Zeta is never outside the realm of suspicion, either by himself or by others. Throughout the book, Acosta underscores Zeta's inability to fully belong, his consistently questionable and questioned motivations and commitments. In an allegory of guilt and commitment, dying for the cause is the ultimate sign of radicalism, and an unimpeachable proof of belonging. Those unwilling to sacrifice become suspect, and as a hedonist, Zeta falls firmly into this category. Early in the narrative, Zeta asks resentfully, "Who in the shit ever said that revolution has to be a drag? Why can't one be serious and have fun at the same time?"[44] His conflicted state—on the one hand inspired by saintly and martyred figures such as Chávez and, on the other, refusing to fetishize self-sacrifice—structures Zeta's ambivalent moral edifice.

Another such moment of ambivalence emerges exactly around Zeta's involvement with the East Los Angeles Chicano Moratorium rally of 1970. After a series of victories, including successfully defending the East L.A. Thirteen for their involvement in the blowouts of 1968, in which thousands of Chicano/a high school students walked out of their schools in protest of substandard conditions and lack of relevant education, Zeta retires to Acapulco to enjoy a lascivious, drug-fueled lifestyle. Zeta is brought back to Los Angeles only by the news of the death of Roland Zanzibar during the Chicano Moratorium rally. Snapped out of his period of self-gratifying hedonism by yet another sacrificial hero, Zeta muses, "Our first martyr, Roland Zanzibar is dead."[45]

Yet his return to Los Angeles is far from triumphant, and he finds his former radical Chicano compatriots dismissive and suspicious about his absence from the movement. The rhetoric they use situates death as the ultimate form of commitment to the cause, next to which all else pales in significance. Death becomes the basis for moral outrage. In response, Zeta articulates another relationship to death that defies such moral absolutes:

"Acapulco!" snorts Waterbuffalo. "Vatos are dying and you're off gettin' a tan."

This is it. With more energy than I have ever used at one time, I shout: SHUT UP!

There is a surprising silence. I calm down, just a little.

"Listen, you guys. I'm no kamakazi! Are you? Do you *want* to die? I'm a writer, yeah, and a singer of songs. I just happen to be a lawyer and a fighter. If I'm not all that, I'm dead! What the fuck are we fighting for? For land and to live just like we want."[46]

He finds that his differently articulated relationship to death alienates him from others in the movement. In the days that follow his declaration, he finds that "some of the men look at me strangely. They know I'm no wimp, but here I am, running around the world, talking of writing and revolution and women and death. Everyone in the room is committed to death. But my commitment to death is different, larger than theirs. It is a night for interrogation and I catch them wondering in the corners of their eyes. I'm different."[47] Zeta's "different," "larger" relationship to death manifests in the undermining of moral absolutes, in the impossibility of a quest for moral purity that the sanctifying of death demands.

While the irony of Acosta's text emerges from the uneasy fit between Zeta's hedonism and the morally earnest affect of nationalism, *So Far from God* critiques Chicano nationalism as a part of undermining a number of sacred metanarratives. The by-turns funny, grotesque, and wrenching tale of the trials and tribulations of a Chicana family in New Mexico, Ana Castillo's *So Far from God* juxtaposes a variety of tones: the fantastical and the sacred exist side by side with the banal and the cynical. The reference to Latin American magical realism in this text has been widely discussed, most specifically by Frederick Luis Aldama.[48] It's not hard to see why: each of the four sisters in this family, as well as all their various friends and relations, lives the most mundane and fantastical of lives and exists similarly in death. Yet these startling juxtapositions, when coupled with a wry, gossipy, and sometimes exasperated narrative voice, produce a formal strategy that is its own significant stylistic mode: an ironic and darkly humorous tone.

B. J. Manriquez situates this use of irony and humor as an instance of postmodernist absurdism.[49] Manriquez understands absurdism as having had its heyday in the 1960s as an epiphenomenon of the postmodern collapse of master narratives.[50] She notes, "The novel of the absurd ignores the ideological, and like *So Far from God*, rebels against essentialist beliefs of both traditional culture and literature . . . because for [Castillo] and for other absurdists, human beings exist in a silent, alien universe that possesses no inherent truth or meaning. Human actions seem senseless and absurd."[51] Manriquez importantly situates parody as a formal strategy that produces this absurdism, or, in her definition, a postmodern critique of a sense of totality. She notes that parody ridicules "any construction that tries to impose direction, order, or meaning upon existence . . . any pretension that life is understandable—literature, history, philosophy, religion."[52] Manriquez lists a series of "cultural beliefs that Castillo ridicules and rejects," highlighting primarily those that decree the sanctity of church and family.[53]

Manriquez's characterization of irony and absurdism as forms that emerge from the collapse of totalizing narratives must be contextualized. This breakdown in totalizing narratives emerged from the challenge that social movements posed to universalizing Enlightenment narratives that were based on colonial political, economic, and epistemological formations. We must understand that the context for the emergence of postmodern irony and critiques of metanarratives is the radical social movements of the post–World War II era that, as Roderick A. Ferguson argues, challenged the universality of Man in Enlightenment thought.[54] One manifestation of this challenge, as I have noted, was oppositional nationalist critique of the hypocrisy of U.S. national culture's claims to universality. Yet oppositional nationalist memorialization of racialized death itself began to act as a metanarrative, a metanarrative about the sanctity of death.

As such, I would add another set of "holy" beliefs to this list of totalizing narratives mocked and deflated by Castillo's text: the social movements of the 1960s and 1970s. To wit, the following passage introduces the family's eldest daughter:

> Esperanza had been the only one to get through college. She had gotten her B.A. in Chicano Studies. During that time, she had lived with her boyfriend Rubén (who, during the height of his Chicano cosmic consciousness, had renamed himself Cuauhtémoc). This despite her mother's opposition, who said of her eldest daughter's unsanctified union: "Why should a man buy the cow when he can have the milk for free?" "I am not a cow," Esperanza responded, but despite this, right after graduation, Cuauhtémoc dumped her for a middle-class gabacha with a Corvette; they bought a house in the Northeast Heights in Albuquerque right after their wedding.[55]

Rather than represent social movements with the usual earnest and rev-
erent canonization, the text subjects them to the same gently mocking
tone, representing them through characters difficult to take seriously,
such as Rubén and his somewhat self-important (and ultimately hypocritical) politicization via Chicano studies. Indeed, we can see Castillo's
Rubén as very much a caricature of the Chicano machismo figure at the
center of Acosta's text, particularly in the ways in which Rubén seems to
regard Esperanza as simply an object for casual sex and self-gratification
and is characterized by a sometimes comical, sometimes exasperating
mix of genuine political conviction and self-indulgent narcissism. The
passage is striking for the way in which it presumes the reader's famil-
iarity with Chicano studies, as well as with what it presents as a clichéd
trajectory of students who are temporarily radicalized by Chicano studies but ultimately end up being absorbed, without much resistance, into
the ranks of the bourgeoisie after graduation.

Further, the text also wryly (though a bit more sympathetically) comments on a kind of Chicana feminism that emerges primarily as a critique
of Chicano masculinity. The text ironically presents a Chicana critique of
machismo through an efficient and perfunctory treatment that makes this
kind of feminism come across as clichéd and not particularly revelatory.
When Esperanza, years later, takes back up with the divorced Rubén, now
engrossed in Native American spirituality, he teaches her "the do's and
don'ts of his interpretation of lodge 'etiquette' and the role of women and
the role of men and how they were not to be questioned. And she concluded as she had during their early days, why not?"[56] Given that the novel
sets up this relationship as so patently unreasonable, it is hardly surprising
when Esperanza finally puts Rubén in his place by unceremoniously dumping him (though, all things considered, it is not an unsatisfying scene).
Yet if the convention in "women's" literature is that feminist moments like
this produce a similarly feminist epiphany in the reader, Castillo's text
interrupts that function by representing this moment with an ironic detachment that makes Esperanza's version of feminism seem rather clichéd.

So Far from God thus puts the sanctimoniousness of cultural nationalist (and liberal feminist) affect in its place. In the same vein, we can see
the text's diverse representations of death, through a number of different

affects, as a marked contrast to the fixity of death under nationalist imaginaries. Like *The Revolt of the Cockroach People*, Castillo's text creates a language for talking about death as a differentiated condition. Rather than death and dismemberment signifying a universal condition of alienation, they are inhabited heterogeneously. Various characters die or are horribly mutilated, but this does not seem to impede their ability to have complex existences, through miraculous resurrections, restorations, or ectoplasmic visitations of one form or another. The eldest, Esperanza, dies while taken as a hostage during the first Iraq war, but comes back to Tome in ghostly form. Unlike most ghosts, Esperanza returns not to silently and mysteriously haunt the living but rather to launch into long-winded, opinionated political discussions with her sister Caridad. Caridad, once a promiscuous beauty prone to "making it in a pickup off a dark road with some guy," is brutally mutilated to the point of near death but is miraculously perfectly restored.[57] Caridad's second "death" occurs when she leaps off the edge of a mesa, hand in hand with a woman with whom she has fallen in love. Yet neither of their bodies is anywhere to be seen and is never found. The youngest sister, La Loca, dies of an epileptic fit in childhood, only to be resurrected at her own funeral. La Loca dies again in adulthood of AIDS but makes "occasional ectoplasmic appearances" at the national and international conventions of MOMAS, or Mothers of Martyrs and Saints, an organization founded by her mother, Sofi. Castillo may be using the conventions of magical realism, but she does so to free herself from the constraints of a nationalist definition of Chicano racialization that limits the responses to death to mourning.

Yet while *So Far from God* resists the totalizing narrative of nationalist mourning, it does not do so categorically. Thus the text does not dismiss the materiality of death as a process to which racialized bodies are particularly vulnerable. One of the four sisters, Fe, dies of cancer caused by the chemicals she is forced to use in her job cleaning weapons parts for a military contractor. Fe's death is recounted thusly:

The rest of this story is hard to relate.

Because after Fe died, she did not resurrect as La Loca did at age three. She also did not return ectoplasmically like her tenacious earth-bound sister Esperanza. Very shortly after her first prognosis, Fe just died. And when someone dies that plain dead, it is hard to talk about.[58]

There are two ways that "hard to talk about" can be read, of course, and I think this passage means them both. There is the idiomatic meaning, in which it is difficult to talk about an event because it is too painful, too emotionally taxing, to talk about something that can only be narrated as tragic. But we can also understand this statement literally; something might be hard to talk about because there is simply no vocabulary, no language, that can describe such a thing. The phrase "it is hard to talk about" in this case describes an epistemological crisis, which, like the autopsy passage from Acosta's text, marks a moment when a Chicano death must be mourned. This is an acknowledgment, in other words, that the process of defeudalization has not been completed and, indeed, has been exacerbated by neoliberalism. As such, oppositional nationalisms' protestations of death must be honored, even as alternative relationships to death must be invented. In that instance, there are no alternative modes of narrating subjectivity except through narratives of wholeness and life, no way to have fun with death and dismemberment. Castillo thus switches between creating a new language for subjectivity and lamenting the lack of such a language. In truth, this is the irony of this text. Insofar as Acosta's text does the same, as demonstrated in the discussion of Robert Fernandez's death, *The Revolt of the Cockroach People* also deploys a kind of irony.

Castillo's and Acosta's texts, then, demonstrate the ways in which U.S. state nationalism's bad-faith demand that we mourn death appropriately produces the very deviations and departures that are so castigated and punished by nationalist definitions of morality. Neoliberalism opportunitistically takes up minority and cultural nationalism by eradicating the heterogeneity of social movements and reducing our memory of what they were. In remembering these social movements differently, these texts highlight the limitations of a politics of recognition that too easily becomes the language by which others are rendered unworthy.

In the chapter that follows, I investigate two authors who likewise interrogate the dangers of recognition and who predicate their politics exactly on being the unworthy: Cherríe Moraga and Audre Lorde. These authors understand deeply the vulnerability to death that attends a practice of deviating from normative valuations of right and wrong. At the same time, they make a compelling case for the political and epistemological importance of inhabiting the space of impossibility that exists in the space of nonrecognition, between life and death.

CHAPTER TWO

On Being Wrong and Feeling Right

Cherríe Moraga and Audre Lorde

But how many lives are lost each time we cling to privileges that make other people's lives more vulnerable to violence?

—Cherríe Moraga, *The Last Generation: Poetry and Prose*

In what way do I contribute to the subjugation of any part of those who I call my people?

—Audre Lorde, "Learning from the 60s"

I began this book with Audre Lorde, in particular her memory and memorialization of the social movements era through the re-narration of Malcolm X's legacy. In the previous chapter, I continued this line of thought, exploring the contradictions of official nationalist memorialization, especially the ways in which nationalism's insistence that mourning is the only proper response to death produces yet disavows a variety of responses, from farce to irony to black humor. I argued that in Oscar Zeta Acosta's *Revolt of the Cockroach People* and Ana Castillo's *So Far from God* an engagement with death becomes the modality through which they critically remember Chicano nationalist movements, in particular the possibilities and limitations of these movements' memorialization of death. While advancing a critique of nationalism, Castillo's and Acosta's texts refuse to jettison completely the political efficacy of the nationalist valuation of life. This ability to maintain contradictory impulses at the same time without resolving them is what is unique to the sphere of culture, and it is what I identify as the impossible politics of difference. In other words, instantiating two ontological, political, and epistemological positions that are constituted as mutually exclusive and mutually negating—two positions that for the purposes of this book I am calling "life" and "death"—and insisting that they be held in suspension alongside each other is to insist on something that should be impossible. In the very process of insisting on impossibility, these texts are able to create, if only contingently, an alternative epistemological, political, and ontological possibility that does not depend on the dichotomizing of life and death.

I see women of color feminism as the most important practitioner of this particular politics, which, as I observed, theorists like Lorde called "difference." In this chapter, I provide readings of texts by two key women of color feminists—Audre Lorde and Cherríe Moraga—who are among the most advanced theorists and practitioners of difference as an affective, embodied, and subjectival practice. Situating their interventions into a neoliberal context in which the racialized ontology of *surplus* becomes increasingly generalized and generalizable, Lorde and Moraga theorize "difference" as a practice that holds in suspension various, mutually exclusive structures of value, and in so doing, constitutes new political (im)possibilities. They do so by theorizing and mobilizing affects such as shame, terror, loathing, and what Lorde famously termed "the erotic," in order to contest the ways in which neoliberal capitalist economies profit from deploying affect as a way of creating surplus, devalued, reviled populations.

As such, I explore the ways in which the "surplus" upon which neoliberal capital is predicated is constituted increasingly through the production of social values (or, in other words, economies of morality) in concert with, but also in excess of, the processes of labor exploitation. To the extent that one, though by no means only, aspect of the liberation movements of the twentieth century was an investment in political radicalism ruled by a binary sense of resistance vs. complicity, this investment has been taken up in the era of neoliberalism as one of a number of criteria for the adjudication of moral personhood. In this era, the moralism of an earlier era, articulated as the injunction to follow norms commensurate to official national culture, is supplemented by a proliferation of *diverse* criteria for moral or ethical conduct.

In this context, criteria for morality such as individualized choice, will, and complicity that we associate with nineteenth-century possessive individualism become remade under neoliberal power. If the classical possessive individual was narrated through the bildungsroman form as eventually resolvable to societal norms, the particularly American version produces criteria for morality that define the moral subject as resistant to societal norms that are articulated as unjust and corrupt. As I have argued in another context, this constitution of a moral subject through the rejection of something described as conventional morality is a particularly American version of the possessive individual, with *The Adventures of Huck Finn* being the paradigmatic example.[1] This operation does not so much displace morality itself as constitute new, unspoken but implicit criteria for morality. As we have seen in chapter 1, minority nationalist movement politics often came to be deployed as a way of disciplining subjects deemed inadequately radical or politicized. Both Lorde and Moraga explicitly challenged such disciplining new moralisms. For example, Lorde remembers in "Listening to the 60s" the ways in which her queer and feminist frustrations with Black politics in the 1960s could be dismissed, even by herself, thinking that "if I was only Blacker, things would be fine."[2] Moraga's entire oeuvre can be read as a critique of how particular aspects of mainstream feminism and nationalist revolutionary movements become wielded to discipline racialized, gendered, and sexualized subjects characterized as insufficiently politicized/radicalized or institutionally naive. As I argued in chapter 1, social movements of the mid-twentieth century were immensely complex and heterogeneous, and cannot be reduced to their single-issue, masculinist, or respectability-focused aspects. However, those aspects have become the dominant memory of these movements in the neoliberal moment. Because neoliberal power operates through the selective remembering of past social movements, a number of queer and feminist projects, scholarly and otherwise, have recently emerged to challenge and contextualize this remembering through a twofold method that both reconstructs lost and erased archives and also insists on the impossibility of any complete reconstruction.[3] I aim to contribute to those efforts by situating the ideas and theories generated by women of color feminists of the 1980s as an alternative mode of memory that contests the epistemological formations of contemporary neoliberal power. Further, women of color feminism can provide an analytic that disinters some of these other occluded and debased subjects who may not be "women of color."[4] In these refusals to base one's politics on the protection of one's own life, we find another, more precarious political ontology that takes seriously the two queries that open this chapter, one by Audre Lorde, and the other by Cherríe Moraga, that resonate deeply with each other. In a context in which individuals are pitted against each other in a desperate effort to deflect the precarious condition of "surplus" through the affective and moralizing dismissal of others, Moraga and Lorde offer, in different but aligned ways, impossible solutions to the conundrum of life and death.

Existential Surplus

In order to understand the shift to racial biopolitics in addition to racial necropolitics, we must understand the liberation movements of the 1960s as marking a fundamental crisis within an earlier instantiation of racial and gendered capitalism and the consequential effects on the relationship between productive and speculative capital. In the industrial period of the late nineteenth and early twentieth centuries in the United States that was organized around production, the contradictions of capitalism were sublated through a particular nexus of gendered and sexualized racialization that emerged through the exploitation of *labor*. As Lisa Lowe observes, in the late nineteenth and early twentieth centuries, the U.S. nation-state required a homogeneous citizenry, while U.S. industrial capital required a heterogeneous workforce, differentiated by categories of race that were always articulated through gender and sexual non-normativity.[5] This contradiction was sublated through the creation of a citizenry defined around whiteness and masculinity, while the racially and gender differentiated labor force was excluded from citizenship, thereby allowing the U.S. nation-state to define itself as homogeneous. While Lowe situates the Asian immigrant as the paradigmatic figure for this racialized and gendered *worker* alienated from citizenship, Mark Rifkin theorizes the creation of the legal category of the "domestic dependent nation" in the nineteenth century as the mechanism through which the U.S. settler colonial state established and legitimated its power to determine sovereignty itself, a power Rifkin calls "metapolitical authority."[6] This power was constituted over and against Native populations, relegating them to a state of "bare habitance."[7] We can see the process by which, in this period, racialization and colonization operated as modes of necropolitical social death; that is, capitalism required the abjection of racialized and colonized subjects as a means of extracting surplus value while the state established its own right to define what a valid state form was through the relegation of Native peoples into a liminal zone of governmentality.

Extending Lowe's argument, Roderick Ferguson identifies *surplus labor* as producing the very forms of racialized, gendered, and sexualized difference that capital requires but cannot entirely manage. Following Marx, Ferguson observes that these differences are necessary to the production of surplus labor. The Marxist term for surplus labor is the industrial reserve army, or the "relatively redundant working populations"[8] who are superfluous during times of contraction but are absolutely necessary in times of growth. Ferguson writes, "In the United States, racial groups who have a history of being excluded from the rights and privileges of citizenship (African Americans, Asian Americans, Native Americans, and Latinos, particularly) have made up the surplus populations upon which U.S. capital has depended."[9] These racialized, gendered, and sexualized differences were "in large part, the outcome of capital's demand for labor," but because of the state's need for a homogeneous citizenry, "the state worked to regulate the gender and sexual non-normativity of those racialized groups,"[10] thus rendering the labor of these groups that much more vulnerable to devaluation and relegation to the category of surplus. As both Lowe and Ferguson argue, these alienated subjects are both produced out of and vitally important to racial state and racial capital, but are in excess of state and capital's capacity to explain or characterize them. Such contradictions are managed through culture. Lowe observes that U.S. national culture claims that the nation-state is able to resolve material contradictions emerging out of racialized, gendered, and sexualized labor exploitation by narrating assimilation to the nation-state as the resolution. Both Lowe and Ferguson observe that this process is contradictory and excessive, and posits culture—Asian American cultural production and the African American novel, respectively—as the site where these repressed contradictions of capital return.

While Lowe and Ferguson identify race, gender, and sexuality as the surplus of material labor, Kara Keeling makes a similar argument in relation to immaterial labor by demonstrating the importance of affective labor to neoliberal capital. In a useful analysis of blaxploitation films, Keeling observes that affective labor is absolutely necessary to "reproduce sociality under capitalism."[11] That is, if as Lowe and Ferguson argue, culture is central to the operations of capital as the sphere in which capitalist social relations are legitimated, Keeling asserts that this process of legitimation also requires the production, circulation, and investment of affect.[12] Keeling's paradigmatic example is the blaxploitation film, which was engineered to produce a "surplus population" of black viewers during the 1970s, when the recessionary economy threatened the mainstream film industry's profitability. Capitalizing on the affective pleasure of Black Power aesthetics and interpellations, blaxploitaiton films allowed Hollywood to carve out a niche audience of black viewers that had previously not existed, and then, when that niche was no longer needed, to absorb them back into the mainstream. Here, black viewership is a form of "industrial reserve army" but for the immaterial labor of affect. Yet affective labor, while set in motion by capital's need to render its own social forms commonsensical and legitimate, "is capable as well of undermining the logic that supports such institutions."[13] For Keeling, as for Lowe and Ferguson, these forms of surplus derived from labor exploitation are both a part of capitalism but in excess of it as well.

Lowe, Ferguson, and Keeling thus help us understand the connection between various forms of surplus labor, both material and immaterial. I extend their analysis by observing that in addition to being produced through capital's need for differentiated labor coming into contradiction with the state's need for a homogeneous citizenry, in our contemporary moment in which the value of speculative capital far outweighs that of productive capital, race, gender, and sexuality are categories created by the process of turning *existence itself* into forms usable for speculative capital, as sheer surplus. If, as Marx observed, circulation of money as capital is an end in and of itself—the very purpose of capitalism, rather than to produce commodities or exploit workers—we might see contemporary neoliberal capitalism, which has been even further unmoored from its already tenuous connection to production and has become centrally a speculative enterprise, as the ultimate manifestation of capitalism. While published almost a decade before the global financial crisis of 2008, Jean Comaroff and John L. Comaroff's description of "a decidedly *neo*-liberal economy whose ever more inscrutable speculations seem to call up fresh specters in their wake"[14] seems particularly prescient right now. They observe, "In the upshot, production appears to have been superseded, as the *fons et origo* of wealth, by less tangible ways of generating value: by control over such things as the provision of services, the means of communication, and above all, the flow of finance capital. In short, by the market and by speculation."[15] If there is one thing that the recent financial crisis reminds us, however, it is that "there is no such thing as capitalism sans production, that the neoliberal stress on consumption as the prime source of value is palpably problematic."[16]

This is not to argue, however, that the category of existential surplus is new. Indeed, the histories of race and settler colonialism constitute the continuity between earlier and later modes of what David Harvey has called "accumulation by dispossession."[17] Seeking to undermine the progressive temporality inherent in Marx's idea of "primitive accumulation," scholars have used Harvey's term to observe that the violent process by which settler colonialism attempts to turn land into property and eliminate the native via extermination and assimilation is not an event long past, but is a process that continues to this day and that structures contemporary state institutions.[18]

In arguing that the long histories of colonialism, enslavement, and settler colonialism exceed Marx's labor theory of value—that is, his idea that all value originates from labor exploitation—Lowe, Ferguson, and Keeling suggest a connection between surplus value derived from labor exploitation and that derived from speculation. In so doing, they help us understand that speculative modes of valuation, which I have defined as value not contingent on labor exploitation, is not unique to the present. That is, the economic extraction of profit is, even in this earlier era,

dependent on the exclusion of certain laboring populations from criteria of value irreducible to labor, criteria that we can call race, gender, and
sexuality. As such, their analyses help us understand forms of surplus
formed not through labor but through other forms of value-creation.
While Ferguson discusses the production of surplus *labor*, his formulation that surplus labor is both "superfluous and indispensible" is useful
for understanding the contemporary production of surplus populations
as *non-laboring* subjects—that is, the populations that are surplus not to
production but to speculation. In other words, "superfluous and indispensible" is not only a way of thinking of differentiated labor but also the
contradictory formation of difference itself in the era of neoliberal racial
capitalism.

We can also understand Lowe's analysis of the shift in the nature of
Asian migration in the post–World War II era as marking the shift from
Asian populations as surplus labor to Asian populations as surplus existence. Lowe observes that while capitalist contradiction expressed itself
through the production of surplus labor in the late nineteenth and early
twentieth centuries, in the post–World War II era, Asian migration to
the United States is generated not only by the need for surplus labor
within a domestic industrializing economy but also as residual effects
of the United States' attempts to manage the pressures of a transnation-
alizing economy. As Lowe observes, in the post–World War II era, capital "required economic internationalism to expand labor and capital, to
secure raw material and consumer markets, to locate areas in which to
invest surplus capital, and to provide a safety valve for domestic ten-
sions."[19] While these needs tended to undermine the traditional influence and coherence of nation-states (for example, rendering borders
more porous to the flow of labor, goods, and capital), Lowe observes that
this new internationalism continued to create incentives that strength-
ened nation-states as well, as these states jockeyed for power "in order
to regulate the terms of that post-war internationalism."[20] Lowe reads
U.S. war-making and neocolonialism in Asia in this era as an attempt to
resolve the contradiction between capital's need for economic internationalism and the U.S. nation-state's need to consolidate itself as a global
hegemon. She notes that "the foreign policy that framed wars in Korea

and Vietnam and neocolonial domination of the Philippines was a liberal hybrid that combined economic internationalism and anti-communism, responding equally to the need to take economic supremacy and to contain the Soviet Union diplomatically."[21] Thus, these wars had both economic *and* necropolitical goals: "Although the U.S. wars in Korea and Vietnam reflected the general desire to incorporate the extractive economies of Asia into the industrial core, the twenty-year period in which the United States vied for power over the rimlands of Northeast Asia, Southeast Asia, and Taiwan also constituted a brutal theater in which the conquest and occupation of Asian countries were the means for the United States to perform its technological modernity and military force in relation to the Asiatic world."[22] Thus, while some of the displaced populations that migrate to the United States as a result of these machinations are certainly later incorporated as labor, their migration is not only impelled by the need for labor. They themselves are the residue or by-product of a geopolitical contest. People as *raw materials, by-products,* or *residues* are examples of existential surplus. This is not to say that these migrants, once in the United States, do not labor (for, of course, many do). Rather, it is to observe that their existence as migrants is not created out of the need for their labor. Many such populations are marked by the category of "refugee," which has historically been defined by the United States as those who flee communist regimes. Those who flee U.S.- and capitalism-friendly regimes like South Korea and the Philippines are more readily called labor migrants, no matter what the actual circumstances of their migration may be.[23] Those fleeing communist regimes like Vietnam, Cambodia, and Laos occupy another role: as those who are valuable for their devalued status. As Lynn Fuijwara has observed, many of these refugees take on the structural role of societal surplus as welfare recipients and other "burdens" on the state.[24]

As such, we can trace in histories of race and colonialism modes of value produced not through the material processes of production but through the immaterial processes of speculation—surplus is generated through the production of surplus populations. If the fundamental characteristic of capitalism is circulation, rather than production, and if contemporary capitalism increasingly has become organized around finance

capital unanchored by production, today's populations are not only surplus *labor* but are also merely surplus: existentially and inherently surplus. While labor exploitation is certainly still an important mode of value
extraction, certain populations are not destined ever to be incorporated
into capitalist production as labor. Jean Comaroff and John L. Comaroff
explain, "'Driven by the imperative to replicate money,' writes David
Korten, 'the [new global] system treats people as a source of inefficiency':
ever more disposable."[25] These conditions require a new definition of
difference. While the non-normativity indicated by race, gender, and
sexuality still indexes the importance of surplus labor, it is also the
marker of *purely surplus* populations, populations who are *existentially
surplus*.

Ruth Wilson Gilmore's analysis of the prison-industrial complex in
California provides a clear and compelling example of the rise of surplus
populations as a result of speculative capitalism's need to continually
expand. Gilmore observes that the boom in prison building, and the corresponding 500 percent increase in the state prison population in California since 1982, is not the result of rising crime rates, as quite the
opposite was happening. Instead, Gilmore traces the ways in which prisons were the solution for a nexus of capitalist needs: the need to invest
an overaccumulation of speculative capital, the need to warehouse African Americans who once had been employed as blue-collar workers in
defense and other industries that had since been relocated overseas, the
need to shift state bureaucracies from Keynesian social welfare to another
governing function, and the availability of rural land.[26] In this context,
Wilson notes, African American prison populations function within the
prison-industrial complex not as *labor* but as raw material. Put differently,
African American criminalization, which is legitimated through narratives of racialized, gendered, and sexualized deviance, is not only a means
of relegating them as surplus labor but also a means of relegating them
to surplus existence.[27]

In the contemporary moment organized around speculation as well
as production, populations are divided into valued and devalued, those
whose lives are protectable and those whose lives are not. To be "surplus" in this moment is to be valueless, unprotectable, and vulnerable.

This is not to say that they are unusable to capital; rather, their value to capital is exactly in their lack of value as labor. That is, while in the earlier period, racial necropolitics existed in order to extract surplus value from labor, in this era, racial necropolitics is created for itself; it is itself a source of value. James Ferguson quotes Larry Sommers, who observes that "the economic logic behind dumping a load of toxic waste in the lowest-wage country is impeccable," and notes that under neoliberalism, certain populations (such as those whose most valuable function in the global economy is to be worthless enough to live among nuclear waste) are most valuable *because* they are worthless.[28] In a very different context, Craig Willse's work on contemporary homelessness demonstrates that while in an earlier era the homeless constituted an industrial reserve army, today the homeless are never destined to labor, no matter how much the economy might expand, and instead, exist only as raw materials for new knowledge industries, particularly the social services sector that administers these populations and the social sciences that study them.[29]

Because Lowe insists on the centrality of culture to the operations of capitalism, she provides us a method for apprehending the ways in which the "surplus" in surplus labor is determined by assessments of which populations are valuable and which are not, determinations that are fundamentally cultural, affective, and ideological in nature. That is, the economic extraction of profit is, in this earlier era, dependent on the devaluation of certain laboring populations and not others. Yet if, as we have seen, surplus emerges not only out of labor exploitation but through the very rendering of certain subjects as the essence of nonvalue, then value is generated not only through labor exploitation but through the production of *values* themselves. In the contemporary era of speculative capital, in which value is produced not through the material processes of production but through the immaterial processes of speculation, surplus is generated through the production of affect.

Being Wrong and Feeling Right: What to Do with Surplus People

With this as context, we can reframe Lorde's and Moraga's theorizations of affect, feeling, and the role of culture as interventions into the specific technologies of neoliberalism. In this section, I read Audre Lorde's foundational book of collected essays and speeches, *Sister Outsider,* as a coherent engagement with the emergence of neoliberal power in the late 1970s and early 1980s, a moment that Lorde diagnosed as mobilizing affect in newly pernicious ways in order to effect biopolitical and necropolitical precarity for subjects rendered "surplus."[30] In this context, Lorde finds power in affects such as terror and loathing, which for Lorde are not categorically different from more celebrated affective registers such the erotic. I then move to Moraga, whose oeuvre Sandra Soto has rightly described as profoundly concerned with abjection, shame, and inadequacy. Moraga, like Lorde, refuses to participate in an economy of abandonment, rejecting the protection that comes with ascribing to the norms that underlie any definition of belonging.

The selective and extreme canonization of certain of Lorde's speeches and essays, most notably "The Master's Tools Will Never Dismantle the Master's House," means that many never read beyond this work—or perhaps even beyond its title. "The Master's Tools" essay is certainly addressed to a white feminist audience, having originated as a speech at the "Second Sex" Conference in 1979, and there is no doubt that the ubiquity of this one essay has cast Audre Lorde's theoretical legacy in certain ways. In addition, a decidedly multiculturalist contingency has taken up, and I would argue, misread Lorde's work in the years after her premature death from cancer in 1992. Yet a tradition of queer of color and women of color feminist scholarship have refused to relinquish Lorde's legacy to multiculturalism and have begun to dislodge the general understanding of her as someone whose political and theoretical interventions were aimed solely or mainly at the white feminist movement.[31] In engaging with Lorde's oft-quoted but rarely deeply analyzed collection of essays and speeches, I imagine myself as contributing to this larger collective project that works to re-center Lorde, who has often been dismissed as a "practitioner," "activist," or "artist" by those for whom these categories are defined in opposition to "theorist," in order to situate her work as a starting point for a queer theory emerging out of a materialist critique of racial capitalism.

I find that Lorde's diagnoses of her contemporary moment are perhaps the most precise and useful descriptions of what I've been calling neoliberalism, descriptions that center affect as foundationally imbricated in the social relations created by neoliberal power. In her essay "Age, Race, Class, and Sex: Women Redefining Difference," which originated as a speech delivered in 1980, she writes, "Institutionalized rejection of difference is an absolute necessity in a profit economy that needs outsiders as surplus people."[32] In "Uses of the Erotic: The Erotic as Power," an essay originally delivered as a speech in 1978, she writes, "The principle horror of any system which defines the good in terms of profit rather than in terms of human need, or which defines human need to the exclusion of the psychic and emotional components of that need—the principle horror of such a system is that it robs our work of its erotic value, its erotic power and life appeal and fulfillment."[33] These two passages epitomize Lorde's theory of what we would now call the biopolitical and necropolitical operations of neoliberal power, as well as her political intervention into that power: what she called the erotic. In these passages, Lorde powerfully describes the ways in which contemporary power operates principally by producing "surplus people"—those whose lives are rendered unprotectable because of their departure from norms—under neoliberal capitalism ("a profit economy") as organized by race and gender as well as sexuality ("institutionalized rejection of difference").

For Lorde, the privileging of some over others can only happen through the deployment of affect. Affect is exactly what prevents us from asking and answering the question that I referenced in my introduction: "In what way do I contribute to the subjugation of *any part of those who I call my people?*" The particular affects that produce consequential difference and prevent us from imagining others as "my people" are, according to Lorde, terror and loathing. Fear, loathing: these are terms that Lorde uses repeatedly, in her many essays, to describe the only *legitimated* affective response to the relation between valued and devalued subjects. For Lorde, feelings are not individual nor free from coercion but rather legislated and enforced as a material structure through which the relational violence marked by "difference" is hidden, and devaluation is legitimated. Years before the "affective turn" in contemporary humanistic scholarship, Lorde theorized what she calls "feeling" as entirely imbricated within the operations of power.[34] While Lorde did not use the term "affect," contemporary theorists' definitions of that term resonate with how Lorde describes the mobilization of fear and loathing. For example, Kara Keeling, following Gilles Deleuze, observes that while "most commonly, we talk about affect as a feeling or emotion . . . it is important to think about affect as also involving the mental activity required to make sense of the world."[35] In Lorde's theorization, "feeling" is most certainly a means to make sense of the world and, further, is turned toward the shaping of a world in which affective judgments of someone's worth determine their claims to life and death. In this way, Lorde's theorization of capitalism's use of affect prefigures Patricia Clough's 2008 observation that "the projection of hate and fear onto a population that makes it into a mythical adversary, may come to function as a support of evaluations of populations, marking some for death and others for life."[36]

In response to capital's mobilization of affect, Lorde's strategy is not to reject "feeling." She says in her famous "The Master's Tools Will Never Dismantle the Master's House" speech: "I urge each one of us here to reach down into that deep place of knowledge inside herself and *touch that terror and loathing* of any difference that lives there. See whose face it wears."[37] This is an idea that she returns to again and again: in "Learning from the 60s," she writes that we must "put our finger down upon that loathing buried deep within each one of us and *see who it encourages us to despise.*"[38] In so doing, Lorde takes these feelings seriously as material, structural, and necessary components of "a profit economy which needs outsiders as surplus people."[39] That is, if contemporary neoliberal capitalism, as I argued earlier, requires a set of existentially surplus people, the mechanism through which populations are rendered surplus—that is, intrinsically devalued—is through the mobilization of terror and loathing against those populations in order to legitimate their disposability. If terror and loathing are the affective modalities through which we justify our own positions of security from violence, and through which we invest in narratives that, in James Kyung-Jin Lee's words, "teach us to abandon people," then Lorde's strategy against this abandonment is to critically interrogate and account for these feelings.[40] Such work, for Lorde, is a *materialist and structural* practice. Returning to the discussion of speculation, if populations are currently rendered disposable and devalued (i.e., racialized, gendered, and sexualized) not only through the process by which capital recruits cheap and vulnerable labor but also through its need for populations that are essentially devalued, how are such populations constituted? How are some populations rendered unworthy of protection? According to Lorde, this crucial operation of neoliberal power occurs through the mobilization of terror and loathing as affective technologies of abandonment.[41]

As I observed in the introduction, Lorde's "Learning from the 60s" speech to the Harvard-Radcliffe BSU asks them—and by extension, us—to take into account the ways in which we are implicated in abandoning others to expendability: "I ask myself as well as each one of you, exactly what alteration in the particular fabric of my everyday life does this connection call for? . . . In what way do I contribute to the subjugation of *any part of those who I call my people?* Insight must illuminate the particulars of our lives: who labors to make the bread we waste, or the energy it takes to make nuclear poisons which will not biodegrade for one thousand years; or who goes blind assembling the microtransistors in our inexpensive calculators?"[42] In this way, Lorde asks us to reckon with the ways in which the "institutionalized rejection of difference" happens *within* African American communities through the very strategies of race-based collectivity that were instituted to protect these communities from the privations of being "surplus people." Instead, she observes, African Americans' rejection of difference ends up contributing to, rather than undermining, the "profit economy" that depends on surplus.

At the same time, a sustained engagement with Lorde's perspective on fear, terror, and loathing demonstrates that she does not advocate the overcoming or negation of these affects. Close scrutiny of her work reveals rather that what one does with terror and loathing is to touch, engage, and acknowledge them. In her essay "The Transformation of Silence into Language and Action," Lorde writes, "I began to recognize a source of power within myself that comes from the knowledge that while it is most *desirable* not to be afraid, learning to *put fear into a perspective* gave me great strength."[43] Likewise, in her interview with Adrienne Rich, Lorde observes, "It's like fear: once you put your hand on it, you can use it or push it away."[44] Instead of rejecting certain affects or fleeing toward an unsatisfying rationality, Lorde's solution is to engage affect.

Her mode of engaging affect is most famously described in her essay "Uses of the Erotic: The Erotic as Power." In this essay, Lorde champions what she calls the "erotic" as a source of power that evades the masculinist, hierarchical relations of domination more conventionally understood as power. Instead, Lorde describes the erotic as centrally located in the sensual and affective; it encompasses the sexual, but is also a more fully saturating category that, unlike what she calls "the pornographic," refuses to compartmentalize the sexual from other aspects of life, thus turning sexuality into a commodity. She writes that "the erotic is not a question only of what we can do; it is a question of how acutely and fully we can feel in the doing."[45] She observes, "Every level upon which I sense also opens to the erotically satisfying experience, whether it is dancing, building a bookcase, writing a poem, examining an idea."[46] In this way, "there is, for me, no difference between writing a poem and moving into sunlight against the body of a woman I love."[47] Lorde's conception of what we might call "sexuality" imagines it not simply as a discrete category created through the production of desire as an operation of power, as in Foucault's analysis, but as a way of being that is an antidote to neoliberal technologies of abandonment. Rather than teaching us to abandon one another, Lorde's erotic enables the full inhabitation of one's self, and as such, the "sharing of joy" that "forms a bridge between the sharers which can be the basis for understanding what is not shared between them, and lessens the threat of their difference."[48] I want to observe here that Lorde does not claim that the erotic will somehow *transcend* or *eliminate* differences—differences that, as I argued earlier, are constituted through *material* processes that differentially protect some from death, disposability, and devaluation at the expense of others. Instead, she envisions a means of "understanding" or clearly apprehending these differences so as to "lessen the threat," perhaps by ensuring that these differences are not met with fear and loathing *as motivators for abandonment*. Put differently, it is not fear and loathing in and of themselves that are the problem, but the harnessing of fear and loathing to structures of abandonment. Further, although Lorde does not explicitly invoke race and class in this essay, instead deploying what might at first seem to be a universalizing category of "women," contexualizing this essay in this way within the larger trajectory of her writings reveals that Lorde's "erotic" engages the racialized, gendered, and sexualized operations of neoliberal power.

As sanguine as Lorde's description of the erotic seems to be here, I want to argue against interpretations that might read the erotic as a simple utopian idealism that minimizes the devastating, life-and-death consequences of necropolitical power. Instead, Lorde expresses over the course of the essays and speeches in *Sister Outsider* an exceptionally complex theory of abjection, affect, and power. In an interview with Adrienne Rich, Rich asks Lorde to clarify what she meant by the "Black mother" in her essay "Poetry Is Not a Luxury," remarking that many read the essay as "simply restating the old stereotype of the rational white male and the emotional dark female."[49] First noting that "leaving rationality to the white man is like leaving him a piece of that road that begins nowhere and ends nowhere,"[50] Lorde goes on to explain what she means by the "Black mother." For Lorde, the "Black mother" is not an actual person or even an identity; rather, she is the figure for all that has been abjected, rendered irrational and disgusting, by modern capitalist relations. Lorde provides a litany of all that the "Black mother" symbolizes: "The terror [and] the chaos which is Black which is female which is dark which is rejected which is messy . . . sinister, smelly, erotic, confused, upsetting."[51] The "erotic" in this context is categorized along with all that modernity has to reject in order to constitute itself. Embracing the erotic, then, is to take on the terrifying prospect of aligning oneself with that which the "profit economy" mobilizes to destroy, and somehow creating connection and community out of the act of rendering oneself open to precarity and devastation. Using the erotic as power, then, is to find a way out of the impossible bind that neoliberal power sets up for us: if we are to refuse to "subjugate any part of those who we call our people," as Lorde asked in "Learning from the 60s," we must embrace, rather than reject, those rendered the most vulnerable and precarious, which means embracing those most vulnerable and precarious aspects of our own existences. This sense of precarity underwrites "the erotic," and as such, living and embodying the erotic is far from easy.

Yet this is the only way to be able to break out of already-colonized definitions of what we can want and do, and of how to live. In the section of the interview with Rich in which Lorde invokes the "Black mother," she says, "The possible shapes of what has not been before exist only in that back place, where we keep those unnamed, untamed longings for something different and beyond what is now called possible."[52] Using the term "that back place" here to describe what she calls "the Black mother," Lorde gestures to the ways in which the erotic operates as what Keeling calls, describing affect, "the felt presence of the unknowable . . . that points toward a different epistemological, if not ontological and empirical, regime."[53]

It is with this understanding of Lorde's theorization of "feeling" as a complex materialist analysis and deployment of affect that we can approach Lorde's use of the phrase "it feels right to me," which comes up in both "Poetry Is Not a Luxury" and "Uses of the Erotic." In "Uses of the Erotic," Lorde writes, "Beyond the superficial, the considered phrase, 'It feels right to me,' acknowledges the strength of the erotic into a true knowledge, for what that means is the first and most powerful guiding light toward any understanding."[54] In "Poetry Is Not a Luxury," in a passage that describes poetry as a means to express feelings that are the only way into "the most radical and daring of ideas,"[55] Lorde writes, "Right now, I could name at least ten ideas that I would have found intolerable or incomprehensible and frightening, except as they came after dreams and poems. This is not idle fantasy, but a disciplined attention to the true meaning of 'it feels right to me.'"[56] If we contextualize Lorde's theorization of "feeling," we can see that Lorde deploys the phrase "it feels right to me" not to claim a form of entitlement based on a preservation or reflexive defense of the self, defined in essentialist terms around an individuated sense of where "feelings" come from. Rather, Lorde describes a process in which the most intolerable, incomprehensible, and frightening ideas—those least societally acceptable, those ideas that defy the limits of normativity and the protection that such normativity promises—find a way to "feel right to me," or, in other words, become assimilable to one's existence, knowledge, and thought. The "true knowledge" that

Lorde refers to above, then, is not a reinscription of an idea of pure knowledge divorced from material relations (what in "Uses of the Erotic" Lorde dismisses as "flattened affect"[57]) but a knowledge that manages to exist despite or perhaps because of societal attempts to render it marginal, dangerous, and mad. In this way, Lorde's definition of "feeling right" resonates with Keeling's description of the processes of affect: "It points toward what escapes recognition, whatever escapes meaning and valuation, exists as an impossible possibility within our shared reality, however that reality is described theoretically, and therefore threatens to unsettle, if not destroy, the common senses on which that reality relies for its coherence as such."[58]

Perhaps no one takes up Lorde's challenge to interrogate the costs of one's own protection more deeply than Cherríe Moraga, whose entire oeuvre is based on creating a politics out of the most precarious and indefensible aspects of herself. If, for Lorde, aligning oneself with what is rendered vulnerable, unprotectable, and unthinkable is crucial to undermining neoliberal power, perhaps no one has so consistently made such a process of self-abjection as central to her artistic or political practice as Moraga. In the two texts I examine in this chapter, *The Last Generation* and *Waiting in the Wings*, Moraga constantly narrates herself as suspended between valued and devalued forms of subjectivity, and does so by staging her complex relationship to biological reproduction.

Biological reproduction has become an immensely important site for marking which subjects are deserving and which undeserving. David Eng insightfully notes the centrality of parenting to contemporary norms of citizenship and social belonging in the United States, writing that "the possession of a child, whether biological or adopted, has today become the sign of guarantee not only for family but also for full and robust citizenship—for being a fully realized political, economic, and social subject in American life."[59] The child becomes the apotheosis of citizenship, the figure that, as Lee Edelman puts it, "alone embodies the citizen as an ideal."[60] In this context, child rearing—whether biologically or through adoption—becomes an avenue, albeit a contentious one, for previously despised gay and lesbian subjects to narrate themselves as deserving, moral, and responsible.

In this framework, procreative temporalities constitute a horizon of legibility and representability, even, or perhaps especially, for gay and lesbian parents. Yet this does not mean that all who procreate are extended this form of protected subjectivity. As Cathy Cohen observes in her foundational essay, "Punks, Bulldaggers, and Welfare Queens," we cannot assume that there is a "uniform heteronormativity from which all heterosexuals benefit."[61] She cites, for example, "the stigmatization and demonization of single mothers, teen mothers, and primarily, poor women of color dependent on state assistance."[62] Likewise, for Moraga, "queer motherhood" does not sit easily. Instead of using motherhood as a way of claiming normativity, she represents herself as engaging with the death and precarity that normativity attempts to banish at the very moment when she seems to be embracing incorporation and affirmation through reproduction. For Moraga, motherhood brings her closer to, not further away from, the kinds of despised subjects who continually face devastation, devaluation, and death: her friends dying of AIDS, her parents' generation who are dying away, their memories and histories fading with their deaths. She does so by marking the ways in which she is constantly in danger of annihilation by being *wrong* in her motherhood. Moraga writes herself into precarity as a mother, not only by being a mother marked as inadequate by her lesbianness but also by foregrounding the ways in which motherhood makes her not radical enough, not butch enough, not nationalist enough, too nationalist, and so on. In this way, Moraga experiences motherhood *both* as a mode of legibility and as a mode of erasure and abjection related to, though not equivalent to, those faced by other non-normative subjects.

As Sandra K. Soto has argued, perhaps no other Chicana feminist has so centrally engaged in articulating a different relationship to the dialectic of power and abjection as Cherríe Moraga.[63] As Soto notes, Moraga's entire body of work, and indeed, the motivating impulse behind her creative process, can be seen to "place a high premium on the public elaboration of private feelings of anxiety, guilt, and fear."[64] Most centrally, Moraga inserts herself in an important Chicana feminist tradition in her arguably most famous essay, "A Long Line of Vendidas" (from *Loving in the War Years*), when she embraces the figure of the traitor by associating herself with the figure of La Malinche.[65] Yet the purpose of this writing is not, as in nationalist mobilizations of such affects, to overcome the losses that produced such feelings: "Moraga's lessons to her students is no self-help healing regimen, nor is it a call to put forth universal truths about the shared pain of being human. Rather . . . Moraga means to inter-twine meaningful personal revelation with ethnonationalist desire . . . ; the more affective and visceral the experience or desire recounted, the more meaningful and tangible the political result."[66] In other words, rather than use loss as a way of justifying a compensatory formation, whether that formation is the patriarchal family or the ethnonational-ist community, Moraga finds her politics in the very location of loss and its attendant affects. This is not to claim, of course, that Moraga does not herself desire these compensatory mechanisms. Soto notes that "there is a nagging sense that in relation to the poststructuralist orienta-tion of queer theory, Moraga's occasional objectification of race, reifica-tion of binary oppositions, refusal to critique models of authenticity, and modernist-inflected conceptions of power and resistance can seem mis-guided, if not flat footed."[67] Yet Soto insightfully argues that because these tendencies in Moraga's work occur in the context of Moraga's con-stant sense of shame over her inadequacy as a racialized subject because of her ability to "pass" as white, her half-white parentage, her lack of Spanish linguistic ability, and her queerness, Moraga's writing can never produce a sense of belonging within an ethnonationalist community or attainment of a nuclear family ideal.

Moraga's *The Last Generation* (1993), a collection of poetry and prose, and *Waiting in the Wings* (1997), a memoir of her experience of mother-hood, are no exceptions to this tendency. Moraga's ruminations on the impossibility of banishing death in the process of bringing forth life are oblique meditations on the exacerbated vulnerability to death that the protection of life mandates. In so doing, in both texts, whether through childlessness or through motherhood, Moraga situates queer Chicana subjectivity as potentially a site for identifying ways of knowing and being both situated in, but in excess of, normative reproduction, generational temporality, and the forms of history that they imply. In contrast to a normative narration of history and generational reproduction, Moraga

describes an epistemological formation that both privileges life and articulates the impossibility of preserving life:

> My family is beginning to feel its disintegration. Our Mexican grand-
> mother of ninety-six years has been dead two years now and la familia's
> beginning to go. Ignoring this, it increases in number. I am the only one
> who doesn't ignore this because I am the only one not contributing to
> the population. My line of family stops with me. There will be no one
> calling me, *Mami, Mamá, Abuelita* . . .
>
> I am the last generation put on this planet to remember and record.
>
> No one ever said to me, you should be a writer some day. But I went
> ahead and did it anyway.[68]

For Moraga, being a Chicana lesbian writer means being able to record
rather than "ignore" the disintegration of this particular version of family. Because Moraga is a lesbian and thus, in her view at this moment,
unable to continue the family line through reproduction, she is given
a kind of vision or awareness: the gift and burden of being unable to
ignore a dying generation by turning her attention to the newly birthed,
by celebrating the fact that the family "increases in number." This generation, the generation of her tíos and tías, Moraga informs us in her
introduction to the volume, will take a particular kind of culture with
them: "Lo mexicano will die with their passing."[69] In *Waiting in the
Wings,* Moraga describes this generation as the "last real generation of
the Mexican-American Moraga clan . . . none of us are as much family
as they. And as my uncle's generation goes, the family goes with it in that
profoundly Mexican sense."[70] Others can ignore this passing by count-
ing children, Moraga says, "but I cannot accept it. I write."[71] In this way,
Moraga articulates the importance of preserving what is lost through
death, but not by producing "life" in the usual, reproductive ways.

Lisa Tatonetti argues that Moraga's association of lesbianism with
loss in *The Last Generation* reproduces the notion of the Chicana lesbian
as "traitor" to her Chicano nation. Tatonetti writes, "An observer rather
than a participant, Moraga contributes to this perceived cultural disintegration by virtue of her same-sex desire: she equates lesbian sexuality

with childlessness, which she represents as familial absence and cultural betrayal. The traditional Chicano portrayal of the lesbian as Malinche, a traitor to her race, is thus fulfilled."[72] In contrast, she reads Moraga's queer motherhood in *Waiting in the Wings* as a means of recuperating the Malinche figure not as traitor but as "the *savior* of Chicano culture."[73] In contrast, I read Moraga's description of her childlessness as not only a sign of "internalized homophobia,"[74] as Tatonetti describes it, but as also a means of seeing and remembering what normative reprosexuality erases. Tatonetti's analysis of Moraga as registering an "internalized homophobia" is symptomatic of the very assessments of moral value that Moraga seeks to evade. That is, Tatonetti's implication that Moraga's utilization of Malinche indexes her insufficiently radical queer politics delineates an unspoken but understood criteria of what constitutes proper queer politics that, while condemning *heteronormative* criteria of value, manifests another set of criteria.

Instead, taking into consideration Soto's argument that Moraga *recuperates* the Malinche figure, we can read queer motherhood in *Waiting in the Wings* as an extension of, rather than a break from, the "traitorous" childlessness of *The Last Generation*. In *The Last Generation*, Moraga imagines the possibilities that emerge out of childlessness, later writing in a poem called "I Was Not Supposed to Remember":

> I am a woman, childless
> and I teach my stories to other
> childless women and somehow
> the generations will propagate and prosper
> and remember pre-memory.[75]

Childnessness in this formulation is not, as Tatonetti argues, a moment where Moraga reproduces the misogyny of the Malinche tradition. Rather, I would argue that childnessness becomes for Moraga a means of imagining other modes of producing culture and of creating community, a way of creating a lineage that does not depend on the erasure of alternative pasts. Instead, the generations created by Moraga and her clan of "childless women" "somehow" queerly exist not through the production of children but through the teaching of "stories." In so doing, these generations "remember pre-memory" or, in other words, that which is not supposed to be remembered, that which normative hetero-reproduction would "ignore" and forget.

Moraga's use of "last," then, gestures to another kind of temporality than that of linear, biological propagation, yet simultaneously situates herself within a generational temporality nonetheless. Moraga posits *herself*, not her tíos and tías, as the "last generation." If she is the last generation who is "put on this planet to remember and to record," this last generation is, definitionally, *queer*. That is, her queerness, her lesbianism, makes her childless, and thus able to see, remember, and write that which those who do bear childen ignore. Rather than the "last" signaling the end of a sequence—a series of generations that ends with her—the "last" instead marks a different inhabitation of time. That she is the "last" does not necessarily imply that there was anyone before her, because her queer way of creating generations is impossible, unexplainable ("somehow"), and so cannot be understood within the mundane conceptions of biologically propagated generations. She is "last" because the work she does as her generation is to remember that which cannot be folded into linear time: "pre-memory." She does so by both celebrating life and documenting death as one and the same act.

Moraga's impetus to preserve this "pre-memory" expands her preoccupation with her immediate blood family to cosmic proportions. Noting that she is completing the book in 1992, "500 years after the arrival of Cristóbal Colón,"[76] she situates the death of this generation of Chicanos as the culmination of centuries of death and destruction following the "violent collision between the European and the Indigenous, the birth of a *colon*ization that would give birth to me."[77] The demise of this generation is the demise of the entire race that was created out of this violent collision. Moraga writes of "a sense of urgency that Chicanos are a disappearing tribe"[78] that spurs her to write. In this way, Moraga does not celebrate or ignore the violences of death, loss, and abjection.

If Chicanos are a disappearing tribe, and this disappearance is the culmination of five centuries of colonialism, Moraga's project in this book is not only to document the end, but also to imagine a new beginning.

What it means for Moraga to revitalize this tribe is to reimagine it as queer. In her essay "Queer Aztlán: The Re-formation of Chicano Tribe," Moraga writes of the need for "a new Chicano movement."[79] She writes, "Chicana lesbians and gay men do not merely seek inclusion in the Chicano nation; we seek a nation strong enough to embrace a full range of racial diversities, human sexualities, and expressions of gender."[80] This is a dangerous line to tread, and is again a manifestation of Moraga's refusal to be affirmed by any criteria or system of value. That is, Moraga is not unaware of, and indeed, is deeply critical of the "dangers of nationalism," its "tendency toward separatism" that can "run dangerously close to biological determinism and a kind of fascism,"[81] and in particular of Chicano nationalism and "its institutionalized heterosexism, its inbred machismo, and its lack of a cohesive national political strategy."[82] It is easy enough to dismiss minority nationalism altogether, in a moment when facile critiques of "identity politics" provide the vocabulary for this dismissal.[83]

Why, then, does Moraga take up nationalism in order to "queer" it? She writes, "I cling to the word 'nation' because without the specific naming of the nation, the nation will be lost (as when feminism is reduced to humanism, the woman is subsumed)."[84] She urges us to "retain our radical naming, but expand it to meet a broader and wiser revolution."[85] Moraga describes this revolution as queer, indigenous, and feminist, and represents this new community as a means of "making culture, making tribe, to survive and flourish as members of the world community in the next millennium."[86] For Moraga, Queer Aztlán is a vision of a new set of possibilities: "As we are forced to struggle for our right to love free of disease and discrimination, 'Aztlán' as our imagined homeland begins to take on a renewed importance. Without the dream of a free world, a free world will not be realized."[87] That is, what is crucial about this notion of a Queer Aztlán is that it names and imagines a possibility that is impossible in the present. It is an example of what José Esteban Muñoz calls "queer utopia": "A structuring and educated mode of desiring that allows us to see and feel beyond the quagmire of the present . . . an insistence on potentiality or concrete possibility for another world."[88] In invoking a millennial cosmology spurred into existence, but ultimately uncontained

by the violence of European colonization, Moraga invokes a different temporality, a temporality not subsumed to the "'dream world' of individualism, profit, and consumerism"[89] that is the inevitable consequence of this
European colonization, but another trajectory, another possible future,
represented by a queer, indigenous, female cosmology. This cosmology
is one in which life and death are not sequential, but coincident. Queer
Aztlán names the possibility of *coexistence* of two radically contradictory
temporalities, one called "life" and the other "death." Thus, in embracing Queer Aztlán, Moraga is not unmindful of the dangers of nationalist
politics. Moraga is, indeed, someone who has consistently challenged
Chicano nationalist imaginaries throughout her oeuvre. Indeed, it is the
very contradiction inherent in "Queer" and "Aztlán" that produces the
possibility of crisis and contradiction.

The potential dangers of such a politics become manifestly evident
in this section, in particular in Moraga's curious lack of ambivalence
around the category of the "indigenous." Unlike lesbian, female, nationalist, mother, or Chicana, all of which Moraga subjects to intense scrutiny as a means of revealing the systems of valuation and devaluation in
which they traffic, Moraga's representation of indigeneity is surprisingly
entirely affirmative. In situating indigeneity as an unqualified and un-
complicated category through which Moraga finds affirmation, she is
not only uncharacteristically departing from the trajectory of her work but
also in many ways replicating the erasure of indigenous peoples that organize both Mexican and U.S. nationalisms. Norma Alarcón argues that
Mexican mestizo nationalism and Chicano nationalism appropriate the
image of the native woman, sanitizing her as a way of making her the
foundation of a mestizo civilization or Chicano community.[90] In contrast,
Alarcón observes that Chicana feminism's recuperation of "La Malinche"
is a means of invoking the native woman *in her abjection* rather than in
an affirmative mode, as with Mexican mestizo nationalism or Chicano
nationalism. In a reversal of some of her earlier work, Moraga posits indigeneity in such uniformly valued terms in *The Lost Generation*, rather
than in the ambivalent terms with which she articulates other categories.

This is particularly striking when we turn our attention to Moraga's discussion of motherhood, which Moraga describes in thoroughly ambivalent

and complex ways. For what happens, then, when this queer Chicana writer becomes a mother, as in *Waiting in the Wings?* Does her foray into motherhood mean that she, too, joins the ranks of those who celebrate the "increase" in the family by "ignoring" the dying, be it the generation of her parents or a generation of queer men? Quite the opposite, we find that *Waiting in the Wings,* while a narrative of the first three years of Moraga's son's life, is nothing less than a sustained meditation on motherhood as not a guarantee of life and value, but as vulnerability to death and devaluation. From the epigraph by Michel de Montaigne that reminds us that "to practice death is to practice freedom" that begins the book, to the very end, Moraga's experience of motherhood, of bringing forth life, is not a way to forestall or banish death. Rather, it is a process haunted continually by the presence of death. Moraga's son Rafael is born three months premature and he is further jeopardized by intestinal conditions that require surgery. Rafael's survival is by no means guaranteed in the first six months of his life, and Moraga writes of the overwhelming terror that Rafael's brushes with death inspire in her.

Yet the text's preoccupation with death is not merely attributable to any parent's terror at the possibility of losing a child but is entirely determined by Moraga's queer Chicana subjectivity. Moraga's effort to create queer of color family means bringing Rafael into the world at the very moment when her friends—her queer family—are dying of AIDS. Interlaced throughout the narrative of Moraga's pregnancy, Rafael's birth and his struggle to survive in an infant ICU, and the changes Rafael's presence brings for Moraga's work as a writer and her relationship with her partner Ella, are the stories of deaths: her friends Tede and Rodrigo and Ronnie, all activists and artists and men who remind her, as Moraga writes in *The Last Generation,* "how rare it is to be colored and queer and to live to speak about it."[91] Moraga finds out that her baby will be a boy just a few days before she learns the news that Tede has AIDS. In that moment before the advent of anti-retrovirals, having AIDS is experienced as tantamount to a death sentence, and Moraga reflects: *"There is meaning in the fact that my fetus has formed itself into a male, a meaning I must excavate from the most buried places of myself, as well as from this city, this era of dying into which my baby will be born."*[92] What does it mean to create a queer family, the text seems to ask, when one generation's birth is accompanied by another generation's premature death?

It is not only queer family whose deaths are connected to Rafael's life, but blood family as well: Moraga's tío, a part of the very generation whose imminent passing inspires Moraga's theorization of queer child-lessness as an alternative way of telling history and marking time in *The Last Generation*, dies when Rafael is two—by then a healthy and pros-pering child. Moraga writes, "I try to write about the impossible, the ordinary beginning of one life and the passing of another. Watching a life enter and another exit within the same brief moment of my family's history."[93] The entire text, in this way, is the evidence of Moraga's attempt to inhabit motherhood and family differently, to produce children and create family not as an attempt to master or overcome death or to recon-cile and thus erase the abjection and loss of death by positing family and children as the epitome of life. If, as Moraga observed in *The Last Gen-eration*, normative biological reproduction and generational temporality is predicated on ignoring death, *Waiting in the Wings* is her attempt to do the "impossible"—which is craft a version of queer motherhood that recognizes the death that inheres in life, and vice versa. For Moraga, queer family means "a relentlessly intimate acquaintance with death,"[94] a kind of death-in-life.

Physical death in this book takes on metaphysical implications. Her tío's death marks the waning of the Last Generation; Tede, Rodrigo, and Ronnie are another generation gone. Moraga traces the "premature" deaths of movements through a rumination on the deaths of César Chávez and Audre Lorde, both of whom die in the year of Rafael's birth. Neither of these deaths are simply the deaths of one individual; instead, they are "the story of [her] own political history as a Chicana and as a lesbian."[95] Yet these two political lineages—the Chicano movement on the one hand, lesbian of color feminism on the other—have very dif-ferent legacies. Moraga "wonders about leadership," and asks "who is there to replace them?"[96] Comparing two photographs, one of Audre, the other of César, she comes to two very different conclusions. César's is a "sad picture," the iconography of a martyred saint. Audre's, in contrast, is "radiant."[97] She observes that "César died in his sleep, a tired man . . .

after thirty years of lucha and no re-emerging movement on the horizon" and wonders if he "died of a broken heart. But not Audre."[98] Audre's physical death, in other words, does not mean the demise of the hopes and dreams of the movement she represented. Unlike César, whose death may have been precipitated by, and allegorizes, the demise of a once-vigorous movement, Audre's death does not close down possibility for a future. Indeed, Audre, whom Moraga calls "the first ancestor of my own colored lesbian tradition,"[99] is narrated as a part of Moraga's present and future, rather than relegated to only her past. Moraga describes a renewed conversation with Audre upon her passing, and imagines her present with Audre: "Tell me about freedom now, sister-poet. Teach me."[100]

This memoir about the birth of her son thus registers the many possibilities that inhere in death. She writes, "Perhaps I have Rodrigo to thank again for this—initiating me to life with the knowledge of death."[101] Rodrigo and his ghostly kin haunt this book. Rafael is one of them: he is initiated into life with the knowledge of death. The book traces a definite progression in her relationship with death. At first, she is horrified: *"I don't understand dying. I don't understand Tede's dying. . . . It is not the death that frightens so, it is the slow humiliating dissolution of the body. I fear the face of death. I am ashamed of my fear."*[102] In this passage, Moraga precisely parses death, acknowledging the ways in which death has multiple meanings. While she holds onto conventional notions of death as the end of meaning *("I don't understand dying"),* she also explores death's multiple meanings and multiple incarnations. Death has a "face"—death's incarnation, its *embodiment,* is apprehensible as the "slow humiliating dissolution of the body." This attack on the body's ability to be whole, to be discrete, to be a *self,* is a form of humiliation, of lessening, of devaluation. The actual fact of death does not produce terror as much as the disintegration of body and self.

In this passage, we see both death's terror and its meaningfulness. As the book progresses, death's meaning expands and widens, provoking Moraga to engage death, rather than repel it. Her meditation on the difference between Audre's death and César's, for example, reveals the myriad ways that death can be inhabited and the different relationships that one can have with the dead. Profoundly, she experiences a turning point or epiphany of sorts about death in the hospital waiting room while Rafael undergoes a surgery to remedy a potentially deadly intestinal infection. She writes, "In the midst of our prayer, I realize suddenly—so profoundly—that my tightest hold against death cannot keep Rafaelito here. The holding itself is what Rafaelito does not need. He needs to be free to decide: to stay or to leave. . . . I only knew my clinging so tightly to my son's waning life could surely crush him and all the heart I had; and there would be no heart left to either mourn or raise a son."[103] At this moment, she decides to accept death, to allow the possibility of death, and to understand death as a form of possibility. After this epiphany in the waiting room, although she still says she *"does not know how to write of death"* she also attests that Rafael's tenuous hold on life has *"introduced me to living with the knowledge of death."*[104] While she didn't "understand death" earlier, Moraga has access to death as "knowledge."

In this scene in the waiting room, Moraga also restages a version of Medea. During her pregnancy, Moraga is commissioned to create a retelling of the Medea story as a Chicana/Mexicana narrative: La Llorona. Moraga comments on the irony: "*I tossed and turned with images of Medea. I still know that this is the play I must write, although I fear it. How is it that I can be pregnant and write the story of killing a child?"*[105] In this moment in the waiting room, Moraga describes herself as surrendering her child to death, to allowing the child to die.

This altered conceptualization of death as possibility means a different understanding of the relationship between life and death. Death is not solely an end, a finality, but also a possibility. This is represented most frequently in the text in the figure of Rafael as the return of the dead. Upon visiting the grave of her grandmother, the matriarch of the family, with a six-month-old Rafael, Moraga wonders, "I wonder . . . if these two did not already know each other. Could Rafael be the messenger boy of the now-dead matriarch?"[106] Moraga also finds meaning in the death of her friend Myrtha's father, whom she learns was named Rafael, and in finding out that Myrtha had a brother who died in childhood, also named Rafael. Moraga writes, "Life and death. Beginnings and endings. Spirits become flesh, then give up the ghost of the body,"[107] and then two pages later, repeats, "Spirits become flesh, then give up the ghost of the body . . .

only to become flesh, again."[108] Unlike the "slow humiliating dissolution of the body" that Moraga associated with death earlier in the narrative, here, she represents the temporality of death as cyclical, rather than linear. Death is the end, the termination of life, but also its beginning. The body is a "ghost"—fleshly, but with its own unreality as well. It no longer takes precedence over the disembodied state. The dissolution of the body into spirit, the disintegration of self, is no longer a humiliation, and the dissipation of human will is no longer a travesty.

In so doing, these texts become her way of imagining, creating, and describing the "impossible" possibilities that emerge out of the condition of *being* surplus. If the contemporary production of surplus creates populations who are, in Audre Lorde's words, "never meant to survive,"[109] Lorde's and Moraga's texts represent this as the very condition of possibility for imagining new (im)possibilities.

CHAPTER THREE

Blues Futurity and
Queer Improvisation

If you can live in the full knowledge that you are going to die, that you are
not going to live forever, that if you live with the reality of death, you can
live. This is not mystical talk; it is a fact. It is a principal fact of life. If you
can't do it, if you spend your entire life in flight from death, you are also in
flight from life.

—James Baldwin, " The Uses of the Blues"

In the above passage from an essay that uses the trope of the blues
to challenge white liberalism's "bubble bath of self-congratulation,"
James Baldwin reminds us that death and life are always mutually dependent.[1] This seeming digression about life and death is anything but,
and this chapter finds inspiration in Baldwin to engage with the structure of disavowal underlying white liberalism, the particular disavowal
of Black death upon which white liberalism is predicated, and the insis-
tent refusal to separate life and death found in Black cultural production.[2]
Further, in invoking the blues, I follow Baldwin in another way. He began
his essay with the following caveat: "The title 'The Uses of the Blues' does
not refer to music; I don't know anything about music. It does refer to the
experience of life, or the state of being, out of which blues come."[3] He
defines the blues as such: "Now I am claiming a great deal for the blues;
I'm using them as a metaphor—I might have titled this, for example, 'The
Uses of Anguish' or 'The Uses of Pain.'"[4] In pointing to the ways in which
the metaphor of the blues has a *use*, Baldwin suggests that this metaphor
is also a method, and this is the method that I take up in this chapter.

Taking Baldwin as inspiration, I examine contemporary Black feminist and queer cultural production to identify a temporality of blues/jazz

improvisation as the formalist expression of the queerness of Black reproduction and kinship. Black feminist and queer scholars have observed that Blackness historically has meant a complex, violent, and violated relationship to normative modes of kinship based on procreation and the temporality of generations based on procreation, a relationship characterized both by forced and foreclosed reproduction. As such, Blackness is and is not representable through the normative mode of individual and collective history narrated through a generational model. Such a condition is not simply an odd accident of history, but instead both comprises and exceeds the very epistemological and ontological bases for modern conceptions of the political subject and the subject of history. In this way, I extend the interrogation of reproduction and temporality in the previous chapter in my reading of Cherríe Moraga by examining generational transmission as a temporality that limits our ability to access disowned pasts and to imagine multiple and alternative futures. Yet this temporality is unstable and incomplete because it is dependent on material relations that alienate racialized and colonized subjects from normative futurity through generational transmission. As I observe later in this chapter, within conversations in both Black studies and queer studies scholarship, this alienation from generationality has been characterized as death. These characterizations, while usefully repudiating the politics of life that are the only legible mode of politics under liberal modernity, must also be supplemented by an understanding of the generative and proliferative aspects of conditions characterized as "death." That is, this distance from normativity produces its own queer temporalities that supplement the more linear temporality of generationality. I thus read Black literary and cinematic texts as enacting memory and constituting community out of the conditions of simultaneously forced and foreclosed reproduction—that is, out of what has been characterized as political and social death. As such, these texts demonstrate that "death" operates as both absence and foreclosure *and* presence and possibility.

The refusal to resolve this tension is best expressed through culture, in particular, through the structure of blues/jazz improvisation, which operates as both metaphor and method in the Black literary and cinematic texts I examine in this chapter. Scholars of blues and jazz have

theorized improvisation as an aesthetic form that enables the simultaneous coexistence of opposite or contradictory tendencies or forces, or
what I have been calling "difference." Through examination of works that
feature representations of the Jazz Age—Gayl Jones's novel *Corregidora*
(1975) and three Black queer films, Isaac Julien's *Looking for Langston*
(1988), Inge Blackman's *B.D. Women* (1994),[5] and Rodney Evans's *Brother
to Brother* (2004)—I posit that improvisation is the aesthetic through
which these texts create alternative temporalities upon which normative
patrilineal temporalities depend but are not able to exhaust.

As I have argued, neoliberalism is a structure of disavowal that claims
that, in the wake of the social movements of the post–World War II
era, racial violence is a thing of the past. Further, as I have outlined in
the introduction, scholars such as Candice Jenkins have convincingly
described the ways in which heteropatriarchal reproductive respectability has been conditionally offered to African Americans in the wake of
desegregation, decolonization, and revolutionary movements of the post–
World War II era.[6] Reading the Moynihan Report as an exemplary text
of neoliberal disavowal, I noted that Black respectability has become an
immensely important structure of erasure, creating a discourse through
which racialized and gendered violence and precarity can be seen not as
structural effects of economies of surplus but as the consequence of irre-
sponsible choices on the part of deviant people devoid of morality. As I
will go on to argue, respectability only comes at the expense of repudiating the long history of racial capitalism's dependence on Black reproductive non-normativity, both in terms of forced and foreclosed reproduction.
Because such populations and practices were rendered deviant *in order
for* racial capital to reproduce itself, this disavowal is ultimately impossible. This raises the following questions: What happens to histories that
are erased both because they are foreclosed from reproduction *and also*
because of forced reproduction, of "compulsory" heterosexuality as not
simply a hegemonic but truly coercive condition? Where and in what
forms do such histories return?

Scholars of social movements have answered these questions by documenting the richness of the activism of Black feminism and women
of color feminism from the 1960s to the present, much of which has

challenged the politics of respectability. The latest instantiation of a centuries-long history of women of color anchoring radical organizations, women of color feminists of the last four decades have tackled everything from welfare reform to anti-sterilization campaigns to prison abolition to gendered and sexual violence.[7] In so doing, these activists not only sought to transform the material conditions wrought by neoliberal abandonment but also instantiated a politics of memory that refused to forget the ways in which the contemporary moment was structured by longer histories of colonialism and racial violence and that resurrected and reconstructed a genealogy of struggle. Maylei Blackwell provides an important analytic through which to apprehend the epistemological interventions of these women of color feminist activists. In her study of an early and influential group of 1960s Chicano/a movement feminists, Las Hijas de Cuauhtémoc, who got their name from a Mexican feminist organization of the early twentieth century, Blackwell argues that Las Hijas deployed a politics of "retrofitted memory" that insisted on the continuity between those movements.[8] Likewise, Zenzele Isoke argues in her examination of contemporary Black feminist activism in Newark that "Black women make direct linkages between past and current realities of black social deprivation and despair—they unearth, invoke, reenact, and most importantly, reenvision historical legacies of struggle against injustice."[9] In this chapter, I read these literary and cinematic texts as an aligned politics of memory that, like these activist projects, insistently refuse the neoliberal imperative to forget.

As I observed in the introduction, neoliberalism's reliance on reproductive respectability is not random; instead, it registers a longer history of political modernity that relies on a category of structuring exclusion that Scott Morgensen has called the "incompletely consanguineous."[10] To restate that argument: Giorgio Agamben observes that the modern state derives its legitimacy from the power of the patriarch, and that consanguinity therefore is the defining logic of political membership. Agamben famously argues that the figure of the *homo sacer,* he whose "bare life" is not protected by the state, is the structuring exception, the figure whose vulnerability to death ensures the protection of life for those within the bounds of consanguinity. While Agamben situates the Holocaust as the epitome of the modern state's dependence on the production of bare life, Morgensen demonstrates that the "incompletely consanguineous" category of Native women and children, who are genocidally rendered non-Native not only through extermination but through forced assimilation, exemplifies the structuring exception that enables political modernity. In other words, Native peoples were eradicated not simply through exclusion from the patriarchal consanguinity of national belonging but also through forced incorporation through rape and intermarriage, which rendered Native women legally non-Native. Bringing Morgensen's analysis together with Christina Sharpe's notion of "tangled"[11] consanguinity, I observe how this condition of an ambivalent, excessive consanguinity characterizes the historical condition of the enslaved woman as well. Black feminist scholarship has documented the ways in which racial capital and the attendant structures of political modernity emerged out of the gendered and racialized exploitation of the enslaved woman, an exploitation that renders concepts such as patriarchy, consanguinity, or inheritance inherently contradictory.

Such arguments revise received theories of the relationship between enslavement and political modernity—most famously, Orlando Patterson's theorization of slavery as social death. While Patterson defines a foundational condition of enslavement to be complete alienation from generational inheritance, the work of Black feminists reminds us that something did get passed down from generation to generation, not patriarchally, but through the enslaved woman: the status of enslavement itself. As Hazel Carby observes, the Black woman's "reproductive destiny was bound to capital accumulation: Black women gave birth to property and, directly, to capital itself, in the form of slaves, and all slaves inherited their status from their mothers."[12] In this context, Hortense Spillers observes, "genetic reproduction is not the elaboration of the life-principle in its cultural overlap, but an extension of the boundaries of proliferating properties."[13] Spillers argues that the particular circumstance in which the captive female found herself—valuable precisely for her ability to bear children to whom she had no social or legal right nor a maternal claim—is what marks her as the "prime commodity of exchange."[14] She calls this "enforced state of breach . . . [a] vestibular cultural formation where kinship loses meaning because it can be invaded at any given and arbitrary moment by property relations."[15] In other words, it is from the very specific circumstances of *her* condition—as the fleshly being that passes on *physical, genetic* life and the political nonbeing that inhabits the position of social death that she also passes on—that capitalism profits from enslavement. In this way, Spillers situates the enslaved female body as exactly the contradictory figure for racial capital modernity, observing that "this open exchange of *female* bodies in the raw offers a kind of Ur-text to the dynamics of signification and representation that the gendered female would unravel."[16]

In the institution of chattel slavery, in other words, the enslaved subject is defined by alienation from kinship through affect as well as alienation from kinship through the property relation. For the enslaved female, the process of *genetic* reproduction and procreation is separated from the social institutions of property relations and rights that allow reproduction to count as "life" in the Western sense, making her the figure that bequeaths genetic life and social death simultaneously. Therefore, the condition of enslavement did not mean simply the *denial* of a history, subjectivity, and "social heritage" through the foreclosure of generational transmission. In this case, generational transmission was *the very means* by which subjectivity and history were denied.

This contradictory, tangled consanguinity complicates and undermines normative temporalities of generational inheritance and the property relations that depend upon them. The historian Jennifer Morgan compellingly describes the ways in which the normative temporality of white, propertied generational inheritance in the Americas depended upon assumptions about speculative futurity—that is, future profits generated from the reproductive capacity of enslaved women, which she calls the "speculative value of a reproducing labor force."[17] Through a compelling reading of wills written by slaveholders in the seventeenth and eighteenth centuries in the Americas, Morgan outlines the ways in which the "relationship between property and progeny" for these slaveholders were predicated on their assumptions about a quite different relationship between property and progeny for the people they enslaved.[18] For example, one will bequeathed one enslaved woman to two children when they reached age of majority; Morgan observes that the division of one enslaved body between two people is impossible unless there is the presumption of that woman's reproductive capacity (i.e., that she might bear a child that could be given to one of the two inheritors). As such, the vision of futurity that comprises the generational transmission of (white) property also situates generational reproduction among enslaved subjects as a speculative source of future income. These two imaginaries around reproduction are both competing and absolutely dependent on each other. As Sara Clarke Kaplan notes, the contradictions inherent in what she calls the "Black reproductive" was and still is a foundational but disavowed condition of possibility for modern definitions of the human.[19]

In situating the Black female subject as what underwrites, yet undoes, the foundations of political modernity, Black feminist theorists make important contributions to contemporary scholarship on social death, thanatopolitics, and bare life, and in so doing, require us to expand upon and extend some of the most important theorizations of Western political modernity. In addition, the Black feminist scholarship on the complexity of Black reproduction complicates a variety of conversations in both Black studies and queer theory that, while coming from very different genealogies of thought, both characterize the exclusion from normative modes of generational transmission and kinship as forms of "death."

In Black studies, this scholarship asks us to reconsider Orlando Patterson's theorization of slavery as social death, which Patterson contends is defined by the foreclosure of generational transmission, by instead observing that enslavement is in actuality marked by the technology of disinheritance and foreclosure of generational transmission *through* forcible reproduction. Patterson's famous definition of social death identifies three constitutive elements of the power relations of enslavement: "At this point we may offer a preliminary definition of slavery on the level of personal relations: *slavery is the permanent, violent domination of natally alienated and generally dishonored persons.*"[20] First, social death is based on the exercise of violence, or brute force. Secondly, social death requires natal alienation, or the removal of the enslaved person from immediate or extended kinship networks. The third, the condition of general dishonor, is contingent on the first two, which are defined by reproduction.

While Patterson's theorization of violence under enslavement does not foreground, and indeed occludes, the ways in which forced reproduction is a form of violence, we may read this effaced history back into his narrative. Patterson observes that the enslaved status is enforced by violence; while the "psychological facet of influence"[21] or "authority" certainly operated in enslaved conditions, the actual use or threat of violence also had to exist as well. Patterson notes that violence inhered not only in the extraction of labor from enslaved persons, but fundamentally in the process of *creating* slaves: "The problem in a slaveholding society, however, was that it was usually necessary to introduce new persons to the status of slaves because the former slaves either died out or were manumitted. . . . Thus, it was necessary continually to repeat the original, violent act of transforming free man into slave."[22]

While he recognizes the production of free man into slave as a form of violence, he is unable to recognize the *reproduction* of enslaved people as violence. He writes, "To be sure, there is the exceptional case of the Old South in the United States, where the low incidence of manumission and the high rate of reproduction obviated the need continually to repeat the violent 'original accumulation' of slaves."[23] In other words, in Patterson's understanding, the violence of enslavement was "obviated" through the procreative function. Yet, of course, this procreative function was often instigated by the systemic and routine practice of rape, a form of violence and violation that Patterson does not remark upon.

The second constitutive element, natal alienation, was entirely organized around reproduction. Slaves were relegated to the condition of social death through natal alienation (or, in other words, through foreclosure from historical memory) in the form of generational temporality. Natal alienation, for Patterson, is the process of severing someone from forms of meaning articulated through normative kinship, so that person no longer has meaning and value as an uncle, a grandchild, a cousin, a son-of-the-tribal-chief, a wife-of-a-tradesman. Instead the slave's only tie to any social group is as the possession of the master. This definitively constitutes the process whereby a living person becomes a commodity. Patterson specifically stresses that "not only was the slave denied all claims on, and obligations to, his parents and living blood relations, but by extension, all such claims and obligations on his *more remote* ancestors and on his descendents."[24] In this way, natal alienation meant that the slave was cut off from "the social heritage of his ancestors."[25] Clearly, natal alienation is a means of being distanced from an experience of history as meaning. A "social heritage," Patterson observes, is not the same as "a past. . . . A past is not a heritage. Everything has a history, including sticks and stones."[26] Natal alienation is therefore a means of imbricating economic and cultural categories; in other words, the importance of this alienation is not solely that one is cut off from the living people who could help one materially or whose wealth could be transmitted through inheritance but also that this economic transmission is just one aspect of a series of connections that imparts *meaning* within a history. Patterson thus defines natal alienation as the absolute denial of a form of selfhood articulated through normative generational transmission.

Thus, we must understand that the condition of social death is itself a social form—that is, it is not so much that the "socially dead" had no social function but rather they performed the social function of representing nothingness itself. Patterson defines reproduction as a "right," or, in other words, the possibility of "claims": "Having no natal claims and powers of his own, he [the enslaved] had none to pass on to his children."[27] This is true if at birth (physical, genetic life) *only* claims and rights are passed on. But for the enslaved, birth was the moment when social death, or the lack of claims and rights, is inherited. The child did "inherit" something from the enslaved woman, but that inheritance was, in Patricia Williams's words, a kind of "disinheritance," the lack of ability to own (oneself, foundationally).[28] Thus, the enslaved passed down the lack of ability to pass down, inherited the lack of ability to inherit. The enslaved *female* was *both* severed *and* connected to her children and they to her, and thus Patterson's assertion that the enslaved is the epitome of natal alienation references an enslaved *male's* inability to pass on his lineage. And if the enslaved male had been born into slavery, he himself had "inherited" his condition from his mother. Thus, the notion that "nothing" had been passed to him is both true and false: something had been passed to him, but that something was the status of *nothingness itself,* social death. In this way, if we bring in the gendered practices of reproduction into Patterson's analysis, we see the ways in which "natal alienation" is a complex category that refers to both the lack of inheritance and the inheritance of lack, or the inheritance of *disinheritance,* as a status. Following the scholarship of Black feminists, then, I conclude that the enslaved Black female was materially necessary to racial capital as the source of reproductive and productive labor, but in that very reproductive role, she threatened to simultaneously undo and reproduce the epistemological separation between social life and social death.

We might call this temporality of incomplete consanguinity described by Black feminist scholars a kind of "queer time." Yet this temporality also departs from certain theorizations of time in contemporary queer theory, particularly those that characterize queer temporality as binaristically opposed to normative, reproductive time. Lee Edelman, for example, situates his deliberate rejection of procreation as a challenge to neoliberal gay and lesbian claims to social and political subjectivity. Edelman takes up the notion, implied by gay and lesbian demands for "family rights," that there is *No Future* without the child, that is, without procreative sexuality. Rather than challenge such an equation, however, Edelman concurs and, indeed, advocates for a queer antipolitics that embraces this foreclosed futurity. In this way, Edelman does not quarrel with the notion that futurity equals procreative sexuality. Instead, he accepts this definition in order to reject it altogether. If the notion of the future is embedded in procreation, then to be queer is to repudiate any notion of the future. He writes, "But there are no *queers* in that future as there can be no future for queers, chosen as they are to bear the bad tidings that there can be no future at all."[29] Edelman takes up the psychoanalytic category of the death drive as the refusal of meaning, the repudiation of narrative resolution. The ultimate form of narrative resolution—of a linear sense of past, present, and future—takes shape as the Child, which he notes is "not to be confused with the lived experiences of any historical children."[30] Thus, the investment in procreation signals a repudiation of the death drive and reflects the desire for meaning and narrative closure that the death drive makes impossible: "To serve as the repository of variously sentimentalized cultural identifications, the Child has come to embody for us the telos of the social order and come to be seen as the one for whom that order is held in perpetual trust."[31] Edelman cannot or will not wrest these two terms—futurity, procreation—away from each other either.

In a related register, Judith Halberstam argues that normative sexualities are fundamentally articulated as relations of time, what she calls "the time of reproduction" and "the time of inheritance."[32] These temporalities are organized around "bourgeois rules of respectability" and "an overview of generational time in which values, wealth, goods, and morals are passed through family ties from one generation to the next." Halberstam writes that heteronormative temporality "connects the family to the historical past of the nation and glances ahead to connect the family to the future of both familial and national stability."[33] In contrast, "queer time" is inhabited by those who "opt to live outside of reproductive and familial time as well as on the edges of logics of labor and production" and who thus "live outside the logic of capital accumulation."[34]

Edelman's adamant rejection of procreative temporality, so extreme that he is willing to reject all claims to a livable and meaningful future, and instead embrace death, meaninglessness, and oblivion, is certainly a bracing critique of gay and lesbian investments in the state and citizenship. Halberstam, too, finds value in deviant temporalities forced out of reprosexuality. Yet Edelman's and Halberstam's schemas cannot account for the ways in which forced consanguinity—that is, forced participation in procreation—was as much a mode of foreclosing futurity and identity as the rejection of procreation. That is, for enslaved and colonized racialized subjects, being excluded from normative modes of inheritance did not make one "outside of capitalist accumulation"; instead, as the Black feminist scholarship outlined above makes manifestly clear, capitalist accumulation was exactly dependent on the process whereby normative modes of inheritance and patrilineality were established via the exclusion through forced inclusion of enslaved and colonized subjects to reproduction and consanguinity. Enslaved procreation, for example, was not valuable because it was organized around the kind of sentimentality and affective investment that Edelman presumes but because it enabled the literal material reproduction of bourgeois society that required the wealth of exploited enslaved labor. As Angela Davis writes,

During the decades preceding the Civil War, Black women came to be increasingly appraised for their fertility (or for the lack of it); she who was potentially the mother of ten, twelve, fourteen or more became a coveted treasure indeed. This did not mean, however, that as mothers, Black women enjoyed a more respected status than they enjoyed as workers. Ideological exaltation of motherhood—as popular as it was in the nineteenth century—did not extend to slaves. In fact, in the eyes of the slaveholders, slave women were not mothers at all; they were simply instruments guaranteeing the growth of the slave labor force.[35]

The sentimentalized protection of childhood within European/American bourgeois society was materially dependent on enslavement, with its thoroughly unsentimental, economic attitude to enslaved procreation. While enslaved procreation was "valued," such valuation happened on a very different register than the bourgeois valuation of procreation that Edelman critiques. While there is evidence that some enslaved people responded to this condition by refusing to procreate, many enslaved people also responded by creating alternative cultural meanings around procreation, family, and kinship that cannot be conflated with bourgeois sentimentality, futurity, and thus with a negation or disavowal of the death drive.[36]

Returning to Baldwin, we can see how he defines Black reproduction as both inside and outside heteropatriarchy, and uses "blues as a metaphor" to describe this state. This Black queer writer and theorist, who never had literal children of his own, provides a description of the radically different subjectivity constituted through Black parenthood in "The Uses of the Blues." He writes:

I'm talking about what happens to you if, having barely escaped suicide, or death, or madness, or yourself, you watch your children growing up and no matter what you do, no matter *what* you do, you are powerless, you are really powerless, against the force of the world that is out to tell your child that he has no right to be alive. And no amount of liberal jargon, and no amount of talk about how well and how far we have progressed, does anything to soften or to point out any solution to this dilemma. In every generation, ever since Negroes have been here, every Negro mother and father has had to face that child and try to create in that child some way of surviving this particular world, some way to make the child, who will be despised, not despise himself.[37]

We may pause to note the stark difference between Baldwin's description of parenthood and that of the parent-as-citizen that constitutes Edelman's horizon of possibility. Baldwin here narrates a kind of parenting that does not even register as parenting in the sentimentalized sense. His theorization of parenting as figuring out "some way of surviving this world" renders both parenting and surviving as complex and contradictory acts. Baldwin's statement leads to the question: What kind of futurity is implied by a mode of parenting constituted by the lack of power and control, when it comprises consistent reminders of one's deep incommensurability with citizenship, rather than one's entryway into the status of citizen? For Baldwin, this contradictory practice of parenting is, for Black people, part and parcel of the basic condition of living and surviving in the midst of death and precarity, and further support to what one scholar of Black culture calls "the fact that the dead and the ways of our dying have been as much a part of black identity as have been the ways of our living."[38] This contradictory existence takes shape, is given form and voice, as the "blues." This is perhaps what Baldwin meant when he described the nature of the blues as paradox, when "Billie or Bessie or Leadbelly stood up and sang about it. . . . And there's something funny—there's always something a little funny in all our disasters, if one can face the disaster. So that it's this passionate detachment, this inwardness coupled with outwardness, this ability to know that, all right, it's a mess, and you can't do anything about it . . . so, well, you have to do something about it."[39]

Baldwin's description of the blues as a set of contradictory imperatives existing simultaneously—"passionate detachment . . . inwardness coupled with outwardness," a situation that "you can't do anything about . . . so you have to do something about it"—is exactly how improvisation has been described. Based on the blues, jazz as a musical form is defined by improvisation in which the musician produces a melodic composition at the very moment of playing, creating a new version of the classic twelve-bar blues progression. While improvisation implies innovation, it is also a bounded and disciplined endeavor. The novelist and critic Albert Murray explains, "By improvisation, of course, I most definitely do not mean 'winging it' or making things up out of thin air. The jazz musician improvises within a very specific context and in terms of very specific idiomatic devices of composition."[40] In other words, improvisation is creating something new *and* repeating something already existing; simultaneously creating tradition and breaking from it. Fred Moten defines Black performance as a whole as "ongoing improvisation of a kind of lyricism of the surplus—invagination, rupture, collision, augmentation. . . . Such Blackness is only in that it exceeds itself; it bears the groundedness of an uncontainable outside. It's an erotics of the cut, submerged in the broken, breaking space-time of an improvisation. Blurred, dying life; liberatory, improvisory, damaged love; freedom drive."[41] Improvisation could be another way of saying difference, as I've been using it in this book.

Based on these theorizations, I situate improvisation as the formal technique ("lyricism") of historical memory for subjects constituted through the condition of tangled and incomplete consanguinity ("the surplus"). What better way of expressing the relationship to reproduction characterized by the forced and foreclosed nature of incomplete consanguinity than "an uncontainable outside"? A different kind of expressive practice is required in order to articulate the fundamental queerness of Black reproduction in its disavowed enabling of normative generational temporalities as well as its demonstrating of normativity's fundamental unsustainability. Such expressive practices demonstrate potential futures existing with, but never of, normative temporality, disavowed and disinherited: Moten's "broken, breaking time-space" that is, as Walter Benjamin promises, never entirely "lost for history."[42] Because Black reproductivity is so inherently "queer," in the sense that Black generational futurity and Black reproduction are both forced and foreclosed, it is possible to connect the contradictions inherent within Black procreation to those that emerge out of non-procreative sexualities.

In order to identify such expressive modes, I turn to literature and film, for culture is where we might find that which has been erased.

These texts take the Jazz Age as their historical methodology as well as the inspiration for their content. Appropriately so, for improvisation can serve as the expression of the temporality of "incomplete consanguinity," of the "vestibular," of "difference." A somewhat unlikely point of departure for my rationale for the importance of culture is Patterson, who compellingly argues that while natal alienation meant the severing of ties to "any formally recognized community, this did not mean that he or she did not experience or share informal social relations. . . . The important point, however, is that these relationships were never recognized as legitimate or binding."[43] As such, these relationships, for Patterson, left no trace. He attests that "we can say little or nothing about the private lives"[44] of either enslaved people or their masters. These private lives would, presumably, encompass their "informal" relationships, but Patterson attests that "we know next to nothing . . . about the way they felt about each other. The data are just not there . . ."[45] For me, Patterson's statements demand a new set of questions. If we "know next to nothing," then what modes of historical remembrance must we deploy besides "knowing"? If the "data are just not there," what besides "data" must we seek out, and how? If that which we can know, that which stands the test of time and becomes legible to history, is represented solely in legitimate forms of kinship and reproduction, how can we access illegitimate relations, relations that are necessary to, but in excess of, these legitimate forms? Can we perhaps call such relations "queer"? What are the archives from which we can recover such relations? Inversely, how are such "queer relations" always, at least in part, empirically unknowable?

Gayl Jones's *Corregidora,* Isaac Julien's *Looking for Langston,* Rodney Evans's *Brother to Brother,* and Inge Blackman's *B.D. Women,* for which the jazz/blues culture of the early twentieth century United States is a unifying trope, suggest that rather than *know,* we might *imagine or improvise.* They suggest that if there are no data, then we might look to fantasies, dreams, and figments. These texts define futurity as the reproduction of social formations through fraught and fragmented attempts to grasp at erased histories, the labor of creating community, and the act of improvising into existence a past and a future that is always fleeting, ephemeral, and without guarantees. A number of Black feminist scholars have addressed the blues as a musical form, arguing that its working-class roots enabled Black women to express challenges to patriarchal and heteronormative ideals and to articulate the complexities of racialized and gendered experience.[46] My argument builds on theirs to examine improvisation as a form of queer of color historical memory. This queer historical memory appears both in the literal representation of jazz and blues as subjects or themes in these texts as well as in the ways in which these texts mobilize formal strategies that we can call improvisational in their simultaneous deployment of seemingly irreconcilable contradictions: the forced and the foreclosed, desire and hate, the already existing and the yet-to-be-made.

Gayl Jones's 1975 novel, *Corregidora,* thematizes historical erasure through the very trope of procreation—or the lack thereof. The narrator is Ursa, the descendent of a line of women whose particularly *sexual* labor, both as prostitutes and as breeders of the next generation of slaves, makes them valuable to their master, Corregidora. *Corregidora* literalizes epistemic erasure: upon the abolition of slavery, "they burned all the slavery papers so it would be like they never had it."[47] In referencing the burning of historical records in Brazil after the abolishment of legalized enslavement, *Corregidora* maintains that history cannot be "what really happened" because those records are gone: they burned the papers. In the face of such erasing gestures, *Corregidora* suggests a number of ways in which the occluded histories of enslavement refuse their relegation to obscurity. Most obviously, the women of *Corregidora* themselves utilize their sexual and procreative capability. By "making generations," they find a way to leave evidence, "because they didn't want to leave no evidence of what they done—so it couldn't be held against them," explains Ursa's great-grandmother. "And I'm leaving evidence. And you got to leave evidence too. And your children got to leave evidence. And when it come time to hold up the evidence, we got to have evidence to hold up."[48]

And yet procreation is not the only mode by which the repressed returns: Jones thematizes an epistemological erasure here, but not simply by positing procreation as a purely resistant practice of memory in opposition to the official history represented by "papers." Indeed, rather than posing the procreative memory of Ursa's maternal line as a purely oppositional formation, Jones suggests that it sustains Corregidora's mastery as much as it subverts it. In one of Ursa's many internal conversations re-created in the text as a kind of blues-like call-and-response refrain, a voice suggests that procreation "could also be a slave-breeder's way of thinking."[49] The very language of having or leaving "evidence," of "bear[ing] witness,"[50] posits a future juridical order, a court or case to which to bring one's claim for justice, a "logic that arises from the unbearable conditions of enslavement" that, as Christina Sharpe insightfully notes, puts the Corregidora women in the "position of believing in the power of the law to free them at the same time that they know that the law is precisely what has kept them enslaved."[51]

As such, replacing a patriarchally organized kinship structure for a matriarchally based one does not evade the perplexed condition of incomplete consanguinity. Madhu Dubey has convincingly argued that *Corregidora* challenges any manifestation of lineage, either the patrilineal model of Oedipalized generational conflict or the matrilineal model of generational continuity initiated by Black feminist writers. Dubey observes that the Black feminist project of creating a matriarchal literary lineage obtained a certain urgency in the wake of the very real threat of utter eradication of culture under enslavement. Yet it is this very threat of eradication that underscores the impossibility of such a lineage. "Reclaiming the power of their wombs, [Corregidora's] women attempt to transfigure the primary site of their oppression into a locus of resistance, wresting their own liberatory story out of the very history of their enslavement."[52] Yet ultimately, Dubey notes, "in making a history for themselves, the Corregidora women become imprisoned in a history that is not of their own making, for what their possession of history gives them is nothing other than the history of their own dispossession."[53] *Corregidora* reveals the consequences of a notion of procreation as the entire horizon of historical possibility, which both repudiates alternative temporalities *and* constitutes the conditions that create them.

It does so by posing the question of what happens when one is unable to "make generations." The narrative begins with Ursa's husband, Mutt, throwing her down a flight of stairs in a fit of jealous rage. Unknowingly pregnant, Ursa loses the child and, further, is rendered sterile by the

doctors who treat her. In the absence of the ability to produce "generations," how can Ursa bear witness to the history of enslavement? The
question remains: is there some other mode of memory obscured by
such a temporality? Ursa cannot bear children, so does this mean that
her story, her memories, her culture, is rendered impermanent by her
own mortality?

Jones's novel uncovers this form of memory in a blues imaginary.
Ursa is a blues singer by trade, and the novel situates her singing as
a form of memory. Yet the novel itself is an act of memory, as it imagines the blues singer and the space of the blues club as a site of possibility. This blues imaginary calls up a "memory" of the 1940s in the
1970s, imagining a continuity between these two moments that cannot
be proved factually and is indeed rendered impossible and invisible by
a concept of historicism that privileges fact. The blues imaginary is a
form of memory that can hold in suspension both procreative and non-
procreative modes of reproduction, one not based only on a mode of historical telling that relies on the linear temporality of *lineage,* but one that
weds that lineage to the deviating, queer, and sometimes perverse relations that are its conditions of disavowed possibility. Unlike the demand
for exactitude that Sharpe identifies in the procreative mode of memory
enacted by earlier generations of Corregidora women, blues enables Ursa
to remember, but in an improvisational manner. Sharpe writes, "Great
Gram and Gram are held in place through their repetitions of their relations with Corregidora; they obey absolutely the compulsion, and they
forbid each other and their daughters to ask the questions that might
begin to alter the repetition."[54] In contrast, Ursa's desire is exactly both
repetition and alteration; she wants to *improvise*: "I wanted a song that
would touch me, touch my life *and* theirs. A Portuguese song, but not
a Portuguese song. A new world song. A song branded with the new
world."[55] Imagining a song that could hold both their struggle against
erasure and her own need to break from that history, a song that would
be both the Portuguese of Corregidora but not, a song "branded with the
new world" in all of its terrible realities and liberatory potentialities, Ursa
describes blues as the impossible becoming possible. *"What do blues do
for you?"* a voice in her mind asks. "It helps me explain what I can't

explain," she responds.[56] In gesturing to this novel's invocation of the blues, I identify a form of cultural *transmission* that is *invention,* a form of *reproduction* that is, at the same time, *production.*

It is this simultaneity of seemingly incommensurable states that makes *Corrigedora* a blues novel, as the blues is characterized by "the ability to contain several sets of contradictions,"[57] or, in other words, paradox as "an ongoing process rather than a problem to be resolved."[58] The book ends with Ursa performing oral sex on Mutt, with whom she reunites after a twenty-two-year separation. While represented as a moment that links Ursa to her great-grandmother, Ursa's fellatio, as Dubey notes, is also a distinctly non-procreative sexual act, one that "can exceed the repro- ductive terms of her maternal ancestor's ideology."[59] Ironically, it is in the moment of engaging in an act that, in its decidedly non-procreative sexuality, flies in the face of her maternal ancestors' injunction to "make generations," that Ursa feels the most direct connection to her great- grandmother: "It was like I didn't know how much was me and Mutt and how much was Great Gram and Corregidora."[60] *Corregidora* thus suggests modes of memory and connection that are both procreative and non-procreative at the same time. The connection between Ursa and her great-grandmother is made both through Ursa's great-grandmother's procreative act, the one that literally created the line that produced Ursa, and also by her replication of a non-procreative one. The connection between Ursa and Great Gram is here both literal/linear/procreative and imagined/nonlinear/queer. That is, when *Corregidora* places blues along- side "generations" as modes of cultural transmission, it imagines cul- ture, history, memory, and futurity being replicated—improvised—in a multiplicity of conflicting and simultaneous ways.

The very last words of the novel are themselves a kind of blues song, and exemplify exactly the bringing together of contradictory impulses that we can call improvisation:

He came and I swallowed. He leaned back, pulling me up by the shoulders.

"I don't want a kind of woman that hurt you," he said.

"Then you don't want me."

"I don't want a kind of woman that hurt you."

"Then you don't want me."

"I don't want a kind of woman that hurt you."

"Then you don't want me."

He shook me until I fell against him crying. "I don't want a kind of man that'll hurt me neither," I said.

He held me tight.

Mutt's statement, "I don't want a kind of woman that hurt you," is ambiguous; while the implication is that he is using "you" to mean the generic pronoun "one," meaning that he doesn't want a kind of woman that would hurt him, the lack of the missing "will" (a kind of woman that *will* hurt you) enables a reading of "hurt" as past tense and "you" as literally referencing Ursa. While Ursa doesn't read his statement this way, adding the "will" in contraction form in her response, if we keep "hurt" in the past tense, it could mean that Mutt doesn't want the kind of woman that hurt Ursa: the Corregidora women, perhaps, whose legacy to her was in part her inability to let go of the past in order to make a future with Mutt. Ursa's repetition of "Then you don't want me" can then be seen as exactly her refusal to let go of the Corregidora women, and by extension, the histories of violence and sex of enslavement. It takes a reprisal of Mutt's original violence against her, but this time with a difference— shaking her until she falls, but catching her with his body—that enables her to break from this maternal lineage and state her own desire, albeit in the negative form, a description of what she does not want. Yet rather than resolving these competing and seemingly mutually exclusive claims on Ursa—her obligation to bear witness to the violence of enslavement and her desire to break from this past—with a promise of a future relationship without hurt, Mutt instead "[holds] her tight," binding them together in what we now realize is the improvisational technique of bringing incommensurabilities together.

Corregidora thus poses a question about how it might be possible to imagine a futurity and a generational connection that is always structured by but in excess of the procreative demand. This procreative demand in the modern era always carries with it the residues of racialized, sexualized, and gendered violence as the disavowed condition of possibility for the law's exclusive premise on consanguinity. Three queer Black films take up this question, albeit in different ways: Isaac Julien's *Looking for Langston,* Inge Blackman's *B.D. Women,* and Rodney Evans's *Brother to Brother.* Because *Corregidora* exists "at the very edges of heterosexuality,"[61] and "render[s] the impossibility of Black heterosexual desire,"[62] *it* acts as a bridge between a Black feminist interrogation of reproduction and a Black queer of color politics of non-procreative futurity by underscoring the fundamental queerness of racialized sexuality as "incompletely consanguineous." These films situate the problem of reproduction for queer Black social formations, and in various ways, *improvise* a history of the Jazz Age, refracted through the Harlem Renaissance. Both inside and outside of procreative time, these formations not only embrace this exclusion, as Edelman and Halberstam propose, but also simultaneously, impossibly, accede to the demands of and desires for inclusion within a temporality of generationality. While many scholars have noted the ubiquity of narratives of heterosexual conflict in the blues,[63] in these films we also see the appropriation of blues as a means of sustaining queer Black imaginaries on both sides of the Black Atlantic.

Looking for Langston, shot throughout in a stylized black-and-white cinematography that beautifully evokes a nostalgic sense of the past, begins with a staged funeral comprising elegantly dressed mourners of a variety of gender presentations who have come to mourn their ancestor. They stand around the open casket of Langston Hughes, played in the film by Isaac Julien himself. We hear the voiceover of a radio broadcast announcing a memorial for Hughes, but memorializing Hughes is more difficult than it may seem. Langston Hughes, rather than serving as the subject of a documentary, is instead a figure that represents both the existence of queer formations and gay subcultures in the Harlem Renaissance and the impossibility of access to that existence. Langston Hughes, in this film, is a ghost. How can we remember Langston Hughes, and by extension, the gay subcultures of the Harlem Renaissance period? Given the paucity of an archive, it is difficult to make a fact-based documentary of Hughes's life as a gay man or the gay subcultures and counterpublics that he may have had access to at that moment. As Isaac Julien notes in an interview with Essex Hemphill, "If one wanted to try to look in an archive to find images of Black gay dance halls, one would be undertaking a journey that would have no beginning because they don't exist."[64] As such, Julien observes, "the choice I made *not to make a documentary* was a very important one."[65] Foreclosed from a recoverable history, *Looking for Langston* juxtaposes a montage of documentary footage of the Harlem Renaissance era interspersed with scenes of a staged fantasy of the Jazz Age. The film reimagines the famed Cotton Club as a site for Black gay club life, replete with dapper Black men in immaculately cut tuxedos, dancing and drinking. These scenes are intercut with dream sequences of a dashing Jazz Age character, Alex, finding his aesthetic and sexual ideal in a character called Beauty.

Looking for Langston, in its refracted, nonreferential manner, gestures to the multiple vectors of forcible forgetting that make a documentary of queer Black life in 1920s Harlem difficult. Such an assessment seems to apply as much to the present day as it does to the Harlem Renaissance era, if various responses to the suggestion of Hughes's homosexuality are any indication. For example, Julien had to re-edit his film for U.S. release, because while the UK publishers of Hughes's work gave the initial copyright clearances for the film, Hughes's estate ultimately did not.[66] One such excised poem was transcribed from the original film by José Muñoz, who reflects upon the "'forgotten' or 'lost' Black queer identity painfully embodied in the hushed tones of Langston Hughes's simple, sorrowful, epitaph-like 'Poem.'"[67] This poem, which simply states, in part, "I loved my friend / He went away from me / There is nothing more to say,"[68] registers, perhaps inadvertently, both the longing and its silencing that are the backdrop to Julien's film. Arnold Rampersad argues in his two-volume Hughes biography that Hughes exercised "an almost fanatical discretion" about his sexual life that makes the empirical verification of his sexuality virtually impossible.[69] Yet Rampersad's and other biographers' reluctance to address Hughes's sexuality cannot be ascribed to this reason alone. As Kobena Mercer notes in his essay on this film, "Langston Hughes is remembered as a key poet of the Harlem Renaissance and has come to be revered as a father figure of Black literature, yet in the process of becoming such an icon, the complexity of his life and the complexity of the Harlem Renaissance itself has been subject to selective erasure and repression by the gatekeepers and custodians of the 'colored museum.'"[70] Such erasure "buries and represses the fact that the Harlem Renaissance was as gay as it was Black."[71]

Yet it is not only Hughes's own secrecy or contemporary investments in his hagiography that explains the lack of an archive. As scholars such as Mercer, José Muñoz, and Manthia Diawara have noted, Julien deliberately addresses the ways in which avant-garde and modernist aesthetics depend on racialized and sexualized notions of taste and beauty. He does so by naming one of its figures Beauty, through the highly aestheticized and stylized black-and-white cinematography, lighting, and set design, and through the inclusion of photographs by Harlem Renaissance portraitist James Van Der Zee and Robert Mapplethorpe. This film demonstrates the ways in which, from the Harlem Renaissance through the present, Blackness has been the fetishized otherness that makes modernist and avant-garde art possible, and in so doing, implies that Black gay life cannot be represented by the avant-garde. In this way, the film represents Langston Hughes as multiply foreclosed.

Yet at the same time, in gesturing to Langston Hughes, the film not only attempts to resurrect the literal Hughes but also endeavors to establish a way of claiming ancestors in the absence of the usual ties of procreation, property, and lineage. It does so by reclaiming a generation of queer Black artists: *Looking for Langston* opens with a dedication to James Baldwin, and Julien has remarked that "one could have easily embarked on a project called *Looking for Jimmy*, James Baldwin."[72] The film's characters Alex and Beauty are from Bruce Nugent's "Smoke, Lilies and Jade," and the portions of this prose poem read in the film act as voiceover for the visual images, including Alex's dream of the fields of lilies and poppies in which he meets Beauty, and his internal meditation on Beauty when he wakes up to find Beauty in his bed. *Looking for Langston* thus advances a way of claiming Hughes, Baldwin, Nugent, and the unnamed and inaccessible queer subcultures that may have surrounded them, and in so doing, asserts the legitimacy of fiction and imagination as a form of claiming.

Throughout, this film imagines connections between past and present that cannot be factually validated or empirically articulated. Julien's use of experimental formal strategies blurs the line between present and past. Contemporary poetry is read over scenes set in the past—both documentary footage from the era and staged scenes evoking the 1920s through costume and set design—in ways that make such poetry seem like the internal thoughts of characters. The image and sound of Bessie Smith singing, which segue seamlessly into the voice of Black queer contemporary musician Blackberri, convey the importance of the blues aesthetic as a mode of historical connection. In these moments, the film imagines into existence, however provisionally, a connection and a history. Mercer highlights the importance of the imaginary when he notes, "Here I would emphasize 'imagined' in Benedict Anderson's term 'imagined community,' because without the notion of a collective historical imagination, how could we understand why a Black British filmmaker whose parents migrated to London from St. Lucia would choose to make a film about a Black American writer from Kansas City?"[73] The connection between past, present, and future, because it is imaginary, can be made across geographical space and in defiance of national allegiance.

B.D. Women likewise begins by commenting on the erasure of queer Black histories. This film intercuts a series of "talking head"-style interviews of contemporary Black queer women with a fictionalized narrative set in the Jazz Age. The opening set of interviews features several of these women discussing the ways in which the queerness of Black history is foreclosed. One of the interviewees, Nasreen Memon, notes, "Black lesbian history repeatedly is erased completely. You get a jazz singer's life story and it completely misses out that she was a lesbian again and again and again and sometimes you get queer history that looks deliberately [sic], overlooks the racism that definitely went on."

This film thus immediately suggests why the invention or improvisation of a queer Black history might be necessary, and then provides just such an invention through the fictionalized narrative. This narrative features a blues singer, whose flirtatious rendition of Ma Rainey's "Prove It On Me Blues" at a Harlem Renaissance jazz club attracts the attention of a dapper Black "butch daddy," as this character is called in the credits. Angela Davis describes the song, featuring lyrics like "Went out last night with a crowd of my friends / They must've been women, 'cause I don't like no men . . . they say I do it, ain't nobody caught me, sure got to prove it on me" as "a cultural precursor to the lesbian cultural movement of the 1970s."[74] Accordingly, the song operates in this film as a marker of the existence of Black lesbian sexualities in the face of their erasure and as a way of creating continuity between those Black queer blues women of the Jazz Age and those speaking in the interview portions of the film. The rest of the fictionalized narrative, involving no dialogue, depicts the blues singer and her butch daddy in a romantic interlude, in which the singer ties her lover to a bed with her stockings. Later scenes find the singer taking her butch daddy to meet her parents: her proper and respectable mother is shocked and will not acknowledge her lover; her father, in a minister's collar, seems less opposed. The narrative concludes with the singer's father presiding over a marriage ceremony for the blues singer and her butch daddy, immaculately dressed, respectively, in a beautiful 1920s-style wedding dress and a tuxedo and top hat. Shot in a sepia-toned print, this fictionalized narrative stylistically references 1920s-era silent film. With no dialogue and no sound except for the soundtrack of Ma Rainey's song, the film uses period-appropriate costumes (flapperish dresses, jeweled headbands, marcelled hair) and art deco furnishings to convey a highly stylized and nostalgic reconstruction of the Jazz Age. One by one, the fictionalized narrative offers conventionally satisfying fulfillments of potentially normative desires, whether through the aesthetic satisfactions of costuming, set design, cinematography, and sound; the narrative satisfactions of romance, tracing the couple's trajectory through flirtation, consummation of desire, and, in the end, marriage; or the possibility of reconciliation with blood kin and a space within a conventional, religiously organized Black community, both represented by the father. The narrative itself establishes referentiality insofar as it is a reproduction of the sentimentalized love story of that (and every) age. Yet it centers a queer butch-femme couple, a crucial difference that produces ironic, erotic, playful, and, at times, poignant moments. The fictionalized narrative manages to convey a simultaneously ironic and nostalgic relationship to this past and to the sentimentalized romantic narrative form. This simultaneity of nostalgia and irony that understands and satisfies the desire for a recoverable, beautiful past, while underscoring the fictitiousness of that past, is what imbues this film with a "blues" imaginary. *B.D. Women* eschews a polemical position, as represented either by an investment in generational continuity or by a dismissal of such investments, in favor of an aesthetic that holds in suspension contradictory relationships to generational, procreative temporality.

The film conveys the importance of both nostalgia and lack, existence and erasure, life and death, by insisting on the importance of fictionality in the narrative of generational continuity. It suggests, and then rejects, the possibility of an empirically verifiable generational connection that could stand in the place of the fictional narrative. In other words, if the opening interview with Menon situates the erasure of history, the film's solution to this is not simple historical recovery. While most of the interviewees are of the same general age—seemingly in their twenties or early thirties—one older woman, Claire Andrews, reminisces fondly about the vibrant subcultures that existed in Britain in the 1960s, discussing with palpable nostalgia the clubs where "everyone enjoyed themselves; it was a good laugh, you know, compared to the clubs of today," referencing perhaps the disciplining nature of contemporary lesbian communities referred to by other interviewees. Yet the film refuses a politics of simple historical recovery, constituting a historical lineage in a purely literal and factual manner, and insists on presenting this alternative, fictionalized narrative *in addition*. The film could very well have been structured around "recovering" Andrew's generation and creating a lineage from her and others of her generation to the younger women in the film. Instead, the connection *B.D. Women* tries to produce is between these women and the fictionalized blues woman of the 1920s. It seems that the act of fictionalizing, of imagining, is vitally important for this film.

Like *Looking for Langston*, *B.D. Women* also emerges from Black British communities. Most of the women in the film are British—both South Asian and Afro-Caribbean—as is the filmmaker. Yet this does not preclude *B.D. Women* from imagining the Harlem Renaissance as a precursor for the community that these women are building in the present day, perhaps remembering and reconstructing the transnational nature of the Harlem Renaissance. Much of the film is devoted to these women's nuanced meditations on the joys and tribulations of creating and inhabiting a queer Black women's community. Their relationships to community are complicated. Navarha Lindsay asserts that her work within gay and lesbian communities makes her "feel loved." "I feel loved. Probably for the first time in my life, I feel loved." Yet we also hear Lenora Rogers-Wright's more critical observation that even within queer Black women's communities, there are unspoken mores and disciplinary injunctions:

> I felt that there were certain things that I wasn't allowed, shall we say, uh, unwritten rules maybe, that I wasn't allowed to do. Having relationships with white women I found difficult. I found like there that there was some unspoken rule, that it was somehow letting yourself down, letting the side down. I found that there were certain areas of sex that I wasn't allowed to mention or bring to forum, particularly around the issues relating to S/M sexuality, or sub/dom sexuality. It was a very, VERY taboo subject.

The work of forming a community is in this way cast as similar to creating historical memory. The interviewees speak of the two in remarkably overlapping terms. Adeola Agbebiyi notes, "Anyone who is different from the mainstream has to create their own family to support them, and so my sense of family is increasingly drawn from people around me, people I've chosen to be there." Similarly, Pamela Sneed—who besides being one of the interviewees also plays the role of "butch daddy" in the fictionalized narrative—describes history as invention: "I feel like we have to invent our history constantly because there is a lack of documentation. I mean, think about trying to figure out how many Black lesbians there were and literally I mean it's difficult to read about. So in that regard a lot of our history has to be fictionalized, a lot of it has to be created." If we think of generationality as the dominant mode of reproduction, and redefine reproduction outside of the constraints of linear time, we might be able to recognize communities created in the *present* as a form of reproduction, but a lateral, not horizontal, version. That is, community building is a form of reproduction that, unlike generational transmission, is not organized around a linear sense of past, present, and future, and for which ephemerality and loss of connection with the past are not indications of failure, but are intrinsic.

Yet this does not mean that the only mode of reproduction is present tense. While this film could most certainly have been made up entirely of these interviews, it insists on incorporating the fictionalized narrative, and thus imagining a past into life. In a manner of speaking, it is itself creating the community, across historical time, that its interviewees describe creating in the present day. In other words, the film's interviewees describe queer community as itself a form of invention, something that has to be *imagined* into existence, much as the film imagines the narrative of the blues singer and her butch lover as a prehistory for these women. In this way, this act of improvisation, of introducing imagination into tradition, is, more than the project of historical recovery, the purpose of this film.

While Rodney Evans's *Brother to Brother*, with a clear central protagonist and narrative arc, is at face a much more conventional feature-length film than the deliberately genre-bending *Looking for Langston* or *B.D. Women*, it likewise both thematizes and subverts the desire for historical recovery. The film imagines a friendship between Perry, a young Black painter, and an elderly and impoverished Richard Bruce Nugent. As Perry negotiates familial and societal rejection as a result of coming out and repudiates a white lover's racial fetishization, Nugent becomes an inspiration and touchstone. Indeed, while this film is marketed as a conventional coming-of-age and coming-out story of Perry coming to terms with his identity as a gay man, what this means in the film is less the fulfillment of individual desire within a coupled relationship and more a reckoning with history and community. As Shawn Anthony Christian notes, "Rather than engage the Harlem Renaissance as a usable past that offers subjects whose experiences help image and articulate Black male, same-sex desire then, and, to a degree, now, Evans privileges and envisions a cross-generational, homosocial rather than homoerotic bond."[75] While Perry states his desire for "someone who's willing to love[him]," and although the film can be read to imply that his friendship with Nugent allows him the personal growth and self-acceptance that would enable him to find a partner, the film ends not with Perry finding romantic love but with him consummating an intergenerational artistic relationship, as Nugent and Perry spend their final evening together painting each others' portraits.

While Evans's film is certainly the most fictional, he too cannot help blurring the lines between fact and fiction. Evans brilliantly uses a scene in one of Perry's classes to insert a documentary interlude within a narrative film; Perry screens a student film made by a friend of his that features grainy images of Black Power movements and gay pride parades. Yet even this "documentary" interlude blurs the line between fact and fiction, as it intercuts these images with an encounter between James Baldwin and Eldridge Cleaver, played by Lance Reddick and Chad Coleman, respectively, that never happened in real life. Shot in black and white and mimicking the documentary style, this brief interlude places a resolute Baldwin against an angry and violent Cleaver, who ends the conversation by standing up and throwing the table between them aside. The scene ends with "Baldwin" and "Cleaver" standing face-to-face, as intimate in their anger as they might be in love. The lines they speak are credited in an intertitle within the film as "from the thoughts and experiences of James Baldwin and Eldridge Cleaver," and the film stages a confrontation between Baldwin and the overtly homophobic Cleaver as a microcosm of the confrontation between those who refuse to define Black and queer as mutually exclusive and the homophobia that structures masculinist Black nationalist politics. Even within the narrow confines of feature-film conventions, Evans takes liberties with the form, innovating an improvisational mode of telling that we can call a blues imaginary.

Improvisation thus provides an imaginary for these texts, and it is the notion of the imaginary that I want to highlight. While these films foreground the ways in which normativity is a practice of memory, obscuring queer relations in the past and the present, none of these texts is prevented from making historical connections by the uncertainty of whether the past described by these texts "truly" happened or if the connections thus described between past and present are "real." As Omes'eke Natasha Tinsley observes, attempting "to convey the drowned, disremembered, ebbing and flowing histories of violence and healing in the African diaspora . . . involve[s] muddying divisions between documented and intuited, material and metaphoric, past and present."[76] Does this blues culture truly hold within it an alternative narrative of history? Is the Jazz Age truly an antecedent to the club culture of the 1980s, as *Looking for Langston* seems to imply? Was the Harlem Renaissance a space and time where a queer Black women's culture existed as a model for such culture in the present day, as *B.D. Women* suggests? Ultimately, it is a blues imaginary of improvisation that *creates* the connection. If the structure of the blues, organized around an improvisational aesthetic of variation-in-repetition, displaces a linear narration of history, we can see how useful it is to queer imaginaries. Queer reproduction is not based on the "real." What such social formations "truly" are may indeed be lost to history. In fact, the archive of the present may well be erased and lost to the future, as unrecoverable to them as Langston Hughes's life as a gay man or the Black lesbian cultures of the 1920s are to us. But perhaps someone, somewhere in the future, will dream our moment into life. Perhaps that is all that we are now and will ever be: the fragments and figments of someone's imagination, of someone's desire for us to exist, much like *Looking for Langston* or *B.D. Women* dreams something in the "past" into existence.

These texts describe a temporality where the connection between past, present, and future cannot be determined with certainty, where one's antecedents are experienced more as ghosts than as fixed entities. Indeed, this form of reproduction is where one haunts one's antecedents as much as one is haunted by them: Langston Hughes haunted by those looking for him. Ursa Corregidora haunted by Gayl Jones. Ma Rainey haunted by B.D. women. Bruce Nugent haunted by all the Perrys of the world. All seeking some sign of the past. And in the seeking, creating it.

CHAPTER FOUR

Bringing Out the Dead

Black Feminism's Prophetic Vision

> The Soothsayers who found out from time what it had in store certainly did not experience time as homogeneous or empty.
>
> —Walter Benjamin, "Theses on the Philosophy of History"

Barbara Christian's 1994 essay, entitled "Diminishing Returns: Can Black Feminism(s) Survive the Academy?," haunts me, almost twenty years after its publication. In this essay, Christian addresses the question of the future of Black feminism by examining the many barriers—material, institutional, intellectual—that deny new generations of African Americans, and African American women in particular, access to college educations, much less graduate degrees that would lead to academic positions. Christian carefully notes that it is not necessarily only African American women who have something to contribute to Black feminism, and situates this condition in light of the seemingly contradictory surge in interest in Black feminism and in African American literature and African American studies. In so doing, she paints a powerful picture of a bleak and ironic future, one in which the university's fetishization of Black feminism as an avenue of intellectual inquiry does not render impossible, and indeed in some ways facilitates, its systemic violence against Black women.[1] She writes, "It would be a tremendous loss, a distinct irony, if some version of Black feminist inquiry exists in the academy to which Black women are not major contributors."[2]

This essay haunts me because I cannot suppress my suspicion that we are indeed facing a moment when this "distinct irony," this "tremendous loss," is occurring, but in a way Christian never might have imagined.[3] I am forced to consider that this bleak future may have come to pass, not only, as Christian so presciently foretold, through the dismantling of redistributive mechanisms that might have enabled current and future generations of Black feminists to enter the academy but also because so many of the Black feminists of Christian's and later generations have died prematurely—struck down by cancer and other diseases—including Christian herself in 2000. June Jordan in 2002. Sherley Anne Williams in 1999. Toni Cade Bambara in 1995. Audre Lorde in 1992. Beverly Robinson in 2002. Endesha Ida Mae Holland in 2006. Claudia Tate in 2002. Nellie McKay in 2006. VèVè Clark in 2007. Toni Yancey in 2013. Stephanie Camp in 2014.[4]

In naming these women, these Black feminists, I respond to James Baldwin's imperative to "bring out your dead."[5] In *The Evidence of Things Not Seen*, a raging meditation on the erasure and disavowal of racialized death, inspired by the murder of at least twenty-one African American children in Atlanta in 1979 and 1980, Baldwin writes,

> Bring out your dead:
>
>   Edward Hope Smith, 14. Reported missing July 20, 1979. Found dead on July 28 of gunshot wounds along a road in a wooded area.
>
> Bring out your dead:
>
>   *Alfred James Evans, 13. Last seen July 25, 1979, waiting to catch a bus. Police identified Evans's body October 13, 1980, after it was found July 28 near the body of Edward Hope Smith. Strangulation.*
>
> Bring out your dead:
>
>   *Milton Harvey, 14. Last seen September 1979. Found dead November 1979. Cause of death: undetermined.*
>
> Bring out your dead.[6]

And the list goes on and on.[7] To bring out your dead is to remember what must be forgotten, to find the "evidence of things not seen": that the notion of American equality in the protection of life is a fallacy, that life is not protected if you are raced and gendered, and that you are raced and gendered if your life is not protected. To bring out your dead is to say that these deaths are not unimportant or forgotten, or, worse, coincidental. It is to say that these deaths are systemic, structural. To bring out your dead is both a memorial and a challenge, an act of grief and of defiance, a register of mortality and decline, and of the possibility of struggle and survival.[8] It is difficult to say and impossible to "prove" that these women suffered early deaths because the battles around race, gender, and sexuality were being waged so directly through and on their bodies.[9] Yet the names bear witness to this unknowable truth.

Let me also pause here to let these untimely deaths resonate with others and to recall other moments when the imperative to call out our dead could not be refused: the twelve Black women and one white woman murdered in Boston in the first half of 1979 and the Combahee River Collective's contestation of the forces that devalued these women's lives.[10] Audre Lorde's poem "Need," dedicated "To Patricia Cowan and Bobbie Jean Graham," two of these dozen Black women, and to "the 100's of other mangled Black women whose nightmare informs my words," is yet another attempt at the impossible: to make words be accountable to and for the deaths that enable us to live.[11] In this poem, Lorde writes: "And how many other deaths / do we live through daily / pretending / we are alive?"[12]

In this chapter I turn the women of color feminist analytic of "difference" toward a meta-analysis of the deeply necropolitical site of the university and interrogate the ethics of deploying women of color feminism and Black feminism as analytics in the context of an academy in which such deployments sometimes legitimate epistemic and physical violence toward Black feminists. The irony of not being a Black feminist myself while deploying Black feminism does not escape me. If what I am doing in this chapter and this book is to have any chance of undermining the structures that replicate such brutalities (rather than just advancing myself professionally within the context of a university that sometimes makes room for and rewards a "women of color feminism" based on the devaluation of actual women of color), I have to recall Lorde's question, the one with which I began this book: "In what way do I contribute to the subjugation of *any part of those who I call my people?*"[13] If I think of "our people" as in part made up by Black feminists in the academy, the question I have to ask is to what extent I am protected by their work, their labor, and their deaths and, as such, whom I am ethically called upon to

protect in turn. This chapter is my necessarily partial attempt at addressing that question.

Christian's essay holds yet another kind of poignancy for me because
it was her presentation of what would become this essay that was the
only occasion I had to see her while she lived. In the first year of my
PhD program in literature, the Modern Language Association (MLA)
annual convention happened to be held in the city where I went to
school. At this convention, Christian was part of what can only be called
a powerhouse panel on "Feminist Criticism Revisited: Where Are We
Going? Where Have We Been?"[14] Every other panelist, as well as the
panel conveners, was a white woman, and the panelists' stature in the
field was such that the audience was enormous—in my admittedly unre-
liable memory, hundreds of people. Taking the opportunity to address
so many in our profession on the question of "Where are we going?,"
Christian powerfully evoked a vision of a future *without* feminism—
Black feminism anyway, or at least not as practiced by Black feminists.
Stunned by this glimpse into a possible futurity, I felt a visceral, immediate, and disturbing sense of the real stakes of being in the academy, of
feminism, and (for the only time in my life) even of the MLA. I remember also that Christian's impassioned presentation, the first on the panel,
was cut off for time by the moderators. I remember thinking that in
cutting her off, they had not accounted for the fact that the panel had
started late. I remember feeling that none of the other presentations for
which Christian had been cut off had the same gravity, consequence, or
urgency, and that the stakes of the other presentations seemed so mild
in comparison. I remember walking out of that panel shaken by the vision
of the future that Christian had painted and disturbed by the vision of
the present represented by that panel, on which Christian seemed to
have been invited as the token woman of color and on which her words
had not received the kind of appreciation that I felt they deserved.

The previous chapter explored women of color feminist and queer
of color enactments of temporality and genealogy that both rely on
and exceed that of normative reproduction. These alternative temporalities and genealogies enable feminist and queer cultures to claim a past
through invention, imagination, and improvisation, a past that has been

foreclosed via more factual, documentable means, because the only documents that remain record normative procreation. This chapter is a meditation on how such an invented or improvised connection to the past might be of use as we attempt to make sense of what the university is to us today, in the midst of racialized and gendered violences. How might a politics of difference help us mourn the premature death of our teachers and colleagues as well as those generations of potential scholars who were never able to be, while at the same time not allowing the university's violences to sever us from those who have been taken from us? While the questions of reproduction and generationality that structured the previous chapter might not seem to pertain to academic life, quite the opposite is true, as Christian herself first observes in another essay. She writes, "[I am] an academic mother to more children than I could have possibly imagined, and to types of children beyond my conjuring . . . at a time when my white counterparts are already academic grandmothers."[15] This chapter, continuing the trajectory of the previous on, ruminates on the effects of racialized and gendered premature death on academic generationality. What happens to Black feminism when normative (academic) reproduction is subverted or even foreclosed not only by the exclusion of the "children," as Christian's essay details, but also by the premature deaths of the "mothers"? What alternative, queer modes of reproduction and memory must be mobilized to forge these connections?

Perhaps as a way of circling back to Christian's prophetic vision, to her calling into being a number of fractured and contingent futures, I return to her words now, many years later, because they challenge how we generally think about the flow of history, highlighting the impossibility of any simple narrative of progress that, in this case, would be evidenced by Black women's increased access to the university. Instead, in this chapter, I use Christian's essay as a guide to examine how it came to be that the U.S. university enacts violence against Black feminists.[16] I build on Christian's insight that epistemological considerations, as much as political and economic ones, constitute this university formation's violence toward Black feminists. That is, Christian importantly connects, in complex ways, questions of access (who is allowed into the university) to questions of knowledge production (what can be said). Christian's essay reveals the ways in which this university formation constitutes particular norms governing what can be validated as scholarly knowledge, and that these norms—in concert with the political and economic structures of racial hierarchy and economic deprivation—become the mechanism by which the university excludes and extinguishes Black feminists. This manifestation of violence toward Black feminists provides, I argue, the clearest perspective of the ways in which this university formation is implicated in the specific processes of racialization and gendering in the contemporary moment. In other words, attending to this university formation's violence against Black feminists gives us insight into its strategies of racial management within the present-day manifestations of global capital.

Yet if the violence toward Black feminist bodies happens through epistemological means, then the obverse is true: a different kind of knowledge production can carve out a space in the academy for Black feminists. Thus I attempt to address how we might reimagine and reconstitute this university formation so that it is no longer so violent toward Black feminists, and by extension, all of "our people." I argue that it is in Black feminist thought that we find the method for reconstituting knowledge production within the university. This is a complex, twofold task. On the one hand, how do we claim the importance of Black feminists' actual lives and bodies without reproducing a reductive positivism that would dismiss questions of knowledge production and epistemology? On the other hand, how do we valorize Black feminist knowledge production in a way that does not inadvertently collude with the casual dismissal of embodied politics as simplistically identitarian, a dismissal that operates to exclude and extinguish Black feminist lives? In order to address this question, I turn to an important intellectual trajectory within Black feminist thought that emphasizes alternative epistemological productions, focusing specifically on the work of Audre Lorde, the Combahee River Collective, and Barbara Christian—referencing the latter's published essays, her unpublished personal and professional papers in her archive housed at the Bancroft Special Collections library, and reflections from a former student. Black feminist *knowledge production* has inherent within it an analytic that connects it to Black feminist *bodies*. As such, rather than utilizing an aestheticized understanding of ideas, we can understand Black feminism as grounded on a theory of analysis as an always materialist practice. As such, we can deploy Black feminism as a means to ensure that there are more Black feminist bodies in the academy, rather than as a ruse to effect their necropolitical excision. In this way, we neither espouse a reductive essentialism that maintains that we only need to get more Black female bodies in the academy (although it is certainly not an unimportant task), nor an equally reductive version of an anti-identitarian critique that insists that bodies are not important and that ignores the material levels at which racism and misogyny organize themselves. Instead of positing epistemological and embodied politics as incommensurate opposites, I follow Christian in arguing that the materialist knowledge production pioneered by Black feminist thought allows us to see them as connected.

In arguing that the examination of the university's violence toward Black feminists allows us to understand the university's implicatedness in neoliberal capital, I build on the analysis of historical transition I elaborated on in the book's introduction, focusing particularly on the university as an institution that is central to the determination of which lives are valuable and which others are not. As Roderick Ferguson argues in *The Reorder of Things*, the university was the laboratory of neoliberalism, as it innovated strategies to contain and manage the student-led social movements of the post–World War II era.[17] State and capital in turn took up these strategies of diversity management.

While institutions of higher education undoubtedly had a variety of functions, and although all universities did not operate similarly, the epistemological structure of Western university education was based on a sense of progress toward a singular and universalizable notion of civilization, represented by a canonical notion of Western culture.[18] This epistemological function was built on, and buttressed, the "founding, financing, and development of higher education in the [American] colonies [that] were thoroughly intertwined with the economic and social forces that transformed West and Central Africa through the slave trade and devastated indigenous nations in the Americas."[19] Because modern universities descend from this rueful history, the university became an important site where the social movements of the post–World War II era challenged these epistemological and material violences.[20] These social movements critiqued the Western European model of the university as an institution that, as the repository of all validated knowledge, represented Western civilization, and that disseminated through the curriculum its norms and ideals. As Ferguson has demonstrated, these new social movements, which in part established ethnic studies within universities across the United States, revealed that white supremacy, articulated through sexualized and gendered norms, was at the heart of the project of Western civilization, and thus that Western civilization was a racial and gendered project.[21] In so doing, they critiqued the very foundations of that earlier formation of global capitalism. Following C. L. R. James, Ferguson has noted that ethnic studies was foremost a critique of Western civilization.[22] James describes Black Studies in his essay "Black Studies and the Contemporary Student" as an intervention into Western civilization as a racial project constituted through the intersecting histories of European slavery, imperialism, and colonization.[23] Ethnic studies programs were established in universities across the country by student activism that intersected with the antiwar, Black Power, and New Left movements of the post–World War II era, and with decolonization movements occurring abroad.[24] Because these student movements approached the university as an institution already implicated in a worldwide system of neocolonial and racialized capitalist exploitation, their efforts were to change the very function of the university. Rather than being a site of knowledge production that legitimated and reproduced U.S. nation-state power—particularly egregious as the United States was engaging imperialist wars in Africa, Asia, and Latin America—the university that these students imagined was a means of redistributing resources, producing counterknowledges, and critiquing white supremacy and imperialism.[25]

Black feminists were central to this struggle. Because the racial project of Western civilization was always a gendered and sexualized project as well, Black feminism emerged as an analysis of the *intersections* of race, gender, sexuality, and class within the context of global colonial capitalism.[26] In the wake of these profoundly transformative social movements of the post–World War II era, technologies of race must operate quite differently. I have elsewhere argued that the emergence of women of color feminism, centrally constituted through the insights of Black feminism, can be read as an important index of the restructuring of the global political economy in the post–World War II era.[27] I argue that the university's violence toward Black feminists is a manifestation of its operations in this neoliberal political economy and that, as such, Christian's critique of the university provides an analysis of this process. The university was profoundly changed by the social movements of the post–World War II era, and its contemporary retrenchment in reaction to these movements—a retrenchment that is most evidently marked on Black feminist bodies—structures its role within contemporary neoliberalism. To recall the argument of my introductory chapter, the social movements of the mid-twentieth century succeeded in rendering untenable the uncritical glorification of Western civilization that was the ideological and cultural basis for the earlier, colonial form of global capital. These social movements did so by critiquing Western civilization's foundations in white supremacy. The logics of racial management shifted toward the rhetoric and policy of neoliberal multiculturalism, which replaced white supremacy as the dominant logic of contemporary globalization. Jodi Melamed has described the "sea change in racial epistemology" in the postwar period in the following manner: "In contrast to white supremacy, the liberal race paradigm recognizes racial inequality as a problem, and it secures a liberal symbolic framework for race reform centered in abstract equality, market individualism, and inclusive civic nationalism. Antiracism becomes a nationally recognized social value, and for the first time, gets absorbed into U.S. governmentality."[28] Melamed calls this new formation "neoliberal multiculturalism," and argues that it organizes racial knowledge and inequity in the post–World War II era.

In many ways, Christian's career exemplified this transition. Christian participated in these early movement-based struggles for ethnic studies and access to education in the student strikes in 1968–69 at the City College of New York, where she was teaching while finishing her PhD at Columbia University.[29] These same struggles were, of course, those that, in Deborah Gray White's words, "pried open the doors of the ivory tower" and "were the causal factors behind the entry of blacks and women into higher education in greater numbers than ever before."[30] Thus, to observe that those of Christian's generation of Black women in the academy have been decimated by premature death is to say that this has happened to the *first* to be able to even be called a "generation." Her activism continued at the University of California, Berkeley, as she worked to establish the African American studies department as well as protect and support ethnic studies, women's studies, and affirmative action programs.[31]

No doubt shaped by these institutional conditions, Christian's research career spanned—and in many ways was an important part of ushering in—a transition in which African American literature, in particular African American women's literature, moved from being dismissed as a narrow and particular category with at best a niche audience to being celebrated as foundational to multicultural literacy. Her attempts at publishing her first book, *Black Women Novelists,* met with rejections or non-responses from a variety of academic and popular presses, including Oxford University Press, the University of Massachusetts Press, and the University of California Press, before Greenwood Press finally released it in 1980.[32] Christian's inquiries to Doubleday were initially met with support: a 1976 letter from the assistant to the West Coast editor, Luther Nichols, asserted that it "sounds like a fascinating study," and that Nichols would be "delighted to see any completed work and outline on Afro-American women novelists."[33] Yet even here, the letter expressed "reservation about its adaptability to the general interest market," a sentiment reiterated in the letters from Oxford and Random House.[34] In 1977, Christian penned a direct request for feedback from Toni Morrison, then editor at Doubleday, about this book, describing a major intervention of the book as ensuring that "black women novelists be seen as craftspersons as well as part of a rich tradition."[35] Despite the fact that the book dealt with two of Morrison's own novels (*The Bluest Eye* and *Song of Solomon*), Morrison could not help get it published. She wrote back in 1978, at which point, she had moved to an editorial position at Random House:

I enjoyed reading BLACK WOMEN NOVELISTS and was very im-
pressed with its clarity and perception. Obviously I wish I could do
something with it here at Random House, but, unfortunately, I cannot. . . . Unless you have some very "hip" (and probably inaccurate)
sociological view to tag on to the literary criticism, it is received with very
little enthusiasm. It is a very bad state of affairs, but that's the case.[36]

However, by the 1990s, after the release of Christian's second book,
Black Feminist Criticism, with Pergamon Press in 1985, the state of affairs
was quite different, with editors at presses from Henry Holt[37] to New
York University Press[38] to Cornell University Press[39] soliciting future
book projects. Christian was even wined and dined by a literary agent,
whose offer of representation she firmly declined.[40] While this might parallel the career trajectories of other distinguished academics who started
off in assistant professor obscurity and rose to eminence, it is also telling
evidence of not only one person's career arc but also the dizzying rise
of "minority literature" as the centerpiece of U.S. multiculturalism. In
1975, Christian's rationale for a grant to create a bibliography of Black
women's writing was that she was "continually receiving letters from
people all over the country who want to teach courses in this area and
need information."[41] In other words, there was such a paucity of information about Black women's writing, much of it coming out of "small
presses and unusual presses,"[42] that faculty members with an interest in
the topic did not even know what existed to teach. Christian went from
this situation to, less than two decades later, penning a congratulations
letter to Morrison for her Nobel Prize in Literature.[43]

Christian's astute institutional analysis of this trajectory of incorporation is evident not only in "Diminishing Returns" but also in her overall
research arc, as well as in the ways in which she described and contextualized her research and teaching in her professional and personal writings. While she consistently maintained the importance of centering
Black women's writing throughout her career, her rationale for doing
this kind of scholarship changed over time. In addition to her original
project of attending to what was marginalized or dismissed, she evinced
a growing ambivalence about the consequences when such literature

was taken up in simply celebratory ways. Christian's analysis of institutionalization highlighted the double-edged sword of multicultural appreciation, which she noted was always coupled with dismissal, starvation,
and attack. Even as she noted the growing acceptance of Black feminism
and Black women's writings, she never stepped back from her focus
on Black women writers, always wary of institutional marginalization
and erasure. However, her analysis of these writers changed, addressing
the changing conditions. While her first book insisted on the existence
and complexity of Black women's literature and her second established
Black literary criticism as a definite and sophisticated practice, her last,
unfinished project, for which she won an ACLS fellowship in 1994,[44]
intended to "explore the pivotal ideas contemporary African American
women writers, Toni Morrison, Alice Walker, Audre Lorde, June Jordan,
and Octavia Butler, have contributed to U.S. social movements such
as the black and women's movements, as well as to global liberation
and environmental movements" as well as how they have "influenced
our intellectual landscape in relation to central ideas such as difference,
the canon, and the construction of female subjectivities."[45] This project
was proposed as an interdisciplinary study based not only on exegetical
analyses of these writers' literary texts but also on "archival materials:
newspapers, media, as well as critical essays."[46] We might understand
this last project as a rejoinder to celebratory, multicultural, or purely formalist analyses of the 1990s that evacuated the political or intellectual
contexts for Black women's literary production.

Accordingly, within the context of the contemporary university, where
"diversity" is tokenistically but not substantively prioritized, racial and
gendered management currently does not occur solely through the den-
igration of Black feminism and Black feminists, but also simultaneously
through a form of valorization and fetishization, albeit of a limited and
facile type. This is the ideological and epistemological formation of *neoliberal* global capital. Black feminists of the 1980s and 1990s, such as
Christian, specifically addressed this new racial and gender formation.
For this very reason, Black feminist thought of the 1980s and 1990s
centrally examines how racist and sexist structures of violence endure
despite this seeming disavowal of overt racism and white supremacy.

In particular, Christian's essay notes that the current neoliberal multicultural moment allows for, and indeed requires, the nominal valorization of Black feminism as a way to deflect charges of racism and misogyny, which does not preclude and in many instances facilitates the institutionalized racist and sexist violence that renders Black feminist lives so precarious. Further, Christian focuses on the ways in which technologies of racial and gender management link knowledge production to demographic and economic processes. In so doing, Christian's essay can be read as a precise diagnosis of the regimes of racial management of our moment and the university's implicatedness in these regimes. Noting that many African American women enter the academy because they are attracted to the possibility of pursuing work organized around alternative models of research, only to be discouraged by the lack of institutional support for such work, Christian writes, "Can we conceive of the idea that sometimes their projects and the ways in which they pursue them might be incomprehensible to our sense of what scholarly enterprises should be about? Can we think about how narrowly defined our own definition of scholarship might be?"[47] Christian thus encourages us to interrogate how we might be reproducing what Patricia Hill-Collins has termed "Eurocentric masculinist criteria for methodological adequacy."[48]

Christian thus importantly connects the question of who has access to the university to the question of what kinds of knowledge are produced. However, this is not presented, in Christian's text, as a reductive essentialism that maintains that African Americans, once in the ranks of the academy, will produce a certain kind of scholarship and espouse a particular kind of politics. Rather, she emphasizes the notion that changes in knowledge production are a *precondition* to the greater representation of African Americans, and African American women in particular, in the university. She makes an important point about the ways in which the *conditions* for knowledge production are determined by assumptions about *what counts as knowledge*. As such the regulation of knowledge production acts as a mechanism of exclusion alongside the oftentimes more acknowledged issues of economic barriers and the racially stratified structures of the U.S. educational system.

The concerns about the pipeline for Black feminists that Christian discusses in "Diminishing Returns" were present from the beginnings of her career. In her first promotion report at the University of California, Berkeley, Christian describes her community service, including being a consultant for the Berkeley public schools. She writes, "One of the major problems high school teachers are facing is an apparent lack of interest in academic matters on the part of Black teenaged women. I have lectured in the schools on the Caribbean and on Black literature. More importantly, I have been presented to these young women as a Black woman who has gone into an intellectual arena. . . . I came into the class as a visitor who was both a mother and a 'career woman.'"[49] Here, Christian explains that for these Black teenaged women, intellectual content must have an embodied context, and that such context is "more [important]" for bringing such students into higher education, underscoring the point she makes in "Diminishing Returns," that the university mobilizes exclusionary tactics on various registers.

As much as she devoted herself to getting Black women into the university, she also worked to extend the university to them, imagining the project of knowledge production and pedagogy beyond existing university structures. In a promotion report written in 1974, Christian describes her three years of work with a project called Universities Without Walls, which she describes as "a multicultural institution designed primarily for students who do not have access to existing colleges and universities. The students at UWW are primarily third world students, many of whom are people who have not wanted to or could not adjust to traditional university structures, as well as older people who have been working for many years and have much experience in the area in which they want a degree."[50]

One such student was Halifu Osumare, now professor of African American Studies at the University of California, Davis. A leading scholar and practitioner of African and African American dance and urban youth culture—in particular, hip-hop dance—Osumare was one of Christian's first UWW students and describes the work she did under Christian's mentorship as the foundation for her creative and academic career trajectory. Osumare's pathway to academia was nontraditional to say the least. With a background in intensive dance training, Osumare enrolled in San Francisco State as a freshman in 1965. In her junior year, inspired by the Black Student Union– and Third World Liberation Front–led strikes of 1968 at San Francisco State, Osumare dropped out of college to tour Europe as a dancer, and built a successful career performing and teaching dance in Copenhagen and Stockholm. Returning to the United States in 1971, she performed with dance companies in Boston and New York before reestablishing herself in the Bay Area. Eager to finish her degree, but reluctant to reenter the classroom, she investigated UWW and was paired with Christian. She recounts, "We had immediate resonance and the rest is history, as they say."[51] Osumare recalls that Christian quickly recognized the validity of her dance career as a source of knowledge:

> Once she assessed the level of experience that I had, she basically said you have enough right here to get your degree. First of all, she started at that level of reassurance that what I needed to do was to document my experience that I obviously had had over the last five years, and that I had enough academic acumen that I could do the culminating paper . . . that would allow me to pull my experience, my research together to make this major statement about Black dance.

Combining secondary sources on African and African American dance with interviews of African diasporic dancers beginning to settle in the Bay Area, Osumane's culminating paper ended up being a twenty-five-page analysis of the continuities between African and African American dance entitled "The Evolution of Black Dance." This argument about the continuities between African and African American dance became what Osumane calls "artistically [her] major contribution to the field of dance," and the title of her paper has lived on as the name of a number of dance performances and demonstrations that Osumane has conducted throughout the United States.

Christian's description of her pedagogy and Osumare's recounting of her experiences under Christian's mentorship are early evidence of a belief Christian more explicitly theorized in her foundational and groundbreaking essay "Race for Theory," published in 1993. She writes in her promotion materials that "part of the process of this kind of non-traditional structure consists in helping students reflect upon and creatively chronicle their practical working experience in order to demonstrate what they have learned while doing them."[52] In other words, Christian developed and honed her argument in "Race for Theory" that "people of color have always theorized—but in forms quite different from the Western form of abstract logic. . . . My folk, in other words, have always been a race for theory" by first putting it into practice as a pedagogical philosophy.[53] In her essay, Christian makes a case for literary production as the site through which people of color have theorized, in stylistically complex ways, "from these groups' reflections on their own lives."[54] In her description of her pedagogical method, she reveals that what it means for her to "teach" these students is exactly to give them the opportunity to theorize—or in her words, "reflect upon and creatively chronicle." In this way, Christian's pedagogy was a way of validating the variety of ways in which people of color produce knowledge, both within and outside the institutions and languages of the academy. Osumare observes, "I think that's why she wanted to be a part of the University Without Walls, because it provided a kind of rubric where those kinds of things could be acknowledged and validated—the world experience and personal experience of different individual students."[55]

Christian's linking of issues of access to issues of judgment, knowledge production, and disciplinary regulation makes clear that we must connect the university's demographic and political economic strategies to its politics of knowledge. Christian's work thus belies the claims of the social theorist Bill Readings, who argues that the university's current configuration around the supposedly contentless and race-neutral privileging of "excellence" marks a decisive break from the earlier organization of the university around the validity of Western civilization, the canon, and "core knowledges." Readings argues that, unlike the earlier era's defense of "core knowledges," the contemporary university's deployment of the rhetoric of "excellence" renders *what* is being said less important than *how* it is being said, making the "content" of knowledge irrelevant: "What gets taught and researched matters less than the fact that it be excellently taught or researched."[56]

Yet in asking us to reconsider "how narrowly defined our own definition of scholarship might be," Christian urges us to understand the ways in which this emphasis on "excellence" implicitly disallows certain forms of knowledge and privileges others. A well-known literary critic once casually remarked that "politicized discourse . . . is sometimes merely an expression of opinion, of good politics but indifferent or redundant scholarship."[57] This scholar evinces a too-common faith in a category of "indifferent or redundant scholarship," with an implied opposing category of "excellent" scholarship, both of which ostensibly can be ascertained through ideologically neutral criteria that exists independently of whatever "political" content this scholarship might espouse. Christian asks us to think more critically about such supposedly neutral forms of evaluation and judgment, suggesting that the very criteria itself is invisibly ideological, validating some forms of knowledge and disallowing others. In so doing, Christian observes, these purportedly neutral criteria not only regulate *what* gets said but also, in making the university an inhospitable place for those African American women seeking alternative models for research, determine *who* can say it.

Christian's emphasis on the connection between questions of access (who makes up the university) and knowledge production (what is getting said and taught) highlights a relationship that is often underappreciated or apprehended too reductively. Knowledge production, for Christian, is absolutely circumscribed by racialized power—in the forms of judgment, discipline, and regulation. That is, the university's management of racialized and gendered *bodies* occurs through its management of racialized and gendered *knowledge*.

Christian's analysis gives us a means to revise Foucault's notion of biopower, which he defines as the dominant contemporary mode of governance in which subjects are ruled through the production of regimes of knowledge, through the management, surveillance, and categorization of the various modes of life: its sustenance, its reproduction, its duration, its embodied manifestations. In this context, norms rather than laws become the regulatory apparatuses of power. For Foucault, race emerges mainly as a way of articulating blood purity, a corollary to his more central preoccupation around the production of norms, which is why, for him, sexuality becomes such a governing and governed site.[58] Yet even after association with Nazism tarnished the notion of blood purity, race continues to have a structuring power, albeit in a different manner. Christian's analysis helps us understand that race, gender, and sexuality function intersectionally to organize how knowledge production regulates bodies in the most minute and thorough ways. If canonical knowledge deployed to demonstrate the superiority of Western civilization was the earlier norm organizing university education, a supposedly contentless excellence that obfuscates the racism and sexism of universities is the new norm within the context of contemporary globalization. These norms are exactly what structures the violence of the university against Black feminists currently. While Christian does not explicitly address such matters, her analysis, in demonstrating the embodied power of knowledge production, gives us an analytic with which to understand how the epistemologies organizing the university might manage racialized and gendered bodies to the point of exhaustion, breakdown, death.

Christian's archive reveals some of her own institutional difficulties that provided the context for her careful theorizations of university power relations. Her tenure process was rendered even more precarious by the fact that she was told of her file due date only two weeks beforehand, unlike other colleagues who were given six months' notice.[59] Subsequent review statements post-tenure reveal a level of university and professional service on committees, on boards of journals, in professional associations, and as chair of the Afro-American studies program, among many other activities, that would defy belief if it were not still so common among women academics of color.[60] Several of her later appeals for leave and funding note that she was the only Black humanities professor at Berkeley at the time and mention health problems even prior to her cancer diagnosis.[61]

And in this context of Christian's own health history, perhaps I might have to reconsider my earlier supposition that when Christian penned "Diminishing Returns," she may not have been thinking about premature death as a "pipeline" issue. Perhaps Christian did sense the impending crisis of premature death and embodied vulnerability for Black scholars and artists of her generation, insofar as she wrote several tributes for dead and dying colleagues, including Audre Lorde, Toni Cade Bambara, and Marlon Riggs, on whose behalf she accepted the Fannie Lou Hamer Award in 1994 as he was lying in a hospital bed dying of AIDS.[62]

As dire as these circumstances are, Christian's essay echoes Foucault's concern over what he called "subjugated knowledges," which he defined as "a whole series of knowledges that have been disqualified as nonconceptual knowledges, as insufficiently elaborated knowledges: naive knowledges, hierarchically inferior knowledges, knowledges that are below the required level of erudition and scientificity."[63] His concern was not simply that these knowledges would be unappreciated by institutions of "science" but that they would become *too* appreciated—appreciable—in their aspirations to be a true "science." In that case, such seemingly subjugated knowledges would be in collusion with the mechanisms of power that constitute hierarchies of knowledge. Foucault cautions that "we should be asking the question, asking ourselves, about the aspiration to power that is inherent in the claim to being a science."[64] While Foucault specifically addressed the fields of Marxism and psychoanalysis, we can see that the study of *race* and *gender* has had this trajectory as well. Indeed, this is exactly the question Christian addresses in another essay that meditates on the promises and perils of institutionalization. In "But What Do We Think We're Doing Anyway?," she offers an intellectual history of Black feminism and meditates on the "positives and negatives of what it means to become institutionalized in universities."[65] In other words, if we are to center the U.S. university as the object of our analysis, we must understand the regulation and disciplining of the study of race and gender as centrally and constitutively organizing its mechanisms of power. Another way of posing this question is: What happens when the study of race and gender is hailed as a sign of the university's "excellence," as the familiar slogan "excellence through diversity" implies? What happens when we who study race and gender ourselves champion a limited notion of "excellence," and in so doing, constrain ourselves from recognizing, as Christian suggested, how "narrowly defined our own definition of scholarship might be"? In so doing, she implies, we are contributing to the very processes that enable the university to be so violent to Black feminists.

While Black feminism has become incorporated, albeit often tokenistically, into many institutions, Black feminists are hampered in these institutions insofar as knowledge production is regulated by the normative
category of "excellence." This category claims to be objective and neutral
because it subjects all scholarly production to the same criteria. Yet Christian's analysis implies that these norms exist in antagonism to Black feminists whose work might not fit such a narrow view of what counts as
knowledge. I would argue that it does so because so much of what Black
feminists produce is the study of what cannot be known. That is, rather
than treat knowledge as transparently available, much of Black feminism has maintained that what counts as knowledge is always ideologically determined. "Black feminism" can be defined not as a discrete and
knowable set of objects, but instead can be deployed as one of the names
for what has been rendered unknown—unknowable—through the very
claim of a totalizing knowledge. While Black feminism has always had
to maintain the validity and existence of alternative forms of knowledge,
an important thread within Black feminist thought also exists that simultaneously gestures toward what cannot be known, what has been erased,
and how. At the moment when this modality of Black feminism fulfills
its project by acknowledging the unknowable, it undermines the norms
of scholarly authority and mastery upon which the university is based.

Yet if the norms of excellence and objectivity are wielded by the university in order to exclude and marginalize Black feminists, this is also the
terrain on which we struggle to reimagine the university as a site where
different kinds of epistemological, methodological, and intellectual projects, as represented in Black feminism, might emerge. Such projects
challenge, rather than reproduce, the norms of the university. Herbert
Marcuse writes, "In order to identify and define the possibilities of an
optimal development, the critical theory must abstract from the actual
organization and utilization of society's resources, and from the results
of this organization and utilization. Such abstraction which refuses to
accept the given universe of facts as the final context of validation, such
'transcending' analysis of the facts in the light of their arrested and
denied possibilities, pertains to the very structure of social theory."[66] The
organization of the university around this "given universe of facts" mar-
ginalizes and devalues the intellectualism of Black feminists.

Yet Black feminism's challenge to the "given universe of facts," its necessary acknowledgment of what cannot be known, can make knowledge production within the context of the university a process that enlivens, rather than extinguishes, Black feminists. As Joy James has argued, Black feminism is not monolithic, but has liberal, radical, and revolutionary trajectories.[67] Yet in the work of Black feminists across a variety of traditions, we see evidence of such epistemological critiques. I have elsewhere provided readings of this critique of epistemological closure and the stability of knowledge in the work of Angela Davis and Barbara Smith, and so in this chapter I will turn my attention to writings by the Combahee River Collective and Audre Lorde.[68]

The Combahee River Collective, in "A Black Feminist Statement," describes revolutionary action as a kind of epistemological unknown: "We might use our position at the bottom, however, to make a clear leap into revolutionary action. If Black women were free, it would mean that everyone else would have to be free since our freedom would necessitate the destruction of all the systems of oppression."[69] This language of the "leap" is evocative; revolutionary action requires a moment where one refuses the status quo. A leap defies the real—the demands of physics, of gravity—in order to be impossibly airborne, even if for a moment. The "clear leap" implies a work of imagination, the ability to believe that a different future might be possible, despite the seeming inevitability of a crushing present. It does not concede the future to the present, but imagines it as something as yet in the balance, something that can be fought over "in order to blast a specific era out of the homogeneous course of history."[70] In this way, the work of culture, of imagining, is revolutionary. Christian takes this leap, imagining the potentiality of a bleak future in order to mark it as something that is hanging in the balance, something over which we can and must struggle. Christian's essay is itself a work of imagination in the tradition of women of color feminism, and as such it "designate[s] the imagination as a social practice under contemporary globalization."[71]

In this tradition, the work of imagination is not a frivolous or superficial activity but rather a material and social practice toward "revolutionary change." Audre Lorde writes in her foundational essay, "Poetry Is Not a Luxury," "Poetry is not only dream and vision; it is the skeleton architecture of our lives. It lays the foundations for a future of change, a bridge across our fears of what has never been before."[72] The imaginative capacity inherent to poetry doesn't merely reflect the material world, nor is it an epiphenomenon of it, but rather it is the "skeleton architecture," its "foundation." In language that resonates with, in order to critique, a Marxist vocabulary for culture, Lorde situates poetry as the *base*, not the superstructure.[73] For Lorde, dismissing as "luxury" the imaginative work of poetry has severe and bleak consequences: "We give up the future of our worlds."

Black feminism reminds us to imagine a different future, for "the future of our worlds" hangs in the balance. So what might our future within the university look like? Is there a version of the university that does not reproduce a "reality" forcibly determined by an invisible ideology of color-blind neutrality, but one that labors mightily against it? If that is what our future might look like, I'd like to propose that perhaps, in fleeting, contingent, and provisional ways, the future is now. In this chapter, I intend to recognize the surviving work of Black feminists, work that does indeed, if even for a moment and with some grave consequences for its authors, make the university a site where a different kind of knowledge is produced. In so doing, these Black feminists imagine the university as a different institution altogether, one that makes central an intellectualism of the type best exemplified by Black feminism. In its redistributive project, Black feminism imagines a university in which a less disciplining definition of knowledge allows more Black feminists to enter, and makes the university a less hostile place for Black feminists. This is the work that Black feminism does now and in the future, for the future, and is the work that we must take up in solidarity.

But this is a joyous responsibility, a life-affirming work. I want to end with another passage from Christian's essay. She writes, "Besides, the point is, and it is an important point, that there is joy in struggle. . . . We will survive in the academy."[74] And she will.

Life, Death, and Everything in Between

I was trying to make sense of what seemed to me the ubiquity of death, from the U.S. wars in Afghanistan and Iraq to the passing of my then-colleague Nellie McKay from cancer, among too many others, and somehow that led to the beginnings of this book. As I finish this book, in August 2014, Israel launches an air and ground attack on Gaza that kills more than two thousand Palestinians, and a police officer shoots and kills eighteen-year-old Mike Brown, whose hands are in the air, in Ferguson, Missouri. So at the end of this book, I'm left where I began, with an array of questions and no satisfying answers.

I have argued that the hallmark of our current moment, which I have been calling "neoliberal," is a structure of disavowal of the ways in which race, gender, and sexuality, operating together, determine the uneven exposure to precarity and violence across people and populations. I have traced the ways, at once immensely systemic and immediately interpersonal, in which these demands for disavowal saturate and infiltrate the very conditions of our living, whether it be the mobilization of mourning as a disciplining apparatus of nationalism, the wielding of affects of fear and terror to legitimate abandonment, the bad faith offer of reproductive respectability in exchange for forgetting the connections between the modes of enslavement of the past and of the present, or the siren song of "excellence" that masks the university's violences. I have done so, however, not to posit this demand for disavowal as inevitable, but so as to better contextualize and highlight the moments when it is exposed, refused, and challenged, and how different ways of attending to the relationship between our lives and others' deaths are invented. It is to recognize the days and weeks and months of protest in Ferguson as the longest working-class rebellion in history, while at the same time remembering that these protests are nonetheless still by and for the living, and that Mike Brown—and many others—are no longer a part of the living. In the previous pages, I have considered the alternative imaginaries that are able to simultaneously suspend and sustain, rather than disavow, contradictory forces and truths—those that require us to build our alternatives by acknowledging that the conditions of our living are based on death. I have called the structure of these alternative imaginaries "difference," using the term in a way that I believe the women of color feminists who mobilized it meant. Difference as a method and a practice can be seen when Audre Lorde claims Malcolm X's legacy as one that defines Blackness as multiple, open to queer, feminist, and transnational politics. It emerges when Chicana feminists identify with all that is rejected and scorned about the figure of La Malinche, when Oscar Zeta Acosta's and Ana Castillo's novels both mourn Chicana/o death and declare that irony and humor are also important responses to death, and when Lorde and Cherríe Moraga embrace the erotic, shame, and inadequacy so as to face, rather than turn away from, the affective forces that relegate whole populations to the neoliberal predations of precarity. Difference appears when Black feminist and queer cultural production improvises ways of forging links across time when traditional, generational modes of transmitting history are made impossible by the legacies of both forced and foreclosed reproduction under enslavement. It also appears when Black feminists in the academy invent similar modes of improvisatory connection because the university as an institution violently interrupts *academic* generationality both through the dismantling of redistributive mechanisms such as affirmative action that might admit future generations and through the distribution of premature death to earlier generations of Black feminists.

I have traced these deployments of difference in order to give context to what is for me an ethical question, a question of reckoning. This reckoning is one that is necessarily never complete; to address the question of life and death requires that we defer resolution, in keeping with the political, epistemological, and ontological practice of difference, and exist in the temporality of suspension. The temporality of social justice is necessarily progressive—a future-directed faith that circumstances can and will change and that the brutalities of the present will not forever constitute our horizon of possibility. In conjunction with this forward-oriented temporality there is another, one that can catch the flickering glimpses of the time that disorganizes the sense of the present, the past, and the future as sequential or causal. This is the time of impossibility, where we work toward another horizon of possibility in the future, and also where there exists a radical forcing of impossible conjunctures *now* so as to acknowledge the unknowable inherent in the present. It is to both claim the future from "modernity's violence,"[1] and to claim the *present* as constituted not only by brutality but also by that which emerges from but exceeds the brutal calculus. It is to mourn death, to understand death as proliferative, and to submit that death escapes meaning, evades mourning, and exceeds understanding.

Difference in the hands of women of color feminists has always contained a radical humility in the face of what we cannot fully know. What I have been describing as an opening up of oneself to devastation as a means of refusing the bad faith promise of protection from precarity could more eloquently be called the "leap,"[2] the "nameless and formless,"[3] the "intolerable or incomprehensible or frightening, except as they came after dreams and poems."[4] It goes by many names: the erotic,[5] love,[6] the blues,[7] ghosts,[8] "the fact that life is complicated,"[9]—which is simply another way of saying "intersectionality."[10] Difference, then, simply means the future, the present, and the past as always simultaneous; it means life and death and all that lies in between.

Acknowledgments

This book exists because I felt called by the dead, and I felt that I had to acknowledge those who died, as a way of reckoning with, to quote Audre Lorde, "the deaths we are expected to live."[1] I think about those whom I have been asked to disinherit in order to exist as I do, and this book is my way of acknowledging them. So first and foremost, those are whom I thank.

But there are many among the living whom I thank as well, for sustenance and support beyond measure and description, and without whom writing this book would have been an impossible and, more importantly, pointless endeavor. I thank my writing group, LOUD Collective, whose membership has changed over the years, but who as individuals and as a group continually inspire and amaze me with their rigorous intellectualism, their generosity and kindness, their ability both to transcend individual hurts and mistakes and to exactingly call them into account, as the situation requires. I have learned so much from them, intellectually, personally, and politically, and this book has taken shape through my conversations and interactions with them in ways that defy accounting.

I thank my friends, colleagues, and interlocutors, who have sheltered me in an intellectual community by reading my work, engaging in conversations with me, entrusting me to read and learn from their fierce and brilliant thoughts, and working side by side with me: Randy Akee, Neda Atanasoski, Maylei Blackwell, Lucy Burns, Yu-Fang Cho, Lisa Kim

Davis, Erica Edwards, Fatima El-Tayeb, Roderick Ferguson, Aisha Finch, Mishuana Goeman, Gayatri Gopinath, Dayo Gore, Yogita Goyal, Sarah Haley, Christine Hong, Julietta Hua, Helen Jun, Kara Keeling, Arlene Keizer, Jodi Kim, Rachel Lee, Sharon Luk, Purnima Mankekar, Curtis Marez, Uri McMillan, Jodi Melamed, Leah Mirakhor, Nick Mitchell, Mignon Moore, Richard Morrison, Lisa Nakamura, Thu-Huong Nguyen-Vo, Kasturi Ray, Chandan Reddy, Shana Redmond, Felicity Amaya Schaeffer, Sarita See, Deb Vargas, Kalindi Vora, K. J. Ward, Randall Williams, Tiffany Willoughby-Herard, and Steven Wu. For the anti-anxiety medications of all types: happy hours, guest bedrooms, workdays in cafés and living rooms, chicken shorwa with extra boiled eggs, late-night phone conversations, sensible advice and outraged commiseration, emergency e-mail requests and panicked texts handled with aplomb, hikes, walks, swims, pedicure dates, potlucks, pastries, and sometimes even actual anti-anxiety medications, thank you.

Lisa Lowe has been, as ever, a guiding light, an inspiration, and a model of integrity, generosity, and intellectualism. I am forever grateful.

The editors at the University of Minnesota Press are exemplars of patience and support. I thank Richard Morrison, whose guidance throughout this project was invaluable; although he has now moved on to Fordham University Press, his mark on this book is indelible. I thank Danielle Kasprzak for seamlessly and expertly stepping in at the later stages and Anne Carter and Scott Mueller for editorial assistance. Many thanks to Shelley Streeby and the second reader for their meticulous, rigorous, and generous suggestions, all of which have only improved this book.

This book has been supported by a number of fellowships and grants. I thank the University of California Humanities Research Institute at which Jodi Kim, Curtis Marez, and I organized a Residential Research Group during the spring quarter of 2012. I have also received grants at crucial stages from UCLA's Institute for American Cultures, Asian American Studies Center, and Council on Research for this project.

I acknowledge with gratitude the opportunity to engage with a number of scholars through presenting and publishing my work. Brenda Gayle Plummer, Myisha Priest, and Cherene Sherrard Johnson gave valuable feedback on chapter 4 in earlier draft form. Don Nakanishi and King-Kok

Cheung provided thoughtful advice about how to direct this project at an early stage. I learned greatly from conversations at presentations, and I thank Karen Brodkin, Keith Feldman, Curtis Marez, Emory Elliott, Gayatri Gopinath, Patrick Anderson, Shefali Chandra, Erica Edwards, Heather Turcotte, Craig Willse, and Min-Jung Kim for invitations to speak. I also thank Halifu Osumare for sharing her memories of Barbara Christian with me.

This book would have been much less thorough without the able assistance of my immensely talented research assistants, who brought their considerable skills to bear on this project from beginning to end: Freda Fair, Lisa Ho, Mary Keovisai, Jacob Lau, Preeti Sharma, and Wendi Yamashita.

The staff in both of my departments at UCLA perform heroic and generally invisible labors on a daily basis, without which I would undoubtedly be lost. In the Department of Gender Studies, I thank Jenna Miller-Von Ah, Van Do Nguyen, Samantha Hogan, and Richard Medrano. In the Department of Asian American Studies, I thank Jessie Singh, Anne Bautista, and Natalia Yamashiro-Chogyoshi.

Victor Bascara makes everything fun and simple and sweet.

With gratitude to my family, Sung Ja Hong, Dai Soon Hong, Christine Heewon Hong, Judy Sungwon Hong, and Olivia Roxie Saddler, who remind me that life prevails.

Notes

Introduction

1. Audre Lorde, "Learning from the 60s," in *Sister Outsider* (Freedom: Crossing Press, 1984).

2. Ibid., 134.

3. For an astute discussion of the consequences of charismatic leadership in African American communities as well as Black feminist theorizations of alternative modes of political struggle, see Erica Edwards, *Charisma and the Fictions of Black Leadership* (Minneapolis: University of Minnesota Press, 2012).

4. Lorde, "Learning from the 60s," 143.

5. Audre Lorde, "Scratching the Surface: Some Notes on Barriers to Women and Loving," in *Sister Outsider* (Freedom: Crossing Press, 1984), 49. Originally published in *The Black Scholar* in 1978.

6. Lorde, "Learning from the 60s," 137.

7. Ibid., 141.

8. Walter Benjamin, "Theses on the Philosophy of History," in *Illuminations* (New York: Schocken Books, 1968), 255.

9. Lorde, "Learning from the 60s," 134.

10. Avery Gordon, *Ghostly Matters: Haunting and the Sociological Imagination* (Minneapolis: University of Minnesota Press, 2008), 25.

11. Lorde, "Learning from the 60s," 135.

12. Ibid.

13. Ibid.

14. Ibid.

15. Ibid., 136.

16. Ibid.

17. Ibid.

18. For a discussion of the ways in which the modern subject of liberal democracy is the injured subject, see Wendy Brown, *States of Injury: Power of Freedom in Late Modernity* (Princeton: Princeton University Press, 1995). In this book, Brown characterizes race-based social movements of the 1960s and 1970s as entirely organized around this politics of *"ressentiment,"* or injury. While I find her critique of liberalism useful, I depart from Brown's argument in my belief that these social movements were heterogeneous, that the only aspects of these movements that could be narrated as injury became institutionalized in the period of containment in the 1970s to the present, and that women of color feminism provided an alternative notion of subjectivity and community not organized around injury.

19. For a recent articulation of this argument, see Frank Wilderson, "Gramsci's Black Marx: Whither the Slave in Civil Society," *Social Identities* 9, no. 2 (June 2002): 225–40.

20. Lorde, "Learning from the 60s," 138.

21. Ibid., 139.

22. Ibid.

23. I thank Erica Edwards for this reading.

24. Jodi Melamed, "The Spirit of Neoliberalism: From Racial Liberalism to Neoliberal Multiculturalism," *Social Text* 24, no. 4 (Winter 2006): 1–24.

25. For a more sustained discussion of women of color feminism as a comparative method, see the introduction to *Strange Affinities*, in which Roderick Ferguson and I argue that women of color feminism provides an analytic of comparison radically different from that of liberal, nationalist epistemologies, one that takes into consideration the ways in which structures of power produce subjects and groups in relation to each other. Grace Kyungwon Hong and Roderick A. Ferguson, "Introduction," in *Strange Affinities: The Gender and Sexual Politics of Comparative Race* (Durham: Duke University Press, 2011).

26. For a recent articulation of this argument, see Jared Sexton, "People of Color-Blindness: Notes on the Afterlives of History," *Social Text* 28, no. 2 (2010): 31–56.

27. See Gloria Anzaldúa and Cherríe Moraga, eds., *This Bridge Called My Back: Writings by Radical Women of Color* (Watertown: Persephone Press, 1981); Angela Davis (interview with Lisa Lowe), "Angela Davis: Reflections on Race, Class, and Gender in the USA," in *The Politics of Culture in the Shadow of Capital,* ed. Lisa Lowe and David Lloyd (Durham: Duke University Press, 1997); Angela Davis and Elizabeth Martinez, "Coalition Building among People of Color," *Inscriptions* 7, http://culturalstudies.ucsc.edu/PUBS/Inscriptions/vol_7/Davis.html; Reagon Johnson, "Coalition Politics: Turning the Century," in *Home Girls: A Black Feminist Anthology,* ed. Barbara Smith (New York: Kitchen Table: Women of Color Press, 1983).

28. For an astute critique of the liberal security state's mobilization of Blackness, see Erica Edwards, "Of Cain and Abel: African American Literature and

the Problem of Inheritance after 9/11," *American Literary History* 25, no. 1 (Spring 2013): 190–204.

29. In situating the social movements of the 1960s and 1970s as a crisis in "racial capitalism," I follow Cedric Robinson in his monumental study *Black Marxism* in which he coins and defines the term "racial capitalism" as the structure against which Black liberation movements are arrayed. Robinson famously defines the Black Radical Tradition as emerging from "a rather more complex capitalist world system" (4) than Marxism can account for. This system of racial capitalism is organized ideologically around the erasure of Europe's genesis from Africa and the exclusion of the African from history, an ideological formation "commensurate with the importance Black labor power possessed for the world economy" (4). Cedric Robinson, *Black Marxism: The Making of A Black Radical Tradition* (Chapel Hill: University of North Carolina Press, 1983). Other scholars of capitalism extend Robinson's argument to demonstrate that racial capitalism is anchored by gender relations. Frances Beal contends that modern capitalism is predicated on the differential gendering of Black men and women, who are held to normative standards but are rendered materially unable to meet them, thus further facilitating their exploitation. Frances Beal, "Double Jeopardy: To Be Black and Female," in *The Black Woman*, ed. Toni Cade Bambara (New York: New American Library, 1970). In arguably the most brilliant elaboration of Marxist contradiction as theorized through race and gender, Angela Davis observes that the Black woman under enslavement was best able to produce and protect the desire for freedom within her community because her domestic labor for other slaves was both a sign of her exacerbated exploitation *and* the means by which she cared for others, and in so doing performed the only form of non-alienated labor available to the enslaved. Angela Davis, "Reflections on the Black Woman's Role in the Community of Slaves," *Massachusetts Review* 13, nos. 1–2 (Winter/Spring 1972): 81–100. Lisa Lowe has importantly proven the significance of Asian difference as a means of repressing or sublating the contradictions between state and capital in the late nineteenth and twentieth centuries; she situates Asian American cultural production as where such unresolved contradictions reemerge. Lisa Lowe, *Immigrant Acts: On Asian American Cultural Politics* (Durham: Duke University Press, 1996). Building on Lowe, Roderick Ferguson observes that racial, gender, and sexual non-normativity are created by capitalism's need for differentiated labor, and punished and regulated by state nationalism, but that these non-normative subjects exceed the terms of their production. Roderick Ferguson, *Aberrations in Black: Toward a Queer of Color Critique* (Minneapolis: University of Minnesota Press, 2004). Kalindi Vora highlights the racialized and gendered nature of contemporary capitalism's dependence on affective and immaterial labor, and traces this dependence as not new but as stemming from an earlier colonial capitalist order that was predicated on the affective and immaterial dimensions of labor. Kalindi Vora, *Life Support: Race, Gender, and*

New Socialities in the Vital Energy Economy (Minneapolis: University of Minnesota Press, 2015). Complicating our understanding of capitalism in this way requires a distinct re-definition of what liberation is to look like, who is to bring it about, and how.

30. Sylvia Wynter, "Unsettling the Coloniality of Being/Power/Truth/Freedom: Toward the Human, After Man, Its Overrepresentation—An Argument," *CR: The New Centennial Review* 3, no. 3 (Fall 2003): 257–337, 262.

31. Ibid., 263.

32. Ibid., 262.

33. Ibid., 263.

34. Foucault's theorization of biopower points to two different ways that the state can legitimate killing. States organized around sovereignty legitimate killing simply as the right of the sovereign to protect himself. Yet the emergence of biopower gives rise to a conundrum—that is, how a power based on the rationale that it protects and proliferates life can legitimate its power to kill. According to Foucault, this conundrum is solved by the invention of modern race. Foucault writes: "When you have a normalizing society, race or racism is the precondition that makes killing acceptable. . . . If the power of normalization wished to exercise the old sovereign right to kill, it must become racist." Michel Foucault, *Society Must Be Defended* (New York: Picador, 2003), 250. Foucault goes on to argue that racism is what finally distinguishes biopower from sovereignty, as racism justifies the putting to death of populations not through war or punishment, but through a *biological* rationale. Foucault recounts such a biological justification in this way: "'The more inferior species die out, the more abnormal individuals are eliminated, the fewer degenerates there will be in the species as a whole, and the more I—as a species rather than individual—can live, the stronger I will be. I will be able to proliferate'" (255). Foucault observes that, in the logic of biopower, "the fact that the other dies does not simply mean that I live in the sense that his death guarantees my safety," as in the logic of sovereignty. Under biopower, "the death of the other, the death of the bad race, of the inferior race (or the degenerate, or the abnormal) is something that will make life in general healthier: healthier and purer" (255). In other words, racism is how power legitimates itself in truly biopolitical ways—that is, by rendering the *quality* of life (rather than the very ability to live itself) dependent on the deaths of others. I would argue that "modern" race always denoted both sovereign and biopolitical legitimations. Thus, I understand these two terms not as discrete and mutually excusive eras, but as modes of power that can and do exist at the same time. If we think of death as always extended by means both sovereign and biopolitical at the same time, I believe that we must center histories of colonialism and race. As such, I depart from Foucault, who, while acceding that racism "first develops with colonization, or in other words, with colonizing genocide" (259), centers anti-Semitism,

culminating in Nazism, as the paradigmatic and most brutal example of the racism that enables biopolitical states to kill.

35. For a discussion of the ways in which the mainstream civil rights movement chose middle-class respectability at the expense of African American working-class and non-normatively gendered and sexualized communities, see Thaddeus Davis, "The Color of Discipline: Civil Rights and Black Sexuality," *American Quarterly* 60, no. 1 (March 2008): 101–28.

36. See Ward Churchill and Jim Vander Wall, *Agents of Repression: The FBI's Secret Wars against the Black Panther Party and the American Indian Movement* (Boston: South End Press, 1988); Kenneth O'Reilly, *Racial Matters: The FBI's Secret File on Black America, 1960–1972* (New York: Free Press, 1991); Nelson Blackstock, *COINTELPRO: The FBI's Secret War on Political Freedom* (New York: Pathfinder Press, 1975).

37. While the mainstream narrative of post–World War II liberation movements tends to domesticate or criminalize them, a number of important works, both scholarly and otherwise, have radically challenged this historical narrative of these movements as simply nationalist, civil rights–based, or organized around the politics of recognition, and instead have crafted a historiography of a Black radical tradition. See Charles Payne, *I've Got the Light of Freedom: The Organizing Tradition and the Mississippi Freedom Struggle* (Berkeley: University of California Press, 1995); Robin Kelley, *Freedom Dreams: The Black Radical Imagination* (Boston: Beacon Press, 2002); Robin Kelley, *Hammer and Hoe: Alabama Communists during the Great Depression* (Chapel Hill: University of North Carolina Press, 1990); Robinson, *Black Marxism*; Cedric Robinson, *Black Movements in America* (New York: Routledge, 1997); Maylei Blackwell, ¡*Chicana Power! Contested Histories of Feminism in the Chicano Movement* (Austin: University of Texas Press, 2011); Dayo Gore, Jeanne Theoharis, and Komozi Woodard, eds., *Want to Start a Revolution?* (New York: New York University Press, 2009); Dayo Gore, *Radicalism at the Crossroads: African American Women Activists in the Cold War* (New York: New York University Press, 2011); Eric McDuffie, *Sojourning for Freedom: Black Women, American Communism and the Making of Black Left Feminism* (Durham: Duke University Press, 2011). See also Karen Tei Yamashita, *I-Hotel* (Minneapolis: Coffee House Press, 2010).

38. Aihwa Ong, *Flexible Citizenship: The Cultural Politics of Transnationality* (Durham: Duke University Press, 1999); Aihwa Ong, *Neoliberalism as Exception: Mutations in Citizenship and Sovereignty* (Durham: Duke University Press, 2006); M. Jacqui Alexander, "Not Just Any(Body) Can Be A Citizen: The Politics of Law, Postcoloniality, and Sexuality in Trinidad and Tobago and the Bahamas," *Feminist Review* 48 (Autumn 1994): 5–23; Cathy Cohen, *The Boundaries of Blackness: AIDS and the Breakdown of Black Politics* (Chicago: University of Chicago Press, 1999). See also Michelle R. Boyd, *Jim Crow Nostalgia: Reconstructing Race in Bronzeville* (Minneapolis: University of Minnesota Press, 2008).

39. For useful critiques of homonormativity, see Martin Manalansan IV, "Race, Violence, and Neoliberal Spatial Politics in the Global City," *Social Text* 84–85 (Fall/Winter 2005): 141–55; José Esteban Muñoz, *Cruising Utopia: The Then and There of Queer Futurity* (New York: New York University Press, 2009); David Eng, *The Feeling of Kinship: Queer Liberalism and the Racialization of Intimacy* (Durham: Duke University Press, 2010). Rickke Mananzala and Dean Spade delineate the homonormativity inherent in mainstream gay and lesbian organizing, and identify similar tendencies in organizing within transgender communities. Rickke Mananzala and Dean Spade, "The Nonprofit Industrial Complex and Trans Resistance," *Sexuality Research and Social Policy* 5, no. 1 (March 2008): 53–71.

40. For an insightful discussion of the ways that contemporary homelessness is mobilized to serve the knowledge-production needs of social science and social services, see Craig Willse, "Neo-liberal Biopolitics and the Invention of Chronic Homelessness," *Economy and Society* 39, no. 2 (2010): 155–84. For a comprehensive study of gendered and racialized stigma around welfare recipients, see Ange-Marie Hancock, *The Politics of Disgust: The Public Identity of the Welfare Queen* (New York: New York University Press, 2004).

41. Sohail Daulatzai, presentation at Race, Politics, and Neoliberalism after 9/11, Black Studies Project, University of California, San Diego, March 5, 2014.

42. For a discussion of contemporary precarity and the limits of mourning, see Judith Butler, *Precarious Life: The Powers of Mourning and Violence* (London: Verso, 2004).

43. Roderick Ferguson, *The Reorder of Things: The University and Its Pedagogies of Minority Difference* (Minneapolis: University of Minnesota, 2012).

44. Scholars of the global prison-industrial complex, for example, have leveled particularly devastating and irrefutable critiques of a historical narrative that would posit a feudal, repressive, coercive mode of power a thing of the past. In an essay about U.S. carceral modes as a form of "neoslavery," Dennis Childs notes that the "Middle Passage never ended" (281) because of the "unsettling reality that the transition from slavery to freedom would lead to an amplification rather than an abatement of injury, living death, and murder for many former slaves" (284) through their incarceration in prisons. This history, Childs contends, "belie[s] any categorical separation of premodern and modern methods of violence and control" (289). Dennis Childs, "'You Ain't Seen Nothin' Yet': *Beloved*, the American Chain Gang, and the Middle Passage Remix," *American Quarterly* 61, no. 2 (June 2009): 271–97. See also Dylan Rodriguez, who writes, "A genealogy of the contemporary prison regime awakens both the historical memory and the sociopolitical logic of the Middle Passage" (239). Dylan Rodriguez, *Forced Passages: Imprisoned Radical Intellectuals and the U.S. Prison Regime* (Minneapolis: University of Minnesota Press, 2006).

45. See Jodi Melamed, "Making Global Citizens: Neoliberal Multiculturalism and Literary Value," in *Represent and Destroy* (Minneapolis: University of Minnesota Press, 2011).

46. For a classic critique of "color blindness" as legal doctrine, see Neil Gotanda, "A Critique of 'Our Constitution is Color-Blind,'" *Stanford Law Review* 44, no. 1 (November 1991): 1–68. For a discussion of whiteness as constituted through a narrative of victimization, see Lisa Cacho, "'The People of California are Suffering': The Ideology of White Injury in Discourses of Immigration," *Cultural Values* 4, no.4 (October 2000): 389–418.

47. See Neda Atanasoski, *Humanitarian Violence* (Minneapolis: University of Minnesota Press, 2014).

48. Jodi Melamed, *Represent and Destroy* (Minneapolis: University of Minnesota Press, 2011).

49. Ferguson, *The Reorder of Things*.

50. See Angela Davis, *Are Prisons Obsolete?* (New York: Seven Stories Press, 2003); Beth Richie, *Arrested Justice: Black Women, Violence, and America's Prison Nation* (New York: New York University Press, 2012).

51. See Gore, *Radicalism at the Crossroads;* Blackwell, *¡Chicana Power!;* McDuffie, *Sojourning for Freedom;* see also Kimberly Springer, *Living for the Revolution: Black Feminist Organizations, 1968–1980* (Durham: Duke University Press, 2005).

52. Lorde, "Learning from the 60s," 138.

53. See Kimberly Springer, *Still Lifting, Still Climbing: Contemporary African American Women's Activism* (New York: New York University Press, 1999); Premilla Nadasen, *Welfare Warriors: The Welfare Rights Movement in the United States* (New York: Routledge, 2004); Felicia Kornbluh, *The Battle for Welfare Rights: Politics and Poverty in Modern America* (Philadelphia: University of Pennsylvania Press, 2007); Lisa Levinstein, *A Movement without Marches: African American Women and the Politics of Poverty* (Chapel Hill: University of North Carolina Press, 2010); Jael Siliman, Loretta Ross, Marlene Garber Fried, and Elena Gutierrez, eds., *Undivided Rights: Women of Color Organizing for Reproductive Justice* (Boston: South End Press, 2004); Rhonda Williams, *The Politics of Public Housing: Black Women's Politics against Urban Inequality* (New York: Oxford University Press, 2004); Jennifer Nelson, *Women of Color and the Reproductive Rights Movement* (New York: New York University Press, 2003); Zenzele Isoke, *Black Urban Women and the Politics of Resistance* (Basingstoke: Palgrave Macmillan, 2012).

54. Gayatri Gopinath, *Impossible Desires: Queer Diasporas and South Asian Public Cultures* (Durham: Duke University Press, 2005), 20.

55. Kara Keeling, "Looking for M—: Queer Temporality, Black Political Possibility, and Poetry from the Future," *GLQ* 15, no. 4 (2009): 565–82, 566–67.

56. Ibid., 576.

57. See Grace Kyungwon Hong, *The Ruptures of American Capital: Women of Color Feminism and the Culture of Immigrant Labor* (Minneapolis: University of Minnesota Press, 2006), xxx–xxxi.

58. Zygmunt Bauman, "Wars of the Globalization Era," *European Journal of Social Theory* 4, no. 1 (2001): 11–28.

59. Gordon, *Ghostly Matters*.

60. Ruth Wilson Gilmore, "Race and Globalization," in *Geographies of Global Change*, ed. R. J. Johnston, Peter J. Taylor, and Michael J. Watts (London: Blackwell, 2002), 261.

61. Roderick A. Ferguson and Grace Kyungwon Hong, "The Sexual and Racial Contradictions of Neoliberalism," *Journal of Homosexuality* 59, no. 7 (2012): 1057–64.

62. Robinson, *Black Movements in America*, 134.

63. Derrick A. Bell Jr., "Brown v. Board of Education and the Interest Convergence Dilemma," *Harvard Law Review* 93 (1979): 533; Mary Dudziak, *Cold War Civil Rights: Race and the Image of American Democracy* (Princeton: Princeton University Press, 2000).

64. Melamed, *Represent and Destroy*, 1.

65. See Wahneema Lubiano, "Black Nationalism and Black Common Sense," in *The House That Race Built: Black Americans, U.S. Terrain*, ed. Wahneema Lubiano (New York: Pantheon, 1997), esp. 248–51.

66. See Hazel Carby, *Reconstructing Womanhood: The Emergence of the Afro-American Woman Novelist* (New York: Oxford University Press, 1987); Angela Davis, *Women, Race, and Class* (New York: Vintage Books, 1983); Sarah Haley, "'Like I Was A Man': Chain Gangs, Gender, and the Domestic Carceral Sphere in Jim Crow Georgia," *Signs* 39, no. 1 (Autumn 2013): 53–77.

67. Candice Jenkins, *Private Lives, Proper Relations: Regulating Black Intimacy* (Minneapolis: University of Minnesota Press, 2007), 10.

68. For important critiques of the Moynihan report and similar ideological mobilizations, see Davis, "Reflections on the Black Woman's Role in the Community of Slaves"; Roderick Ferguson, "Something Else to Be," in *Aberrations in Black*; Wahneema Lubiano, "Black Ladies, Welfare Queens, and State Minstrels: Ideological War by Narrative Means," in *Race-ing Justice, Engendering Power: Essays on Anita Hill, Clarence Thomas, and the Construction of Social Reality*, ed. Toni Morrison (New York: Pantheon Books, 1992).

69. One exception is Ferguson's chapter "'Something Else to Be," in his book *Aberrations in Black*. For scholarship on neoliberalism, see Milton Friedman, *Capitalism and Freedom: Fortieth Anniversary Edition* (Chicago: University of Chicago Press, 2002), originally published in 1962, which established the key terms of neoliberal thought, in particular the idea that free trade and competitive capitalism enhances political freedoms and liberal democracy. For useful critiques, see David Harvey, *A Brief History of Neoliberalism* (Oxford: Oxford University Press, 2005); Gérard Duménil and Dominque Lévy, *Capital Resurgent: Roots of the Neoliberal Revolution* (Cambridge: Harvard University Press, 2004), and *The Crisis of Neoliberalism* (Cambridge: Harvard University Press, 2011); Ong, *Neoliberalism as Exception*; Jean Comaroff and John L.

Comaroff, eds., *Millennial Capitalism and the Culture of Neoliberalism* (Durham: Duke University Press, 2001).

70. Ferguson, *The Reorder of Things*.

71. For scholars who have followed Karl Marx's theorizations of capital as a world-historical process, and in particular as a means of understanding the contemporary moment, see Ernest Mandel, *Late Capitalism* (London: Verso, 1978); Immanuel Wallerstein, *The Modern World System* (New York: Academic Press, 1976); David Harvey, *The Condition of Post-Modernity* (Oxford: Blackwell, 1989); Giovanni Arrighi, *The Long Twentieth Century: Money, Power, and the Origins of Our Times* (London: Verso, 1994).

72. United States Department of Labor Office of Policy Planning and Research, "The Negro Family: A Case for National Action" (Washington, D.C.: Superintendent of Documents, US Govt. Printing Office, 1965), n.p.

73. For important discussions of the connections between social movements and race politics in the United States and decolonization movements abroad, see Robin Kelley, "'But a Local Phase of a World Problem': Black History's Global Vision," *Journal of American History* 86, no. 3 (December 1999): 1045–77; Cynthia Young, *Soul Power: Culture, Radicalism, and the Making of a U.S. Third World Left* (Durham: Duke University Press, 2006); Gore, *Radicalism at the Crossroads*; Cheryl Higeshida, *Black Internationalist Feminism: Women Writers of the Black Left* (Urbana: University of Illinois Press, 2011).

74. Sara Clarke Kaplan, "Love and Violence / Maternity and Death: Black Feminism and The Politics of Reading (Un)Representability," *Black Women, Gender, and Families* 1, no. 1 (Spring 2007): 94–124.

75. As Lisa Lowe has argued, bourgeois notions of intimacy that emerged in the eighteenth and nineteenth centuries in European and American liberal humanist thought disavowed its dependence on the processes of settler colonialism, indentured labor, and enslavement that produced other, less evident forms of intimacy and admixture among enslaved, indentured, and colonized populations. Lisa Lowe, "The Intimacies of Four Continents," in *Haunted by Empire: Geographies of Intimacy in North American History*, ed. Ann Laura Stoler (Durham: Duke University Press, 2006). African chattel slavery on which modern racial capital is predicated was organized around the differential management of reproduction. Hazel Carby demonstrates the ways in which the nineteenth-century Cult of True Womanhood constituted white womanhood as pure, proper, and respectable over and against the figure of the lascivious, unwomanly Black enslaved female, as the context in which Black women novelists emerged. See Carby, *Reconstructing Womanhood*. Jennifer Morgan traces the ways in Black women's reproductive labor, in particular their ability to reproduce capital in the form of their children, became materially and ideologically central to New World slavery in the Americas. See Jennifer Morgan, *Laboring Women: Reproduction and Gender in New World Slavery* (Philadelphia: University of Pennsylvania Press, 2004).

76. Jenkins, *Private Lives, Proper Relations,* 24.

77. Melamed, *Represent and Destroy,* 1.

78. For an important critique of military humanitarianism, see Atanasoski, *Humanitarian Violence.*

79. See Alexander, "Not Just (Any)Body Can Be a Citizen." Ding Naifei reveals the complicity between feminism and the state against which sex workers in Taiwan organized in the 1990s in "Parasites and Prostitutes in the House of State Feminism," *Inter-Asia Cultural Studies* 1, no. 2 (August 2000): 305–18. Hans Tao-Ming Huang similarly critiques state feminism in his discussion of AIDS organizing in Taiwan in *Queer Politics and Sexual Modernity in Taiwan* (Hong Kong: Hong Kong University Press, 2011). Jodi Melamed critiques the cosmopolitanization of liberal feminism in Azar Nafisi's *Reading Lolita in Tehran* in her chapter "Making Global Citizens: Neoliberal Multiculturalism and Literary Value," in *Represent and Destroy.*

80. Loïc Wacquant importantly connects the carceral state and the welfare state in *Punishing the Poor.* For analyses of the neoliberal and U.S. imperialist deployments of the Model Minority discourse, see Victor Bascara, "Cultural Politics of Redress: Reassessing the Meaning of the Civil Liberties Act of 1988 after 9/11," *Asian Law Journal* 10 (2003): 185–214; Grace M. Cho, "The Fantasy of Honorary Whiteness," in *Haunting the Korean Diaspora: Shame, Secrecy, and the Forgotten War* (Minneapolis: University of Minnesota Press, 2008); Kamala Viswesaran, "Diaspora By Design: Flexible Citizenship and South Asians in U.S. Racial Formations," *Diaspora* 6, no. 1 (Spring 1997): 5–29; Helen Jun, "Black Surplus in the American Century" and "Asian Americans in the Age of Neoliberalism," in *Race for Citizenship: Black Orientalism and Asian Uplift from Pre-emancipation to Neoliberal America* (New York: New York University Press, 2011). For an analysis of Asian class development and U.S. militarism, see Jin-Kyung Lee, *Service Economies: Sex Work and Migrant Labor in South Korea* (Minneapolis: University of Minnesota Press, 2010). For discussions of the emergence of the Black bourgeoisie, see Cohen, *The Boundaries of Blackness;* Boyd, *Jim Crow Nostalgia.* For an analysis of the warehousing of poor Black populations, see Ruth Wilson Gilmore, *Golden Gulag: Surplus, Crisis, and Opposition in Globalizing California* (Berkeley: University of California Press, 2008). For scholarship on the criminalization of welfare, see Dorothy Chunn and Shelly A. M. Gavigan, "Welfare Law, Welfare Fraud, and the Moral Regulation of the 'Never Deserving' Poor," *Social and Legal Studies* 13, no. 2 (June 2004): 219–43; Kaaryn Gustafson, *Cheating Welfare: Public Assistance and the Criminalization of Poverty* (New York: New York University Press, 2011); Frances Fox Piven and Richard Cloward, *Regulating the Poor: The Functions of Public Welfare* (New York: Vintage, 1971); Sharon Hays, *Flat Broke with Children: Women in the Age of Welfare Reform* (Oxford: Oxford University Press, 2003).

81. See Incite!, *The Revolution Will Not Be Funded: Beyond the Non-Profit Industrial Complex* (Boston: South End Press, 2009); Soo-Ah Kwon, *Uncivil*

Youth: Race, Activism, and Affirmative Governmentality (Durham: Duke University Press, 2013); Willse, "Neo-liberal Biopolitics and the Invention of Chronic Homelessness."

82. For useful critiques of homonormativity, see Chandan Reddy, "Asian Diasporas, Neoliberalism, and the Family: Reviewing the Case for Homosexual Asylum in the Context of Family Rights," *Social Text* 84–85 (Fall/Winter 2005): 101–19; Anna Agathangelou, Daniel Bassichis, and Tamara Spira, "Intimate Investments: Homonormativity, Global Lockdown, and the Seductions of Empire," *Radical History Review* 100 (Winter 2008): 120–43; Craig Willse and Dean Spade, "Freedom in a Regulatory State: *Lawrence*, Marriage, and Biopolitics," *Widener Law Review* 11 (2004/5): 309–29.

83. Roderick Ferguson, "'Something Else to Be.'"

84. Patricia Williams, *The Alchemy of Race and Rights: Diary of a Law Professor* (Cambridge: Harvard University Press, 1992).

85. I use the term "women of color feminism" to describe an intellectual and political formation, sometimes used alongside or interchangeably with the term "Third World feminism," that emerged out of and in relation to the social movements of the 1960s and 1970s. In using this term, I am indebted to the work of Chandra Mohanty, who has theorized women of color or Third World feminism not as an identitarian or sociological category that describes a discrete set of people but rather as "imagined communities of women with divergent histories and social locations, woven together by the *political* threads of opposition to forms of domination that are not only pervasive but systematic." Chandra Mohanty, "Introduction," in *Third World Women and the Politics of Feminism*, ed. Chandra Mohanty, Ann Russo, and Lourdes Torres (Bloomington: Indiana University Press, 1991), 4. By using this term, I reference a group of writers, theorists, scholars, and activists including Angela Davis, the Combahee River Collective, Barbara Smith, the Third World Women's Alliance, Frances Beal, Audre Lorde, and Cherríe Moraga, as well as many others. However, I do not mean to imply by my use of this term or my identification of a set of common analytics and politics that there is a clear and definable set of texts, authors, or activists, as these are always contested and fluid categories.

86. Nick Mitchell, "Curricular Objects: 'Women of Color,' Feminist Anti-Racisms, and the Consolidation of Women's Studies," University of California President's Post-doctoral Fellows Retreat, October 6, 2012.

87. "Intersectionality," a term coined by Kimberlé Crenshaw in 1989, refers to an idea that predates the term. See Crenshaw, "Demarginalizing the Intersection of Race and Sex: A Black Feminist Critique of Antidiscrimination Doctrine, Feminist Theory, and Anti-Racist Politics," *University of Chicago Legal Forum* 140 (1989): 139–68. This idea can be seen earlier in, for example, the Combahee River Collective's "Black Feminist Statement," first published in 1978, in which they declare, "The most general statement of our politics at the

present time would be that we are actively committed to struggling against racial, sexual, heterosexual, and class oppression and see as our particular task the development of integrated analysis and practice based upon the fact that the major systems of oppression are interlocking." Combahee River Collective, "A Black Feminist Statement," in *Capitalist Patriarchy and the Case for Socialist Feminism,* ed. Zillah Eisenstein (New York: Monthly Review Press, 1978), 362.

88. A number of scholars, including Kara Keeling, Roderick Ferguson, Fatima El-Tayeb, and others have begun the work of analyzing the intellectual and discursive complexities of women of color feminist theorists such as Audre Lorde, Cherríe Moraga, Angela Davis, Barbara Christian, June Jordan, Toni Cade Bambara, and others, and of theorizing this body of work as a useful analytic for contemporary modes of power. Kara Keeling and Roderick Ferguson have individually used women of color feminism as a means of engaging with but also supplementing classical post-structuralism, in particular Gilles Deleuze (Keeling) and Jacques Derrida (Ferguson). Cathy Cohen first argued that contemporary queer of color critique and activism shares a genealogy with women of color feminism rather than with white queer theory and activism. See Cathy Cohen, "Punks, Bulldaggers, and Welfare Queens," *GLQ* 3, no. 4 (1997): 437–65; Kara Keeling, *The Witch's Flight* (Durham: Duke University Press, 2007); Ferguson, *Aberrations in Black;* Fatima El-Tayeb, *European Others* (Minneapolis: University of Minnesota Press, 2011); Grace Kyungwon Hong, "The Future of Our Worlds," *Meridians* 8, no. 2 (2008): 425–45; Grace Kyungwon Hong, "The Ghosts of Transnational American Studies," *American Quarterly* 59, no. 1 (March 2007): 33–39; Melamed, *Represent and Destroy;* Chandan Reddy, *Freedom with Violence* (Durham: Duke University Press, 2011).

89. In referencing "queer of color," I follow the scholarship of Cathy Cohen, Roderick Ferguson, José Esteban Muñoz, M. Jacqui Alexander, and Chandan Reddy, who have theorized this term. These scholars helpfully describe the ways in which racialization, colonization, and sexuality are interrelated processes; they define queerness through non-normative sexual formations that do not necessarily correlate with "gay" and "lesbian" identities, queering such figures as Black women on welfare and the Black transgender prostitute; they also insist that queer of color theory and activism can be traced not to white queer/ LGBT formations, but what we might more readily call "women of color" feminism, looking to Audre Lorde, the Combahee River Collective, and Barbara Smith as important theorists of non-normative sexualities. See Cohen, "Punks, Bulldaggers, and Welfare Queens"; Ferguson, *Aberrations in Black;* José Esteban Muñoz, *Disidentifications: Queers of Color and the Performance of Politics* (Minneapolis: University of Minnesota Press, 1999); Alexander, "Not Just (Any)Body Can Be a Citizen."

90. Gopinath, *Impossible Desires,* 11.

91. Cohen, "Punks, Bulldaggers, and Welfare Queens," 437–65.

92. Previously, the role of the sovereign was simply to determine life or death, either by recruiting his subjects as soldiers to wage war against external enemies, or by subjecting his subjects to death if they were themselves unlawful. In the eighteenth century, however, a new mode of power emerged, *biopower*, which took as its responsibility the management—and thus the extension of—human life. Such problems as how long people were living, in what state of health, how many children they were bearing, etc., which had previously been the provenance of God, were began to be understood as within the control of men, and the maintenance of life became the responsibility of the sovereign. The sovereign function, then, also extended away from just the state itself to a number of nonstate institutions as sites of knowledge production dedicated to ascertaining exactly how best to extend and proliferate life.

93. Giorgio Agamben, *Homo Sacer: Sovereign Power and Bare Life* (Stanford: Stanford University Press, 1998).

94. Ibid., 8.

95. Foucault observes that this attention to the preservation of life has in fact enabled the exacerbation of death: "Yet wars were never as bloody as they have been since the nineteenth century, and all things being equal, never before did regimes visit such holocausts on their own populations. . . . The power to expose a whole population to death is the underside of the power to guarantee an individual's continued existence." Michel Foucault, *The History of Sexuality*, vol. 1 (New York: Pantheon Books, 1990), 137. An important implication of Foucault's theory is that biopower operates productively, creating desires and entitlements, rather than merely through repression. As such, Foucault famously argues that resistance to repression through the expression of a supposedly prohibited desire is not an overturning of power, but is a way of submitting even more fully to regulatory modes of control. In other words, for Foucault, *affirmation* ("power organized around the management of life" [147]), more so than repression ("the menace of death" [147]), is where power inheres.

96. Mbembe uses the examples of the plantation and the occupied territory of Palestine, which he calls "the most accomplished form of necropower" (27), to make the point that the colony is the site of the death and violence that is disavowed by European political culture organized around "reason" but on which this culture is based, materially and ideologically. Mbembe notes that if one takes into account the history of colonialism, one can see the ways in which contemporary regimes of power are based on the active deployment of death, "in the interest of maximum destruction of persons and the creation of *death-worlds*, new and unique forms of social existence in which vast populations are subjected to conditions of life conferring upon them the status of *living dead*." Achille Mbembe, "Necropolitics," *Public Culture* 15, no. 1 (2003): 40.

97. Ibid., 25.

98. Patterson describes social death as constituted through the total domination of master over slave, the slave's natal alienation (or his inability to accrue

or pass on value through kinship, inheritance, and procreation), and the slave's generalized dishonor, a condition that constitutes an economy of honor for those who are not enslaved. Orlando Patterson, *Slavery and Social Death* (Cambridge: Harvard University Press, 1982).

99. While Patterson observes that slavery as an institution existed prior to the modern era, he differentiates between what he calls personalistic and materialistic idioms of power. Unlike under the personalistic idiom of power in which the hierarchies between people are demystified and acknowledged, societies organized around materialistic idioms of power disavow these hierarchies, instead claiming strict binaries between freedom and enslavement. For Patterson, the separability of social life and physical life is important because it explains how it can be that in Western societies freedom becomes inextricably dependent on enslavement. In contrast, for Agamben, this separation addresses the question of how modern political entities enable mass death through precisely the mechanism that it constitutes to define and protect life. Foucault's interest is not in ruminating on the separability of physical and political life, but rather on examining the moment when the political began to concern itself with biological life, and the consequences of this interest on modern power.

100. This analytic, articulated by feminist and queer scholars of race and colonialism, that centers racialized reproduction as the structure of modern power helps to highlight underappreciated aspects of Mbembe's and Patterson's theories—that is, that they do not posit the racialized, colonized, or enslaved figure as entirely *outside* the structures of Western modernity but rather highlight the ways in which exclusion is the structuring process that creates Western modernity. Patterson's notion of "social death," for example, does not describe a figure outside of society, but instead describes a social position, but one that stands in for *nothingness.* Social death, in other words, must be understood as a category of exclusion or exception upon which modern politics depends.

101. Agamben, *Homo Sacer,* 4.

102. Ibid., 7. Agamben writes, "Bare life has the particular privilege of being that whose exclusion founds the city of men."

103. Ibid.

104. Scott Morgensen, "The Biopolitics of Settler Colonialism: Right Here, Right Now," *Settler Colonial Studies,* no. 1 (2011): 52–76. Scott Morgensen critiques the tendency to erase indigenous histories by scholars who ignore the gendered and sexualized politics of settler colonialism. While the main targets of his essay are Agamben and Foucault, he also demonstrates the ways in which scholars of race and colonialism like Mbembe naturalize settler colonialism, demonstrating the need for a relational analysis across racial and colonized histories that does not perform such erasures.

105. Ibid., 71.

106. Ibid., 53.

107. Ibid., 66.

108. Hortense Spillers, "Mama's Baby, Papa's Maybe: An American Grammar Book," in *Black, White, and in Color: Essays on American Literature and Culture* (Chicago: University of Chicago Press, 2003).

109. Ibid.

110. See ibid.; Carby, *Reconstructing Womanhood;* Morgan, *Laboring Women.*

111. Examining settler colonialism, enslavement, and labor migration and imperialism as relational modes of epistemological, representational, and political difference, simultaneously inarticulable and hypervisible, is not to utilize a comparative model, but a relational one. Yu-Fang Cho's book *Uncoupling American Empire: The Cultural Politics of Deviance and Unequal Difference, 1890–1910* (Albany: State University of New York Press, 2013) produces such a relational analytic exactly centering the institution of marriage as that which mediated access to citizenship by race, gender, class, and sexuality. Cho develops a relational analyses of Asian American/Asian immigrant, African American, and U.S. colonial racial formation through what could be called, following Morgensen, "incomplete consanguinity."

112. Spillers, "Mama's Baby, Papa's Maybe," 224.

113. Gordon, *Ghostly Matters,* 19.

114. Gayatri Spivak, "Bonding in Difference: Interview with Alfred Arteaga," in *The Spivak Reader,* ed. Donna Landry and Gerald MacLean (New York: Routledge, 1996), 14.

115. Saidiya Hartman, "Venus in Two Acts," *Small Axe* 12, no. 2 (June 2008): 1–14, 2.

116. Gordon, *Ghostly Matters,* 25.

117. Hartman, "Venus in Two Acts," 2.

118. Saidiya Hartman, *Lose Your Mother: A Journey along the Atlantic Slave Route* (New York: Macmillan, 2008), 133.

119. Lorde, "Learning from the 60s," 134.

120. Hartman, "Venus in Two Acts," 2.

121. Ibid, 11.

122. G. Cho, *Haunting the Korean Diaspora,* 10–11.

123. Lorde, "Learning from the 60s," 135.

1. Fun With Death and Dismemberment

1. Ana Castillo, *So Far from God* (New York: Penguin, 1993), 19.

2. Oscar Zeta Acosta, *The Revolt of the Cockroach People* (New York: Vintage Books, 1989).

3. Ian Haney López, "Protest, Repression, and Race: Legal Violence and the Chicano Movement," *University of Pennsylvania Law Review* 140, no. 1 (2001): 4.

4. L. Lowe, *Immigrant Acts*.

5. Donald Lowe, *History of Bourgeois Perception* (Chicago: University of Chicago Press, 1982).

6. Benedict Anderson, *Imagined Communities: Reflection on the Origin and Spread of Nationalism* (London: Verso, 1991), 11.

7. Ibid.

8. Lorena Oropeza, *¡Raza Sí! ¡Guerra No! Chicano Protest and Patriotism during the Viet Nam War Era* (Berkeley: University of California Press, 2005), 114–15.

9. Rosalío Muñoz, "Speech Refusing Induction," *La Raza*, December 10, 1969, 6.

10. Dionne Espinoza, "'Revolutionary Sisters': Women's Solidarity and Collective Identification among Chicana Brown Berets in East Los Angeles, 1967–1970," *Aztlán* 26, no. 1 (2001): 37. The East Los Angeles–based Las Adelitas de Aztlán was composed of women who were formerly members of the Brown Berets but left the organization in protest of masculinism and male supremacism. As we can see by their mobilization of a nationalist affect of mourning in the Chicano Moratorium march, they still adhered to nationalist ideologies and principles even after their departure from the Brown Berets. However, as Espinoza argues, within the context of cultural nationalist rubrics both during their participation in the Brown Berets and after their departure, these women invented their own agendas and analytics, took on leadership positions and maintained autonomy, and resignified discourses of family away from heteropatriarchal models toward women-identified ones. Espinoza calls this form of negotiation "feminist nationalism" (42).

11. *La Raza* 1, no. 3 (n.d.).

12. "The Murder of Ruben Salazar," *La Raza* 1, no. 3 (n.d.): 38; Arturo Sanchez, "La farsa del 'inquest,'" *La Raza* 1, no. 3 (n.d.): 53.

13. Norma Alarcón, "Chicana Feminism: In the Tracks of the 'Native' Woman," in *Between Woman and Nation: Nationalisms, Transnational Feminisms, and the State*, ed. Caren Kaplan, Norma Alarcón, and Minoo Moallem (Durham: Duke University Press, 1999), 69.

14. Ibid.

15. Ibid.

16. Blackwell, *¡Chicana Power!*

17. Ana Nieto Gomez, "Chicana Feminism," in *Chicana Feminist Thought: The Basic Historical Writings*, ed. Alma Garcia (New York: Routledge, 2014), 52–53. Originally published in *Caracol* 2, no. 5 (1976): 3–5.

18. Blackwell, *¡Chicana Power!*

19. Many Chicana feminist critiques of cultural nationalism can be said, following José Muñoz, to *disidentify* with cultural nationalism to different degrees. That is, Chicana feminist critiques are not complete rejections of Chicano movement politics and of the nationalism that was a founding ideology of

the movement, nor are they a complete dismissal of so-called identity politics. Instead they tend to articulate nationalism and feminism as sometimes contestatory, sometimes overlapping ideologies that address similar sets of historical circumstances, albeit in different ways. In their earliest writings, Chicana feminists such as Marta Cotera spoke *from within* and to the Chicano movement. When these authors, in their early writings, traced an alternative genealogy of Chicana feminism, which they imagined as something that is organic to Chicana and Mexicana participation in Mexican and Chicano/a anticolonial and antiracist struggles, they were doing so within a conversation inside the Chicano movement, to refute detractors who narrated feminism as a corrupting outside ideology created by white women. In her essay "Our Feminist Heritage," Cotera traces Mexican feminist activities, beginning with the participation of women in the Mexican Revolution, and articulates a parallel, rather than causal, relationship between white women's movements and Chicana feminism, explaining that "a [white] women's *movement happened to come on the scene* when Chicanas were ready to take the step toward stronger development and realistic approaches to family problems." Marta Cotera, "Our Feminist Heritage," in *Chicana Feminist Thought*, originally published in *The Chicana Feminist*, ed. Marta Cotera (Austin: Information System Development, 1977), 44 (emphasis mine). In reference to Las Hijas de Cuauhtémoc, an influential Chicana feminist organization founded by Ana Nieto Gomez, Maylei Blackwell coins the term "retrofitted memory" to describe a similar reappropriation of Mexican and Chicano history to invent a Chicana feminist tradition. In the context of the Yucatan's El Partido Liberal Mexicano during the Mexican Revolution, Emma Perez's "feminism-in-nationalism" describes the ways in which Mexicana working women used the terms of an incipient Mexican nationalism to articulate their specific concerns. In so doing, Perez argues, they created a "third space," which, even (or perhaps especially) in the moments when they attempted to faithfully reiterate Mexican nationalist sentiments, created a dissonance or contradiction. Dionne Espinoza distinguishes between "feminism-in-nationalism," which operates within the terms of nationalism, and feminist nationalism, which creates a new narrative that borrows from nationalism but is not entirely of it. In her essay about the twin figures of Guadalupe and Malinche, Alarcón notes that La Malinche has been an important figure for Chicana feminists, and notes that "in order to break with tradition, Chicanas, as writers and political activists, simultaneously legitimate their discourse by grounding it in the Mexican/Chicano community and by creating a 'speaking subject' in their reappropriation of Malintzin." Norma Alarcón, "Chicana's Feminist Literature: A Re-vision through Malintzin; or, Malintzin: Putting Flesh Back on the Object," in *This Bridge Called My Back*, 71. In other words, Alarcón argues, although Malinche allows Chicana feminists to undermine the bounds of "tradition," she does so from *within* Mexican and Chicano cultural reference. Sandra Soto's analysis posits a slightly different kind of disidentification with Chicano nationalism. Soto sees Moraga as thoroughly undermining the stable subject of ethnonationalism, but notes that Moraga does so *by reproducing ethnonationalist and essentialist idioms and affects*, albeit through shame and alienation in a way that does not allow for resolution. In this way, Soto's argument is aligned with Perez's, insofar as they both argue that even seemingly faithful reproductions of nationalist sentiments necessarily exacerbate nationalism's inherent contradictions. Yet others also *implicitly* characterize Chicana feminism as undermining any sense of coherent subjectivity or "voice" by underscoring the fundamentally invented nature of Chicana feminism, which subverts any stable sense of origins or heroic narrative of historical progress. See Maylei Blackwell, "Contested Histories: Las Hijas de Cuauhtémoc, Chicana Feminisms, and Print Culture in the Chicano Movement, 1968–1973," in *Chicana Feminisms: A Critical Reader,* ed. Gabriela F. Arredondo, Aída Hurtado, Norma Klahn, Olga Nájera-Ramírez, and Patricia Zavella (Durham: Duke University Press, 2003). On a faith in language as reflective of meaning (as in Chicano nationalism), see Alarcón, "Chicana's Feminist Literature." In a number of ways, then, these queer and feminist Chicana scholars and activists simultaneously refute cultural nationalist claims that Chicana feminism colludes with racist modes of power, and also undermine white feminist or postmodernist analyses that would dismiss all antiracist nationalisms as only reactionary and social movement actors as dupes of nationalist articulations of power. See Muñoz, *Disidentification;* Cotera, "Our Feminist Heritage"; Emma Perez, *The Decolonial Imaginary: Writing Chicanas into History* (Bloomington: Indiana University Press, 1999); Espinoza, "'Revolutionary Sisters'"; Norma Alarcón, "Traddutora, Traditora: A Paradigmatic Figure of Chicana Feminism," *Cultural Critique* 13 (1989): 57–87.

20. An essay that rigorously critiques minority nationalism for its maintenance of heteropatriarchy, Lubiano's "Black Nationalism and Black Common Sense," first observes, in the African American context, that "black nationalism is of inestimable ideological—commonsensical—importance given the reality that U.S. blacks, in their 'being-as-a-group,' control no means of production, no land mass, and until about thirty years ago, were excluded from meaningful participation in formal, political politics. Necessarily, culture has been our terrain of struggle." Lubiano, "Black Nationalism and Black Common Sense," 233.

21. Wendy Brown, in *States of Injury,* tends to see antiracist mobilizations and critiques by people of color as a reductive sense of identity politics entirely motivated by a ressentiment that simply reinvests the state with power. My argument in this essay, which sees Chicano/a cultural production as *both* reinscribing nationalist mourning *and* articulating its limits and contradictions, is partly an attempt to contest arguments like Brown's.

22. Rosalind Morris notes, in the context of contemporary Thai nationalism, the commonness of news stories about the resolution of deaths through

proper burial, whether it be "the processes by which a body is recovered, a death reconciled with its corpse, or burial accomplished long after the fact of mortality." Rosalind Morris, "Returning the Body without Haunting: Mourning 'Nai Phi' and the End of the Revolution in Thailand," in *Loss: The Politics of Mourning*, ed. David Eng and David Kazanjian (Durham: Duke University Press, 2002), 29. Morris argues that such stories are allegories of the process by which nationalism gives meaning and existence to the present, but only in retrospect, in the same way that deaths are rendered meaningful by their after-the-fact proper treatment. Morris observes: "This suggests to us that nationalism is itself a formation produced in the space of loss or at least in the space of anticipated loss." Morris, "Returning the Body without Haunting," 30.

23. Ibid.

24. Alarcón, "Traddutora, Traditora," 69, 70.

25. Ibid., 68–69.

26. Ibid., 70. Guadalupe herself, as the figure that must represent "ritualized repetition," or, in other words, the woman who faithfully reproduces Mexican/Chicano communities and traditions without her own subjectivity, is a sacrosanct figure, which sheds light on why queer and feminist Chicanas have found it useful to take up, in complicated and critical ways, the Virgen, as well as why such controversy ensues. For a thoughtful analysis of how such refigurations of the Virgen, in particular by the queer Chicana artist Alma Lopez, enable the articulation of queer Chicana desire in the face of Chicano nationalist attempts to discipline desire, see Luz Calvo, "Art Comes to the Archbishop: The Semiotics of Contemporary Chicana Feminism and the Art of Alma Lopez," *Meridians* 5, no. 1 (2004): 201–24.

27. Alarcón, "Traddutora, Traditora," 68.

28. Ibid.

29. Alarcón, "Chicana Feminism," 68.

30. Acosta's masculinism has been critiqued by many scholars. Carl Gutiérrez-Jones, *Rethinking the Borderlands: Between Chicano Culture and Legal Discourse* (Berkeley: University of California Press, 1995), offers a particularly insightful reading of *The Revolt of the Cockroach People* in which he convincingly recounts the homosocial bonding that forms the basis of Acosta's nationalism, a relationship organized between men and through heterosexism, misogyny, and homosexual panic. That is, Gutiérrez-Jones notes that Acosta's definition of Chicano identity is organized around a "conflation, which joins the desire for partners and the quest of revolutionary righteousness. . . . Thus, in the logic of this narrative, to be a Chicano (male) means to sleep with Chicanas." Gutiérrez-Jones, *Rethinking the Borderlands*, 130. Ultimately, for this nationalist masculine formation, women are mere units of exchange between men. The instrumentalist view of women found in Chicano nationalism results from its organization around homosocial bonding, which, as Gutiérrez-Jones observes, "is not the same as to argue that such a group is latently homosexual. . . . In

fact, as Sedgwick argues, how a man succeeds in the patriarchal environment, in the world of men granting entitlements to men, depends fundamentally on how well he manipulates this gray area" (133). Arguing that we must pay attention to not only "overt examples of sexism, but also . . . the sharing of that sexism among Chicano males" as the necessary bond that organizes Chicano nationalism, Gutiérrez-Jones insightfully points out this text's "disturbing vision in which the law promulgates homosocial bonds in such a way as to limit revolutionary actions by setting marginalized groups into patterns of self-inflicted violence" (133). In other words, Gutiérrez-Jones argues that the homosocial organization of Chicano nationalism is its limit, the point at which its radical politics are reined in by its nationalism.

31. Acosta's own mysterious disappearance in 1974 has been the subject of much speculation. He was last heard from just prior to boarding a boat for a trip along the California coast, and was never heard from again, though rumors that he was still alive have circulated since then.

32. Acosta, *The Revolt of the Cockroach People*, 25.

33. Ibid., 22.

34. Ibid., 28.

35. Ibid., 42.

36. Oscar Zeta Acosta Papers, CEMA 1, Department of Special Collections, University of California, Santa Barbara Library.

37. Acosta, *The Revolt of the Cockroach People*, 89.

38. Ibid., 104.

39. Ibid., 201.

40. Ibid., 102–3.

41. Ibid., 102.

42. Ibid., 44.

43. Ibid., 47.

44. Ibid., 85.

45. Ibid., 197.

46. Ibid., 207.

47. Ibid., 211.

48. Frederick Luis Aldama, *Postethnic Narrative Criticism: Magicorealism in Oscar "Zeta" Acosta, Ana Castillo, Hanif Kureshi, and Salman Rushie* (Austin: University of Texas Press, 2003).

49. B. J. Manriquez, "Ana Castillo's *So Far from God*: Intimations of the Absurd," *College Literature* 29, no. 2 (2002): 37–49.

50. For the most-cited articulation of this definition of postmodernism as the critique of metanarratives, see Jean-Francois Lyotard, *The Postmodern Condition: A Report on Knowledge* (Minneapolis: University of Minnesota Press, 1984).

51. Manriquez, "Ana Castillo's *So Far from God*," 39.

52. Ibid., 44.

53. Ibid.

54. Ferguson, *The Reorder of Things.*

55. Castillo, *So Far from God,* 26.

56. Ibid., 36.

57. Ibid., 27.

58. Ibid., 186.

2. On Being Wrong and Feeling Right

1. Hong, *The Ruptures of American Capital.*

2. Lorde, "Learning from the 60s," 137.

3. See note 37 in the introduction.

4. For a women of color/queer of color analysis of the racialization and gendering of her cousin Brandon Martinez, see Lisa Cacho, "Racialized Hauntings of the Devalued Dead," in *Strange Affinities.*

5. Lisa Lowe, "Immigration, Citizenship, Racialization: Asian American Critique," in *Immigrant Acts.*

6. Mark Rifkin, "Indigenizing Agamben: Rethinking Sovereignty in Light of the 'Peculiar' Status of Native Peoples," *Cultural Critique* 73 (Fall 2009): 88–124, 90. Rifkin observes that U.S. sovereignty is based not simply on establishing the particular deployments of the "state of exception" but also on the constant, performative reestablishment of its *exclusive* right over the process of determining the state of exception.

7. Ibid., 90.

8. Karl Marx, *Capital,* vol. 1 (London: Penguin Classics, 1990), 782. Quoted in Ferguson, *Aberrations in Black,* 15.

9. Ferguson, *Aberrations in Black,* 15.

10. Ibid., 14.

11. Keeling, *The Witch's Flight,* 96.

12. That is, culture "works" precisely through inspiring affective investments, "(re)produc[ing] cultural value via investments in social forms and ideas that serve to solidify and sustain the categories and institutions that today enable and support the reproduction of capitalism, such as race, family, religion, heterosexuality, and the law." Ibid., 98.

13. Ibid. While observing that some of the surplus value becomes reintegrated as a kind of affective venture capital that provides "some of the start-up required for such projects as Quentin Tarantino's *Pulp Fiction,* Snoop Doggy Dogg's star image, and Darius James' book *That's Blaxploitation!*" (106), Keeling also identifies "nonreproductive, nonheterosexual, and nonheteronormative, queer" circulations of the affective surplus value generated through blaxploitation. She does so by tracing the ways in which Pam Greer's career is haunted by the residues of "a potential or implied lesbian sexuality" (108) that her blaxploitation films both capitalized upon but also violently disciplined. This residue makes it such that Greer's presence leaves open the possibility of "racialized

nonheteronormative working-and under-class forms of sociality" (117) through her performances in even such staunchly homonormative texts as *The L Word*.

14. Comaroff and Comaroff, *Millenial Capitalism and the Culture of Neoliberalism*, 2.

15. Ibid., 5.

16. Ibid., 7.

17. David Harvey, "The 'New' Imperialism: Accumulation by Dispossession," *Socialist Register* 40, no. 40 (March 19, 2004): 63–87.

18. Patrick Wolfe, "Settler Colonialism and the Elimination of the Native," *Journal of Genocide Research* 8, no. 4 (2006): 387–409.

19. L. Lowe, *Immigrant Acts*, 15.

20. Ibid.

21. Ibid., 18.

22. Ibid.

23. See Ji-Yeon Yuh, "Moved by War: Migration, Diaspora, and the Korean War," *Journal of Asian American Studies* 8, no. 3 (2005): 277–91.

24. See Lynn Fujiwara, *Mothers without Citizenship: Asian Immigrant Families and the Consequences of Welfare Reform* (Minneapolis: University of Minnesota Press, 2008).

25. Comaroff and Comaroff, *Millenial Capitalism and the Culture of Neoliberalism*, 10.

26. Gilmore, *Golden Gulag*.

27. For an analysis of the ways in which racialized criminalization legitimates abandonment by producing social value as a form of morality, see Lisa Cacho, *Social Death: Racialized Rightslessness and the Criminalization of the Unprotected* (New York: New York University Press, 2012).

28. James Ferguson, "De-moralizing Economies: African Socialism, Scientific Capitalism, and the Moral Politics of Structural Adjustment," in *Global Shadows: Africa in the Neoliberal World Order* (Durham: Duke University Press, 2006), 69.

29. See Willse, "Neo-liberal Biopolitics and the Invention of Chronic Homelessness," 155–84.

30. Audre Lorde, "Age, Race, Class, and Sex: Women Redefining Difference," in *Sister Outsider* (Freedom: Crossing Press, 1984), 115.

31. Within the humanities, scholars such as Kara Keeling, Roderick Ferguson, Fatima El-Tayeb, and others have begun the work of re-reading the intellectual and discursive complexities of women of color feminist theorists such as Audre Lorde, Cherríe Moraga, Angela Davis, Barbara Christian, June Jordan, Toni Cade Bambara, and others. We have argued that some of the most important theoretical innovations within humanistic study have indeed been presaged by such theorists. See Keeling, *The Witch's Flight*; Kara Keeling, "'I=Another': Digital Identity Politics," in *Strange Affinities*; Ferguson, *Aberrations in Black*; El-Tayeb, *European Others*; Hong, "The Future of Our Worlds," 425–45; Hong,

"The Ghosts of Transnational American Studies," 33–39; Melamed, *Represent and Destroy*.

32. Lorde, "Age, Race, Class, and Sex," 115.

33. Audre Lorde, "Uses of the Erotic: The Erotic as Power," in *Sister Outsider* (Freedom: Crossing Press, 1984), 55.

34. Lorde's discussion of affect both resonates with and departs from other theorists of affect under capitalism. Like such theorists, Lorde makes a distinction between emotion and what she calls "feeling," a category closer to the ways in which affect theorists describe affect, as pre-subjectival, embodied but not necessarily recognizable, and producing pre-linguistic forces and connections between bodies. For important work in affect studies, see Patricia Clough and Jean Halley, *The Affective Turn* (Durham: Duke University Press, 2007); Melissa Gregg and Gregory Seigworth, *The Affect Studies Reader* (Durham: Duke University Press, 2010); Katherine Stewart, *Ordinary Affects* (Durham: Duke University Press, 2007); Sara Ahmed, *The Cultural Politics of Emotion* (New York: Routledge, 2004). Brian Massumi helpfully describes the U.S. security state's mobilization of fear in the post-9/11 era in ways similar to Lorde's analysis; as I argue in the body of this chapter, Lorde goes on to connect state mobilization of fear to capitalist accumulation through the production of surplus existence. See Brian Massumi, "Fear (The Spectrum Said)," *Positions: East Asia Cultures Critique* 13, no. 1 (Spring 2005): 31–48.

35. Keeling, "Looking for M—," 566.

36. Patricia Clough, "The Affective Turn: Political Economy, Biomedia, and Bodies," *Theory, Culture, and Society* 25, no. 1 (2008): 1–22, 18.

37. Audre Lorde, "The Master's Tools Will Never Dismantle the Master's House," in *Sister Outsider* (Freedom: Crossing Press, 1984), 113.

38. Lorde, "Learning from the 60s," 142 (emphasis mine).

39. Lorde, "Age, Race, Class, and Sex," 115.

40. James Kyung-Jin Lee, *Urban Triage: Race and the Fictions of Multiculturalism* (Minneapolis: University of Minnesota Press, 2004), xxviii.

41. For analyses of neoliberal, late liberal, and late capitalist productions of abandonment, see Zigmunt Bauman, *Wasted Lives: Modernity and Its Outcasts* (Malden: Blackwell, 2004); Elizabeth Povinelli, *Economies of Abandonment: Social Belonging and Endurance in Late Liberalism* (Durham: Duke University Press, 2011); Cacho, *Social Death*.

42. Lorde, "Learning from the 60s," 139.

43. Audre Lorde, "The Transformation of Silence into Language and Action," in *Sister Outsider* (Freedom: Crossing Press, 1984), 42.

44. Audre Lorde, "An Interview: Audre Lorde and Adrienne Rich," in *Sister Outsider* (Freedom: Crossing Press, 1984), 95.

45. Lorde, "Uses of the Erotic," 54.

46. Ibid., 57.

47. Ibid., 58.

48. Ibid., 56.

49. Lorde, "An Interview," 100.

50. Ibid.

51. Ibid., 101.

52. Ibid.

53. Keeling, "Looking for M—," 567.

54. Lorde, "Uses of the Erotic," 56.

55. Audre Lorde, "Poetry Is Not a Luxury," in *Sister Outsider* (Freedom: Crossing Press, 1984), 37.

56. Ibid.

57. Lorde, "Uses of the Erotic," 56.

58. Keeling, "Looking for M—," 566–67.

59. Eng, *The Feeling of Kinship*, 101.

60. Lee Edelman, *No Future: Queer Theory and the Death Drive* (Durham: Duke University Press, 2004), 11.

61. Cohen, "Punks, Bulldaggers, and Welfare Queens," 437–65, 453.

62. Ibid., 455.

63. Sandra K. Soto, "Cherríe Moraga's Going Brown: 'Reading Like a Queer,'" *GLQ* 11, no. 2 (2005): 237–63.

64. Ibid., 254.

65. Cherríe Moraga, "A Long Line of Vendidas," in *Loving in the War Years* (Boston: South End Press, 1983). See chapter 1 of this book for a more extended discussion of the figure of La Malinche in Chicana feminist thought.

66. Soto, "Cherríe Moraga's Going Brown," 255.

67. Ibid., 238.

68. Cherríe Moraga, *The Last Generation: Prose and Poetry* (New York: South End Press, 1993), 9.

69. Ibid., 2.

70. Cherríe Moraga, *Waiting in the Wings: Portrait of a Queer Motherhood* (Ithaca: Firebrand Books), 119.

71. Ibid., 2.

72. Lisa Tatonetti, "A Kind of Queer Balance: Cherríe Moraga's Aztlán," *MELUS* 29, no. 2 (Summer 2004): 227–47, 244.

73. Ibid., 240 (emphasis in original).

74. Ibid.

75. Cherríe Moraga, "I Was Not Supposed to Remember," in *The Last Generation: Prose and Poetry* (New York: South End Press, 1993), 98.

76. Cherríe Moraga, "The Last Generation," in *The Last Generation: Prose and Poetry* (New York: South End Press, 1993), 1.

77. Ibid., 2 (emphasis in original).

78. Ibid.

79. Cherríe Moraga, "Queer Aztlán: The Re-formation of Chicano Tribe," in *The Last Generation: Prose and Poetry* (New York: South End Press, 1993), 164.

80. Ibid.

81. Ibid., 149.

82. Ibid., 148–49.

83. For example, see Wendy Brown's narration of "politicized identity" as simply Nietzschean *ressentiment* in *States of Injury*, 66–76.

84. Moraga, "Queer Aztlán," 150.

85. Ibid.

86. Ibid., 174.

87. Ibid., 164.

88. Muñoz, *Cruising Utopia*, 1.

89. Moraga, "The Last Generation," 4.

90. Alarcón, "Chicana Feminism."

91. Cherríe Moraga, "Tribute," in *The Last Generation: Prose and Poetry* (New York: South End Press, 1993), 177.

92. Moraga, *Waiting in the Wings*, 32 (emphasis in original).

93. Ibid., 118.

94. Moraga, "Tribute," 177.

95. Moraga, *Waiting in the Wings*, 42.

96. Ibid.

97. Ibid.

98. Ibid.

99. Ibid.

100. Ibid.

101. Ibid., 177.

102. Ibid., 32 (emphasis in original).

103. Ibid., 64.

104. Ibid.

105. Ibid., 33 (emphasis in original).

106. Ibid., 92.

107. Ibid.

108. Ibid., 94.

109. Audre Lorde, "A Litany for Survival," in *The Black Unicorn* (New York: Norton, 1978).

3. Blues Futurity and Queer Improvisation

1. James Baldwin, "The Uses of the Blues," in *The Cross of Redemption: Uncollected Writings* (New York: Vintage Books, 2011), 74.

2. Karla F. C. Holloway argues in her study of African American practices of death and mourning that "African Americans' particular vulnerability to an untimely death in the United States intimately affects how black culture both represents itself and is represented." Karla F. C. Holloway, *Passed On: African American Mourning Stories* (Durham: Duke University Press, 2003), 2.

3. Baldwin, "The Uses of the Blues," 70.

4. Ibid.

5. Inge Blackman now goes by Campbell X; however, *B.D. Women* was made prior to the change in name. I therefore use the name to which the film is credited in this chapter.

6. Cohen, *Boundaries of Blackness;* Jenkins, *Private Lives, Proper Relations.*

7. Nadasen, *Welfare Warriors;* Kornbluh, *The Battle for Welfare Rights;* Levin-stein, *A Movement without Marches;* Jael Siliman et al., *Undivided Rights;* Nelson, *Women of Color;* Gilmore, *Golden Gulag.*

8. Blackwell, *¡Chicana Power!,* 2.

9. Isoke, *Black Urban Women and the Politics of Resistance,* 2.

10. Morgensen, "The Biopolitics of Settler Colonialism," 66.

11. Christina Sharpe observes that in the intersection of incest and amal-gamation as the legacy of African enslavement we can see the mechanisms through which acts of reproduction become classified—some as kin, others as property. The violation of the taboo against reproduction between "kin" is called incest; yet reproduction between master and slave, owner and property, even if they are related by blood, can only be termed amalgamation. Sharpe outlines the contradictions of modern politics based on a fallacious notion of consanguinity—the idea that one's political identity accrues by way of a state constituted on the premises of patriarchally organized kinship. She does so by highlighting the ways in which patriarchally organized kinship itself, within the history of modern racial capitalism, is fundamentally premised on a prop-erty system that must preclude kinship relations (i.e., the possibility of incest) even when blood ties exist. Christina Sharpe, *Monstrous Intimacies: Making Post-slavery Subjects* (Durham: Duke University Press, 2011).

12. Carby, *Reconstructing Womanhood,* 24–25.

13. Spillers, "Mama's Baby, Papa's Maybe," 220.

14. Ibid.

15. Ibid. Expanding upon Spillers, Alexander Weheliye observes that Spill-ers's notion of the *flesh* allows for an understanding of the Black body that displaces the *human,* instead providing "a version of the human unburdened by shackles of Man" (66). In other words, Weheliye situates in Spillers's notion of "flesh" the possibility of pain as a kind of freedom that exceeds representa-tion because it both sustains and exceeds the violence that produces that pain. Alexander Weheliye, "Pornotropes," *Journal of Visual Culture* 7, no. 65 (2008): 65–81.

16. Spillers, "Mama's Baby, Papa's Maybe," 220 (emphasis in original).

17. Morgan, *Laboring Women,* 3.

18. Ibid., 71.

19. See Sara Clarke Kaplan, "Our Founding (M)other: Erotic Love and Social Death in *Sally Hemings* and *The President's Daughter,*" *Callaloo* 32, no. 3 (Sum-mer 2009): 773–91.

20. Patterson, *Slavery and Social Death,* 13 (emphasis in original).

21. Ibid., 1.

22. Ibid., 3.

23. Ibid.

24. Ibid., 5.

25. Ibid.

26. Ibid.

27. Ibid., 9.

28. Williams, *The Alchemy of Race and Rights*.

29. Edelman, *No Future*, 30.

30. Ibid., 11.

31. Ibid.

32. Judith Halberstam, *In a Queer Time and Place: Transgender Bodies, Subcultural Lives* (New York: New York University Press, 2005), 5.

33. Ibid.

34. Ibid., 10.

35. Davis, *Women, Race, and Class*, 7.

36. For a discussion of different relationships to procreation in slave societies, see Morgan, *Laboring Women*; Rhoda Reddock, *Women, Labour, and Politics in Trinidad and Tobago: A History* (London: Zed Books, 1994). See also Darlene Clark Hine and Kate Wittenstein, "Female Slave Resistance: The Economics of Sex," in *The Black Woman Cross-Culturally*, ed. Filomina Chioma Steady (Cambridge: Schenkman, 1981), 289–300. For a discussion of African American family formation, see Herbert Gutman George, *The Black Family in Slavery and Freedom, 1750–1925* (New York: Pantheon Books, 1976); Brenda E. Stevenson, *Life in Black and White: Family and Community in the Slave South* (New York: Oxford University Press, 1996); and Wilma Dunaway, *The African-American Family in Slavery and Emancipation* (New York: Cambridge University Press, 2003).

37. Baldwin, "The Uses of the Blues," 73.

38. Holloway, *Passed On*, 8.

39. Baldwin, "The Uses of the Blues," 74.

40. Albert Murray, "Improvisation and the Creative Process," in *The Jazz Cadence of American Culture*, ed. Robert G. O'Meally (New York: Columbia University Press, 1998), 112.

41. Fred Moten, *In the Break: The Aesthetic of the Black Radical Tradition* (Minneapolis: University of Minnesota Press, 2003), 26.

42. Benjamin, "Theses on the Philosophy of History," 254.

43. Patterson, *Slavery and Social Death*, 6.

44. Ibid., 11.

45. Ibid.

46. See Angela Davis, *Blues Legacies and Black Feminism: Gertrude "Ma" Rainey, Bessie Smith, and Billie Holiday* (New York: Pantheon Books, 1998). See also Hazel Carby, "It Just Be's Dat Way Sometime: The Sexual Politics of

Women's Blues," in *The Jazz Cadence of American Life,* ed. Robert O'Mealley (New York: Columbia University Press, 1998).

47. Gayl Jones, *Corregidora* (Boston: Beacon Press, 1975), 9.

48. Ibid., 14.

49. Ibid., 22.

50. Ibid., 10.

51. Sharpe, *Monstrous Intimacies,* 49.

52. Madhu Dubey, "Gayl Jones and the Matrilineal Metaphor of Tradition," *Signs: Journal of Women in Culture and Society* 20, no. 2 (1995): 245–67, 260.

53. Ibid., 252–53.

54. Sharpe, *Monstrous Intimacies,* 56.

55. Jones, *Corregidora,* 59.

56. Ibid., 56.

57. Madhu Dubey, *Black Women Novelists and the Nationalist Aesthetic* (Bloomington: Indiana University Press, 1994), 82.

58. Ibid., 81.

59. Dubey, "Gayl Jones and the Matrilineal Metaphor of Tradition," 252.

60. Jones, *Corregidora,* 184.

61. Dubey, "Gayl Jones and the Matrilineal Metaphor of Tradition," 258n11.

62. Ibid., 258.

63. Dubey, *Black Women Novelists and the Nationalist Aesthetic,* 81. See also Sherley Anne Williams, "Comment on the Curb," *Black Scholar* 10, nos. 8–9 (May–June 1979): 49–51, 51.

64. Essex Hemphill, "Brother to Brother" (interview with Isaac Julien), *Black Film Review* 5, no. 3 (Summer 1989): 14–17, 16.

65. Ibid., 15 (emphasis in original).

66. Ibid.

67. José E. Muñoz, "Photographies of Mourning: Melancholia and Ambivalence in Van Der Zee, Mapplethorpe, and *Looking for Langston,*" in *Race and the Subject of Masculinities,* ed. Harry Stecopoulos and Michael Uebel (Durham: Duke University Press, 1997), 337–58, 342.

68. Ibid.

69. Arnold Rampersad, *The Life of Langston Hughes, Vol. II, 1914–1967: I Dream a Life* (New York: Oxford University Press, 1986), 336.

70. Kobena Mercer, "Dark and Lovely Too: Black Gay Men in Independent Film," *Cineaction,* no. 32 (Fall 1993): 51–62, 59.

71. Ibid., 59.

72. Hemphill, "Brother to Brother," 14.

73. Mercer, "Dark and Lovely Too," 58.

74. Davis, *Blues Legacies and Black Feminism,* 40.

75. Shawn Anthony Christian, "Between Black Gay Men: Artistic Collaboration and the Harlem Renaissance in *Brother to Brother,*" in *The Harlem*

Renaissance Revisited: Politics, Arts, and Letters, ed. Jeffrey O. G. Ogbar (Baltimore: Johns Hopkins University Press, 2013), 180.

76. Omise'eke Natasha Tinsley, "Black Atlantic, Queer Atlantic: Queer Imaginings of the Middle Passage," *GLQ* 14, nos. 2–3 (2008): 191–215, 194.

4. Bringing Out the Dead

1. In so doing, Christian was one of the first, but certainly not the last, to reflect on the specificities of the experience of the academy for Black women and for women of color. For later engagements, see Gabriella Gutiérrez y Muhs, Yolanda Flores Niemann, Carmen G. Gonzalez, and Angela P. Harris, eds., *Presumed Incompetent: The Intersections of Race and Class for Women in the Academy* (Boulder: University Press of Colorado, 2012); Deborah Gray White, ed., *Telling Histories: Black Women Historians in the Ivory Tower* (Chapel Hill: University of North Carolina Press, 2008); Lois Benjamin, ed., *Black Women in the Academy: Promises and Perils* (Gainesville: University Press of Florida, 1997).

2. Barbara Christian, "Diminishing Returns: Can Black Feminism(s) Survive the Academy," in *Multiculturalism: A Critical Reader,* ed. David Theo Goldberg (Boston: Blackwell, 1994), 173. This essay is also republished in a landmark collection of Christian's writings: see Gloria M. Bowles, Giulia Fabi, and Arlene Keizer, *New Black Feminist Criticism, 1985–2000* (Urbana: University of Illinois Press, 2007).

3. I wrote the first version of this chapter as an article in 2005. I had hoped that in the intervening years the moment I was diagnosing, in which we had so many Black feminist deaths to mourn, had passed, and this article would become an artifact. I cannot in all honestly say that that has happened, but I hope that it will soon.

4. In listing these women in this way, I do not aim to be comprehensive, although I do not relish the thought that there are more Black women intellectuals who have died about whom I do not know. Instead, I mean to impress upon us the magnitude of this crisis. If we keep in mind that most of these women listed are literary critics, the extent of the crisis becomes even more staggering, since this list, being mostly of women from one particular field, is undoubtedly partial. I also mean to pay tribute to these women (a few of whom I knew personally but most of whom I know only through their work), all of whom have enabled me to do my own work in ways both direct and oblique. For an eloquent commentary on the phenomenon of Black feminist deaths, see Myisha Priest, "Mourning Vital Links to Our Culture," *Crisis* 111, no. 2 (2004): 54. There have been a number of published memorials for individual Black feminists who have died. For a tribute to Claudia Tate, see Nell Irwin Painter et al., "Symposium on the Works of Claudia Tate," *Journal of African American History* 88, no. 1 (2003): 59–81. For a memoriam for Christian, see June Jordan, "In Memoriam: Barbara Christian (1943–2000)," *Callaloo* 23, no. 4 (2000): 1172–73. See also Ula Taylor's meditation on the deaths of Christian

and Jordan in "The Death of Dry Tears," in *Telling Histories: Black Women Historians in the Ivory Tower* (Chapel Hill: University of North Carolina Press, 2008). For a collection of moving and thoughtful essays about Nellie McKay and her work, see Joycelyn Moody et al., "Nellie McKay Tribute," *African American Review* 40, no. 1 (2006): 5–38. See also Nell Irwin Painter, "The Praxis of a Life of Scholarship: Three Nellie McKay Letters from 1995," *African American Review* 40, no. 1 (2006): 9–12.

5. In naming an epidemic of premature deaths among Black feminists, I hope to provide an analytic that illuminates, rather than erases, other premature deaths. In that vein, I mean for this essay to also be a tribute to Gloria Anzaldúa, Clyde Woods, Manning Marable, Lindon Barrett, José Esteban Muñoz, Rosemary Marangoly George, and others that I may not mention by name here.

6. James Baldwin, *The Evidence of Things Not Seen* (New York: Henry Holt, 1985), 39.

7. I wrote this section of this chapter prior to having read Priest's. When I found Priest's moving tribute to Black women intellectuals, I found to my amazement that "the list goes on and on" was a phrase she used as well. There was apparently something that resonated about this phrase for both of us. While I would, in other circumstances, remove it so as to avoid any seeming impropriety or plagiarism, I have decided to include it here to retain this resonance, with this acknowledgment that Priest's use was the earlier written and published.

8. For a Black feminist theorization of "survival," see Alexis Pauline Gumbs, "The Shape of My Impact," *The Feminist Wire*, October 29, 2012, http://the feministwire.com/2012/10/the-shape-of-my-impact/.

9. For accounts of Black women's experiences with health, sickness, and the academy, see Chana Kai Lee, "Journey Toward a Different Self: The Defining Power of Illness, Race, and Gender," in *Telling Histories*. I thank Sarah Haley for this reference.

10. See the Combahee River Collective, "Why Did They Die? A Document of Black Feminism," *Radical America* 13, no. 6 (October–November 1979): 41–50. For a reading of this pamphlet, see Grace Kyungwon Hong, "Introduction," in *The Ruptures of American Capital*.

11. Audre Lorde, "Need," in *The Collected Poems of Audre Lorde* (New York: Norton, 1997). For a discussion of this poem and the context of the murder of Black women in which it arose, see Alexis De Veaux, *Warrior Poet: A Biography of Audre Lorde* (New York: Norton, 2004), 240. I thank Cynthia Rich for directing my attention to this poem and for giving me her copy of an early draft that Lorde had sent her and her late partner Barbara MacDonald. The correspondence from Lorde to Rich/MacDonald is now a part of the Cynthia Rich and Barbara MacDonald papers housed at the Schlesinger Library on the History of Women in America at the Radcliffe Institute for Advanced Study.

12. Lorde, "Need," 349.

13. Lorde, "Learning from the 60s," 135.

14. The program for that year's convention, as for all years, is published in its entirety in the MLA's official publication, *PMLA*. See "Program," *PMLA* 109, no. 6 (November 1994): 1162–83. The listing for the panel to which I refer is on page 1236.

15. Barbara Christian, "Polylogue on Feminism and the Institution," *Differences: A Journal of Feminist Cultural Studies* 2 (Fall 1990): 57.

16. I realize that, in using the term "the university," I risk implying that there is only one monolithic university formation, which is certainly untrue. Within each university there are localized operations of racial and gendered management that might differ based on whether a university is public or private, research or teaching oriented, well funded or underfunded, or a historically Black college or university (HBCU) or, as the majority tend to be, a historically white institution. There are institutions that are organized around religious faiths (mainly Catholic or Jewish), one university for the deaf, and another for Native American students. Certainly, how Black feminists and Black feminism might fare in these varied sites will surely differ. While HBCUs cannot be exempted from critiques of sexism and male-dominated organization, and while Black feminism undoubtedly faces challenges of different sorts in HBCUs than in historically white colleges and universities, the attacks on affirmative action have made HBCUs that much more important for the education of African American students currently. Indeed, Beverly Guy-Sheftall's account of the successful establishment of Black feminism as a central component to the curriculum at one historically Black college—Spelman College—leaves open the possibility that HBCUs may become the center of Black feminist teaching, theorizing, and knowledge production within the academy in the future. See Beverly Guy-Sheftall, "A Black Feminist Perspective on Transforming the Academy: The Case of Spelman College," in *Theorizing Black Feminisms: The Visionary Pragmatism of Black Women* (New York: Routledge, 1993). It is an important and worthwhile project to examine the differentiated histories of Black feminism within the various kinds of institutions that make up the American academy, though such a project is not within the scope of this article. In this essay, when I refer to the university as a formation, I am speaking mainly about historically white, research or liberal arts institutions in the context of which many of these Black feminist deaths have occurred, and in which affirmative action rollbacks have severely impacted the recruitment and retention of African American students. Yet on a larger level, I am tracing the "university" as an institutional logic and administrative technology, emerging out of Western liberal democratic culture and shaped in relation and in contradiction to first industrial and then neoliberal capitalism, which organize all universities in the United States.

17. Ferguson, *The Reorder of Things*.

18. See Bill Readings, *The University in Ruins* (Cambridge: Harvard University Press, 1996). See particularly chapter 5, "The University and the Idea of Culture."

19. Craig Steven Wilder, *Ebony And Ivy: Race, Slavery, and the Troubled History of America's Universities* (New York: Bloomsbury Press, 2013), 1–2.

20. Of course, the university was not the only site radically transformed by these movements. Even within educational institutions, scholars have noted the ways in which the earliest and most radical movements for self-determination for students of color and for a curriculum relevant to these students emerged not at the university level but in high schools and community colleges. See Dolores Delgado Bernal, "Grassroots Leadership Reconceptualized: Chicana Oral Histories and the 1968 East Los Angeles School Blowouts," *Frontiers: A Journal of Women Studies* 19, no. 2 (1998): 113–42, for a useful analysis of the role of Chicana leadership in the 1968 East Los Angeles "blowouts," in which over ten thousand Chicano/a students staged a walkout to protest the poor conditions at their high schools and middle schools.

21. Ferguson, *The Reorder of Things.*

22. Roderick Ferguson, "African American Studies," in *Encyclopedia of Lesbian, Gay, Bisexual, and Transgender History in America,* ed. Mark Stein (New York: Charles Scribner's Sons, 2005), 78.

23. C. L. R. James, "Black Studies and the Contemporary Student," in *The C. L. R. James Reader,* ed. Anna Grimshaw (Cambridge: Blackwell, 1993), 397.

24. For a brilliant accounting of the many ways in which activists of color in the United States in the post–World War II era situated themselves in alliance with decolonization struggles in the Third World, see Young, *Soul Power.*

25. For an analysis of the movement for ethnic studies at San Francisco State University that makes the connection between this movement and larger decolonizing struggles evident, see Mike Murase, "Ethnic Studies and Higher Education for Asian Americans," in *Counterpoint: Perspectives on Asian America,* ed. Emma Gee (Los Angeles: UCLA Asian American Studies Center, 1978).

26. Several useful anthologies and collections of black feminism exist. An early collection is Toni Cade Bambara, ed., *The Black Woman* (New York: Penguin Books, 1970). Barbara Smith has been one of the most important editors of such collections; her *Home Girls* and *Some of Us Are Brave* are foundational texts. See Barbara Smith, ed., *Home Girls: A Black Feminist Anthology* (New York: Kitchen Table: Women of Color Press, 1983); and Gloria T. Hull, Patricia Bell Scott, and Barbara Smith, eds., *All the Women Are White, All the Blacks Are Men, But Some of Us Are Brave* (Old Westbury, N.Y.: Feminist Press, 1982). The most comprehensive collection is Beverly Guy-Sheftall, ed., *Words of Fire: An Anthology of African-American Feminist Thought* (New York: New Press, 1995), which collects African American feminist theory beginning from 1831. Joy James and T. Denean Sharpley-Whiting, eds., *Black Feminist Reader* (Malden: Blackwell, 2000), collects more recent work from the 1970s onward.

27. See Hong, *The Ruptures of American Capital.*

28. Melamed, "The Spirit of Neoliberalism," 2. For insightful discussions of multiculturalism, see Avery Gordon and Chris Newfield, *Mapping Multiculturalism* (Minneapolis: University of Minnesota Press, 1996). See also Lee,

Urban Triage, for a discussion of the "long decade" of the 1980s in which multiculturalist celebrations of the cultural production (particularly literary) of people of color did little to alleviate, and instead obscured and legitimated, the economic and political assault on racialized communities. Christian's "Diminishing Returns" essay was clearly her intervention into a politics of multiculturalism, and was published in a volume specifically addressing this topic. See David Theo Goldberg, *Multiculturalism: A Critical Reader* (Boston: Blackwell, 1994).

29. Christian discusses her participation in the City College strikes in "Camouflaging Race *and* Gender," in *Race and Representation: Affirmative Action*, ed. Robert Post and Michael Rogin (Boston: Zone Books, 1994). For an incisive account of the City College struggle, see Ferguson, *The Reorder of Things*, especially chapter 3.

30. White, *Telling Histories*, 17.

31. Promotion report, 1998, Barbara Christian Papers Collection, Bancroft Library, BANC MSS 2003/199, Carton 2, Folder 24.

32. Letter from John Wright, editor at Oxford University Press, April 25, 1977; letter from Doris Kretschmer, editor at University of California Press, February 24, 1978; letter of inquiry from Christian to Leone Stein, editor at University of Massachusetts Press, February 18, 1975, Barbara Christian Papers Collection, Bancroft Library, BANC MSS 2003/199, Carton 1, Folder 26.

33. Letter from Ellen Bry for Luther Nichols, editor at Doubleday, Barbara Christian Papers Collection, Bancroft Library, BANC MSS 2003/199, Carton 1, Folder 26.

34. Ibid.

35. Letter to Toni Morrison, editor at Doubleday, Barbara Christian Papers Collection, Bancroft Library, BANC MSS 2003/199, Carton 1, Folder 26.

36. Letter from Toni Morrison, editor at Random House, April 5, 1978, Barbara Christian Papers Collection, Bancroft Library, BANC MSS 2003/199, Carton 1, Folder 26.

37. Letter from Tracy Sherrod, editor at Henry Holt, Barbara Christian Papers Collection, Bancroft Library, BANC MSS 2003/199, Carton 8, Folder 5.

38. Letter from Niko Pfund, editor at New York University Press, Barbara Christian Papers Collection, Bancroft Library, BANC MSS 2003/199, Carton 8, Folder 7.

39. Letter from Bernhard Kendler, executive editor at Cornell University Press, Barbara Christian Papers Collection, Bancroft Library, BANC MSS 2003/199, Carton 8, Folder 12.

40. Printout of computer file, letter to Barbara Lowenstein, Barbara Christian Papers Collection, Bancroft Library, BANC MSS 2003/199, Carton 12, Folder 20.

41. Grant proposal addressed to Robert Lee Grant, Chairman, University of California, Berkeley Budget and Finance committee, January 15, 1975, Barbara

Christian Papers Collection, Bancroft Library, BANC MSS 2003/199, Carton 1, Folder 26.

42. Ibid.

43. Printout of computer file, letter to Toni Morrison, December 13, 1993, Barbara Christian Papers Collection, Bancroft Library, BANC MSS 2003/199, Carton 12, Folder 20.

44. Printout of computer file, letter to Douglas C. Bennett, ACLS Vice President, March 24, 1995, Barbara Christian Papers Collection, Bancroft Library, BANC MSS 2003/199, Carton 12, Folder 20.

45. Printout of computer file, abstract, ACLS grant proposal, Barbara Christian Papers Collection, Bancroft Library, BANC MSS 2003/199, Carton 12, Folder 21.

46. Ibid.

47. Christian, "Diminishing Returns," 187.

48. Patricia Hill-Collins, "The Social Construction of Black Feminist Thought," *Signs* 14 (1989): 753. For an analysis of how the "epistemological racism that limits the range of possible epistemologies considered legitimate within the mainstream research community" affects the retention, promotion, and tenure rates of scholars of color, see Dolores Delgado Bernal and Octavio Villalpando, "An Apartheid of Knowledge in Academia: The Struggle over the 'Legitimate' Knowledge of Faculty of Color," *Equity and Excellence in Education* 35, no. 2 (2002): 169–80. See also Gloria Ladson-Billings, "Racialized Discourses and Ethnic Epistemologies," in *Handbook of Qualitative Research,* 2nd ed., ed. N. K. Denzin and Y. S. Lincoln (Thousand Oaks: Sage, 2000); J. J. Scheurich and M. D. Young, "Coloring Epistemologies: Are Our Research Epistemologies Racially Biased?," *Educational Researcher* 26, no. 4 (1997): 4–16.

49. Promotion report, 1974, Barbara Christian Papers Collection, Bancroft Library, BANC MSS 2003/199, Carton 2, Folder 24.

50. Ibid. Although Christian's name did not end up on the massive three hundred–plus page accreditation report of UWW-Berkeley written for the Western Association of Schools and Colleges, it is clear from her promotion materials that she was substantively involved in this program. See Barbara Christian Papers Collection, Bancroft Library, BANC MSS 2003/199, Carton 11, Folder 15 for the report.

51. Halifu Osumare, Skype interview with the author, November 17, 2014.

52. Promotion Report, 1974, Barbara Christian Papers Collection, Bancroft Library, BANC MSS 2003/199, Carton 2, Folder 24.

53. Barbara Christian, "Race for Theory," *Cultural Critique* 6 (Spring 1987): 51–63, 52.

54. Ibid., 54.

55. Halifu Osumare, Skype interview with the author, November 17, 2014.

56. Readings, *The University in Ruins*, 13.

57. John Guillory, "Preprofessionalism: What Graduate Students Want," *ADE Bulletin* 113 (1996): 7 (also available at www.mla.org/adefl_bulletin_d_ade_113_4.pdf).

58. Foucault writes, "Beginning in the second half of the nineteenth century, the thematics of blood was sometimes called to lend its entire historical weight toward revitalizing the type of political power that was exercised through the devices of sexuality. Racism took shape at this point (racism in its modern, 'biologizing,' statist form); it was then that the whole politics of settlement *(peuplement)*, family, marriage, education, social hierarchization, and property, accompanied by a long series of permanent interventions at the level of the body, conduct, health, and everyday life, received their color and their justification from the mythical concern with protecting the purity of the race and ensuring the triumph of the race." Foucault, *The History of Sexuality,* 1:149.

59. Tenure review statement, Barbara Christian Papers Collection, Bancroft Library, BANC MSS 2003/199, Carton 2, Folder 24.

60. Promotion report, 1998, Barbara Christian Papers Collection, Bancroft Library, BANC MSS 2003/199, Carton 2, Folder 24. The tradition of exceptional service stretches back to the very first women of color with PhDs, as Deborah Gray White documents in her introduction to *Telling Histories.* She observes that the eulogies of Marion Thompson Wright, the first Black woman to receive a PhD from an American institution, "suggest that Wright gave much, perhaps too much, to academe. One tribute celebrated . . . the numerous at-large committees that sought and received her help; and the time she gave to students and friends. It noted that she was willing to give up her leisure time to help prevent student failure, provide remedial experiences, and alleviate difficulties in college adjustment." White, "Introduction: A Telling History," in *Telling Histories,* 16.

61. Letter to Margaret Wilkerson, chair of African American Studies, requesting research assistant, May 17, 1994, Barbara Christian Papers Collection, Bancroft Library, BANC MSS 2003/199, Carton 12, Folder 20.

62. Printout of computer file, draft of speech, Barbara Christian Papers Collection, Bancroft Library, BANC MSS 2003/199, Carton 12, Folder 24. The essay on Audre Lorde was originally published as "Remembering Audre Lorde," *The Women's Review of Books* 10, no. 6 (March 1993): 5–6. It is reprinted in the *Berkeley Women's Law Journal* as "Your Silence Will Not Protect You—A Tribute to Audre Lorde," *Berkeley Women's Law Journal* 8, no. 1 (1993): 1–5.

63. Foucault, *Society Must Be Defended,* 7.

64. Ibid., 10.

65. Barbara Christian, "But What Do We Think We're Doing Anyway: The State of Black Feminist Criticism(s); or, My Version of a Little Bit of History," in *Changing Our Own Words: Essays on Criticism, Theory, and Writing by Black Women,* ed. Cheryl Wall (New Brunswick: Rutgers University Press, 1989), 73.

66. Herbert Marcuse, *One-Dimensional Man: Studies in the Ideology of Advanced Industrial Society* (New York: Beacon Press, 1991), xi.

67. Joy James, "Radicalizing Black Feminism," *Race and Class* 40 (1999): 15–31. Much of this essay also appears in some form throughout her later work *Shadowboxing.* I cite from the essay version.

68. See Hong, *The Ruptures of American Capital,* xxx–xxxi, for a discussion of Davis, and Hong, "The Ghosts of Transnational American Studies," 36–39, for a discussion of Smith.

69. Combahee River Collective, "A Black Feminist Manifesto," reprinted in Anzaldúa and Moraga, *This Bridge Called My Back,* 213.

70. Benjamin, "Theses on the Philosophy of History," 263.

71. Ferguson, *Aberrations in Black,* 117.

72. Lorde, "Poetry Is Not a Luxury," 39.

73. For a description of the traditional Marxist characterization of culture as the "superstructure" to the economic "base," see Raymond Williams, *Marxism and Literature* (London: Oxford University Press, 1977).

74. Christian, "Diminishing Returns," 177–78.

Epilogue

1. Gordon, *Ghostly Matters,* 19.

2. Combahee River Collective, "A Black Feminist Statement," 213.

3. Lorde, "Poetry Is Not a Luxury," 36.

4. Ibid., 37.

5. Lorde, "Uses of the Erotic."

6. bell hooks, *All About Love: New Visions* (New York: William Morrow, 2001).

7. Baldwin, "The Uses of the Blues."

8. Gordon, *Ghostly Matters.*

9. Williams, *The Alchemy of Race and Rights.*

10. I thank Sarah Haley for this insight.

Acknowledgments

1. Lorde, "Poetry Is Not a Luxury," 38.

Index

abandonment, Lorde's discussion of, 78–93

accumulation, existential power and, 69

Acosta, Oscar Zeta: death in writing of, 31–32, 35–36, 48–56, 63, 148, 173n30; disappearance of, 174n31

Adventures of Huckleberry Finn, The (Twain), 65

affect: Lorde's discussion of, 74–80, 177n34; research on, 177n34; theorization of impossibility and, 15

African Americans: death practices of, 179n2; educational barriers for, 125–46; Moynihan Report on families of, 18–22; prison warehousing of, 72–73

African American Studies, 132

Agamben, Giorgio, 25–29, 98–99

Agbebiyi, Adeola, 121

"Age, Race, Class, and Sex: Women Redefining Difference" (Lorde), 75–94

AIDS, Moraga's discussion of, 89–93

Alarcón, Norma, 43–44, 46–47, 88, 170n19

Aldama, Frederick Luis, 56

Anderson, Benedict, 37–38, 118

antiracism, neoliberalism and, 18–19

antiwar movement, Chicano Moratorium and, 39–42

Asian migration: existential surplus and, 70–73; racial capitalism and, 157n29; racial difference and, 169n111

Autobiography of a Brown Buffalo (Acosta), 48–56

Baldwin, James, 95, 106–8, 117, 123, 126

Bambara, Toni Cade, 126, 143

Barrera, Elma, 44

B.D. Women (film), 33, 97, 109, 115, 118–24

Beal, Frances, 157n29

Bell, Derrick, Jr., 18

Benjamin, Walter, 108–9, 125

biopolitics: Lorde's discussion of, 75–81; Moraga's discussion of, 81–93; racial politics and, 10, 19, 158n34

Black British communities, images of, 119–24

191

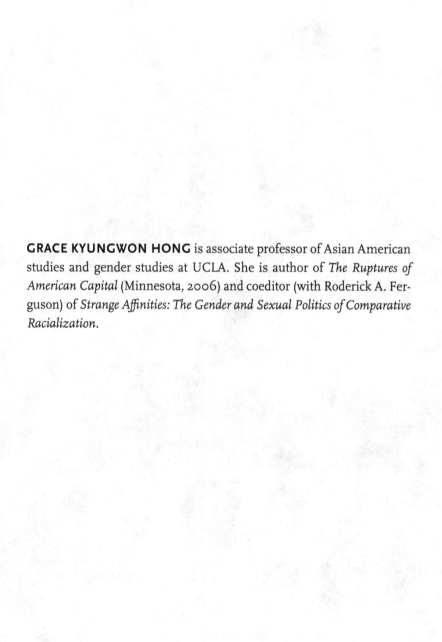

GRACE KYUNGWON HONG is associate professor of Asian American studies and gender studies at UCLA. She is author of *The Ruptures of American Capital* (Minnesota, 2006) and coeditor (with Roderick A. Ferguson) of *Strange Affinities: The Gender and Sexual Politics of Comparative Racialization.*